WHEN A CONGREGATION
IS BETRAYED

When a Congregation Is Betrayed

Responding to Clergy Misconduct

Beth Ann Gaede, Editor

AUTHORS
Candace R. Benyei
E. Larraine Frampton
Nancy Myer Hopkins
Patricia L. Liberty
Deborah Pope-Lance

THE
ALBAN
INSTITUTE

Library of Congress Cataloging-in-Publication Data
When a congregation is betrayed : responding to clergy misconduct / edited by Beth Ann Gaede ; authors, Candace R. Benyei . . . [et al.].

   p. cm.

   Includes bibliographical references.

   ISBN 1-56699-284-2

   1. Pastoral theology. 2. Sexual misconduct by clergy. 3. Sexual abuse victims— Pastoral counseling of. 4. Clergy—Deposition. I. Gaede, Beth Ann. II. Benyei, Candace Reed.

   BV4392.5.W44 2005

   253'.2 dc22   2005031703

09 08 07 06 05   1 2 3 4 5

CONTENTS

FOREWORD

Pamela Cooper-White

THE PUBLICATION OF THIS VOLUME marks an important milestone in the prevention of and intervention in clergy sexual misconduct. How far we have come in a little over 15 years! Twenty years ago, as the stories of survivors continue to tell us, the church community was largely deaf and blind to the sexual exploitation of parishioners by their clergy. Victims kept silent out of shame, self-blame, and a fear that no one would believe what happened. When cases of abuse were brought to the attention of church authorities, the situations were all too often handled as anomalies to be hushed up or explained away. Sexual abuse of children was minimized or denied, and sexual exploitation of adults was more often framed as adultery and a personal moral lapse, rather than a professional matter of ethics, fiduciary responsibility, and boundaries. Deals were cut in bishops' offices, clergy were quietly moved on to new assignments with a verbal admonition to do better next time, and congregations were left unaided to cope with rumors, suspicions, confusion, unconscious dynamics of splitting and secrecy, eventual membership decline, or a repeating cycle of hiring charismatic, narcissistic clergy.

Although things are by no means perfect now, and the pull in church systems will probably always be toward denial—as with all trauma[1]—this book signals that new understandings have not only been raised up, but indeed, are now being integrated into the standards of care and leadership across many denominations and faith traditions. It is part of the welcome mainstreaming of what began as a kind of resistance movement. In the late 1960s, other forms of abuse began to be uncovered, and by the late 1980s, clergy-abuse survivors began to tell their stories aloud, in the context of small, grass-roots support groups. Sexual abuse by clergy was being recognized as belonging on the spectrum of other forms of abuse and trauma, and the dynamics of clergy abuse came to be understood as not a matter of personal morality, but of professional ethics and the exploitation of power.[2]

Research in the past two decades on the prevalence of clergy misconduct has begun to provide evidence for what was once a shameful secret. Self-reports of sexual boundary crossings range from 5.8 to 38.6 percent, and when clergy were asked to report not on themselves but on their knowledge of other ministers who had had sexual contact with a parishioner, as many as 70 percent responded affirmatively.[3] In my own recent research among pastoral counselors, 42 percent reported that a colleague had told them of committing sexual misconduct, and 87 percent had treated a client who had been sexually abused by a pastor, and many had treated five or more clients with similar reports.[4] Myths persist about sexual exploitation being committed equally by women, as well as child abuse by homosexual priests (thus displacing responsibility from the actual perpetrators), but empirical research continues to validate that the vast preponderance of sexual misconduct (90+ percent) is committed by heterosexual male clergy, implicating the continuing systemic gender inequality and patriarchal indifference of institutional religion.

The result of such research is that we have all heard the painful truths that perhaps we were loathe to hear, and have been forced—in part by our ethical mandate as people of faith to promote care and justice, and in part by the recognition of legal liability—to take the issue of clergy sexual misconduct seriously. It is now clear that we must advocate at a systemic level for justice for women and children, and begin in concrete ways to implement effective policies for screening, training, prevention, reporting, and intervention and healing for both individuals and congregations.

This book, then, represents yet another step beyond recognition, and beyond front-line prevention and intervention, to addressing the sorrow and anger that is left in the wake of clergy misconduct. By assembling a team of writers geared to educate and support "afterpastors" (those who are called to congregations in the aftermath of violation) and judicatory leaders, Beth Gaede has done the faith community an important service. Experts, some of whom are represented among the contributors to this volume, have identified a number of congregational symptoms in the aftermath of clergy misconduct,[5] including reactivity, divisiveness, preoccupation with caring for the offending clergyperson without similar apparent regard for victims, a climate of gossip and conjecture, embarrassment, preoccupation with matters of sex, "symbolic fights"[6] in which aspects of the building or program become arenas for acting out conflicts about the unspoken abuse, nostalgia or idealization of a former time, despair, fear, cynicism, and disillusionment about religious faith.

Not only individual victims, but congregations and communities are betrayed by clergy misconduct. Congregations therefore need and deserve sophisticated, thoughtful, and empathic intervention, including ample, appropriate disclosure; opportunities for well-facilitated public discussion and education about appropriate professional boundaries, expectations of clergy, the misuse of power inherent in clergy sexual misconduct, and a theological framing of the issues; access to the most recent policies and procedures; and education and support for going through various stages in the congregational healing process—similar to trauma debriefing.[7]

Those for whom this book is written are responding to a specialized and demanding vocation, requiring courage, vision, nonreactivity, and above all, hope. Anger is often displaced onto congregation staff members, interims and afterpastors, and judicatory executives. Inviting people to share their grief, anger, and betrayal is a sacrificial work, with real danger over time of succumbing to "compassion fatigue" and secondary traumatization. Self-care, collaboration with other experts, and consultation for oneself is crucial. Yet the rewards are also great. Violated congregations that do not receive skilled intervention are like a closed-up house with a toxic, polluted river running beneath its floorboards. The environment is poisoning the people inside, but no one can say where the fumes are coming from. More than anything else, it is the task of afterpastors and denominational leaders to listen—to throw open the windows to let in light and air (permission to see, to know, and to speak), and the doors to let in new life (new ideas, new insights, even new people). More than anything, these facilitators "hear the congregation into speech," to borrow the words of Nelle Morton.[8] In so doing, they (in other words, you, the reader!) are bearers of hope, and partners with the Holy One who is always present, even in the most toxic and violated places, whispering, "Behold, I am doing a new thing!" So read on—and take nourishment for the journey!

PREFACE

Beth Ann Gaede, Editor
For the Contributors

ONCE A CLERGYPERSON HAS BETRAYED A CONGREGATION'S TRUST, what can be done to help everyone affected respond effectively, experience healing, and fulfill their roles and responsibilities in the congregation and elsewhere? Specifically, how can a congregation that has been betrayed heal—that is, integrate the event into its history, identity, and ongoing life?

When a Congregation Is Betrayed offers strategic resources to help clergy and lay leaders answer these questions—and ultimately to survive and serve well in congregations where clergy misconduct has occurred. Many books, videos, curricula, and organizations address clergy misconduct and its effects on congregations, and the resource section at the end of this volume lists a number of valuable tools recommended by the contributors. In the earliest conversations that led to the development of this book, however, we asked ourselves, "What is missing? What do congregation leaders need to know that no one else has covered?" During many hours of telephone conference calls held over the course of about a year, it became clear we were being called to write a book that focuses on misconduct by *clergy* involving *adult* victims.

Those who have contributed to this volume are well aware that some misconduct in congregations involves neither clergy nor adult victims. Anyone who has paid attention to news reports in recent decades has read or heard tragic accounts of clergy who have abused children and whose misconduct has often been covered up by church authorities. Numerous books have also been written about the problem. Little has been written, however, about clergy misconduct involving adults, a more complex issue. Many people have a hard time recognizing misconduct involving adult victims for what it is—not a matter of a "relationship" gone awry but an abuse of power. A differential of power between two adults seems subtler and more difficult to understand than the obviously unequal power between an adult and a child. Of course, we could easily blame the media for failing to cover power dynamics in clergy relationships and for focusing instead on abuse of children, an issue whose drama can be captured in headlines and sound bites. But it seems apparent to us that church leaders themselves—clergy, lay leaders, denominational officials—have little interest in wrestling with the implications of this fact: whatever their ministry setting, clergy have power and authority that can be abused. Rather than address yet again clergy abuse of children and youth, we focus instead in this resource on the abuse of adults, an issue that has gotten little attention among the general public.

The other decision we made when developing this book, one already implied, was to focus on misconduct by clergy, although we recognize that other leaders in a congregation can betray members' trust. Youth directors, musicians, childcare or Sunday school teachers, bookkeepers, and financial secretaries—anyone, paid or volunteer, who is entrusted with a responsibility or has authority over others—can violate the privilege of the role. And no matter what the offender's position, the fallout in a congregation when misconduct occurs can be deep and long lasting. Still, clergy play a unique role in the congregational system. As Rabbi Edwin Friedman, family systems therapist, explains: "The overall health and functioning of any organization depend primarily on one or two people at the top, and that is true whether the relationship system is a personal family, a sports team, an orchestra, a congregation, a religious hierarchy, or an entire nation."[1] In a congregation, the pastor is usually one of the people "at the top" on whom the well-being of the entire system depends. No one else in a congregation fills the *office* of the pastor, a role that grants power, authority, and responsibility to the clergyperson not available to any other person in the congregation.

As the outline for this book evolved, another need became clear to us. Although many resources discuss the dynamics of clergy misconduct, nothing had been written about what we came to call "strategic survival tactics" for leaders of congregations where clergy misconduct has occurred. These leaders include both "afterpastors"—clergy (interim or settled) who follow offending pastors, and lay leaders who may themselves have witnessed or been victimized by the offending clergyperson. Both groups of leaders, as well as the judicatory staff who support them, need guidance about how to assess and effectively respond to the misconduct, so that they as individuals and the congregation as a whole can maintain personal wellness, care for the victim/survivor, and carry out the mission and ministry to which the congregation has been called.

The large majority of clergy serve their congregations with great integrity. A relatively small percentage—by most estimates, somewhere between 10 and 15 percent—will choose to abuse the power inherent in their role. This abuse of power, or misconduct, may be sexual and may range from hugging too long or making inappropriate comments to severe offenses, such as engaging in sexual intercourse with other staff, members, and even children. Misconduct may also involve financial misdealings, including embezzling congregation funds or arranging to receive a member's estate upon the member's death. Some misconduct would probably strike observers as merely foolish or incompetent, such as attending to personal commitments and "skipping out on" a major congregation event, perhaps the annual children's Christmas pageant. This book is not primarily concerned with the lesser offenders on this continuum but rather with that small percentage of clergy who have had complaints brought against them and have been found by a careful and fair disciplinary process to be unfit for ministry in a congregation.

The contributors to this volume have all worked with betrayed congregations as afterpastors or consultants, and several have also taught and written about clergy misconduct. In this book, they draw on their professional expertise to provide nontechnical guidance for the leaders in congregations where misconduct has occurred. They write not only for people who are professionally interested in the betrayed congregations, but for those who must deal day to day with the aftermath of clergy misconduct. They give readers tools to engage congregation members in the issues surrounding clergy misconduct, so real healing can occur; provide resources to help congregations understand the victim's/survivor's experience; and offer strategies to help afterpastors and other leaders survive personally, thrive and serve well, and manage situations that might never be good.

Congregations are called to be instruments of healing in a broken world. When a congregation is betrayed by clergy misconduct, however, its capacity to bring about that healing is greatly diminished. Although all healers are in some way wounded, congregations that have been betrayed are dealt a blow that can nearly consume their energy and drain resources into activities that feed unproductive, internal anguish. Such congregations—as a body and as individuals—can no longer carry out the work God calls them to do.

Those who have contributed to this volume remind us, however, that God is all about relationships, and therefore, so are we. We follow Jesus, who has modeled for us how to be in relationships in a way that allows people to reach their greatest potential, to live authentically and ethically as they serve God and neighbor, and ultimately, to prepare for the reign of God among us. We offer this book with hope—hope for the members and leaders of congregations that have been betrayed by clergy, that they may be healed and may one day be restored to the mission and ministry to which God calls them.

INTRODUCTION

Deborah Pope-Lance

CLERGY WHO SERVE A CONGREGATION OR ORGANIZATION after a predecessor's misconduct are called afterpastors. The term, coined by a group of clergy in Minnesota who met regularly for mutual support,[1] describes clergy who minister in the aftermath of a betrayal of pastoral trust. Some clergy find the rhyme in the word humorous and appreciate the clearer perspective laughter and language provide. Other clergy, perhaps unaccustomed to referring to themselves as "pastor," find the word ill fitting but nonetheless recognize it accurately describes their experience. This book was primarily developed for afterpastors, as well as the congregation and judicatory leaders who work with them, to help them understand and address the needs of the congregation where clergy misconduct has occurred. The primary contributors who developed the outline for this book often referred to it during early discussions as "a strategic survival manual" for afterpastors.

A predecessor's betrayal of trust can involve a variety of misconduct—unethical conduct as described by professional codes; conduct unlawful by state or federal statute; sexual exploitation; harassment or abuse of individuals; sexualized relationships, behavior, or speech; abuse of authority, office, or power; financial malfeasance or embezzlement; violations of role or appropriate boundaries; or unfulfilled responsibility. Often more than one type of betrayal of trust has occurred, creating a constellation of boundary and trust violations. The fact that these violations tend to occur in clusters demonstrates that misconduct is not merely a specific behavior or event. Rather, it is a process of interactions by which trust is betrayed in a ministerial relationship. Artifacts of this process and individual and systemic responses to this betrayal generate the unique challenges of serving in the aftermath of misconduct.

Some afterpastors know before beginning their service with a congregation that a predecessor engaged in some type of misconduct. Denominational or congregational leaders have straightforwardly provided them with an accurate, complete history of the congregation's relationships with ministers. Some clergy discover they are afterpastors only by accident. Perhaps a congregant comes to them for counseling and outlines a story, and then another with a similar story comes, and another. Or a ministerial colleague, realizing the afterpastor has not been told what happened, shares what is known or rumored. Sometimes an afterpastor learns the congregation's story only after serving for some time. Some learn by reading newspaper articles alleging improprieties, others by being subpoenaed for testimony when a legal or civil suit is filed against the predecessor and the congregation.

Some clergy come to know they are afterpastors when they experience unsettling interactions with members or inexplicable events in their work. Perhaps a pattern of organizational dysfunction thwarts their and lay leaders' efforts at change. Or individuals challenge boundaries in a variety of ways, great and small—for example, consistently calling the cleric at home or repeatedly failing to issue staff paychecks on time. Other clergy will never know for certain whether the congregation they now serve was betrayed by a predecessor but will nonetheless experience many of the unique challenges in ministry routinely described by afterpastors.

Common Experiences of Afterpastors

In my years working as an afterpastor, consulting with congregations where clergy misconduct has occurred, and researching clergy misconduct for my work in a doctoral program, I have found several clear patterns in afterpastors' experience. Afterpastors say relationships and interactions in their ministries are frequently characterized by distrust and suspicion. Rather than being treated with respect and confidence, they are met with doubt and misgivings. They often feel misheard or unheard by lay leaders and congregants. One afterpastor reported, "I attended meetings where I might as well have been invisible and mute, because no one ever acknowledged what I said." Some describe being treated rudely or being the object of inexplicable anger and even rage from congregants.

Afterpastors report feeling manipulated, coerced, and sabotaged by lay leaders or seeing decisions co-opted or corrupted by poor process or underhanded leadership. One afterpastor explained, "Sometimes I'd be the last one to know a meeting was cancelled, or sometimes I'd show up, not having been told the location had been changed. Then I'd be ridiculed for being so obviously inept at keeping my commitments straight." Communication was quite erratic and confused in this congregation, even apart from direct communications with this afterpastor. Often, regardless of who had authority or responsibility, people simply did whatever they wanted to do, neither seeking approval nor hearing disapproval from anyone. Other afterpastors report deliberate, planned undermining of their ministries. For example, an afterpastor recounted how he was asked by lay leaders to represent the congregation at a denominational gathering. At the meeting, the lay leaders appeared and contradicted everything they had asked him to say. Another reported how a church treasurer who consistently neglected to pay her on time lied to board members for months about their interactions, saying that the minister yelled at and belittled the treasurer at every turn and that he was afraid of the minister.

Less dramatic sabotage reported by afterpastors includes: misrepresenting a previous meeting's decision, changing worship plans made by the minister, misquoting the minister, and discussing concerns about the minister with nearly everyone but the minister. One afterpastor, having planned a service according to the lectionary, inquired about a change in the bulletin—the children's Bible story no longer matched the day's reading. He was told he was mistaken; there had been no change. Many afterpastors say they are often criticized without cause or unwarrantedly berated for incompetence. One afterpastor, who had long led preaching seminars for new ministers, was regularly criticized by members of the pastor-parish relations committee for her poor sermons. Later, after she learned she was an afterpastor, she discovered that one committee member's spouse had been a victim of the minister's misconduct, and another had persuaded the minister to leave, lest the abuse be discovered.

Confusion about a minister's role and authority can present difficulties to an afterpastor. Not a few have indicated that they were welcomed into their new congregation with undue reverence and dependence, "as if everything I said was gospel and nothing I said could be questioned," described one. In one congregation, an afterpastor learned that the bylaws gave the minister sole discretion and oversight for an endowment fund that subsidized the summer Sunday school camp. After her predecessor was accused of sexualizing relationships with camp teachers, it was later discovered that he had also used funds from this endowment for his personal use. Other congregations, however, demand that an afterpastor stay far away from the church's affairs. One afterpastor, who was also an intentional interim, said that when she showed up an hour before Sunday service began, as was her custom, she was questioned about what she imagined she needed to do, arriving so early. Another discovered that some issues were being settled in premeeting board meetings, so that he could not participate in the discussions.

Nearly all afterpastors describe a general reactivity to their presence or position that encumbers their work and relationships. In one congregation, a minister merely had to casually mention a fondness for something and the thing was produced, whether the item was popcorn at vestry meetings or a designated parking space. In another, an afterpastor came to realize that if he expressed an interest in something being approved, reasonable or not, the board swiftly defeated the idea. A few describe reactivity so acute that it made them lightning rods for every upset, conflict, and complaint—large or small—in the congregation. When news of a predecessor's alcoholism and sexual abuse of teenage girls first reached the membership in one church—information the afterpastor learned for the first time by reading it, as they had, in the newspaper—the vestry blamed her for not being sufficiently capable to manage keeping the information secret. In another congregation, a minister reported that no error in his daily rounds, no matter the scale, went unnoticed or undiscussed. Some congregations have had a succession of ministers with these same experiences. Repeatedly, each minister is blamed for whatever is not right in the congregation.[2]

More often afterpastors are triangulated in petty, perennial conflicts or caught in webs of mixed messages. Not a few afterpastors indicate that nearly every interaction contains some element of reactivity, confrontation, disrespect, and challenge. Communications are characterized by boundary challenges, power struggles, threats, and coercion. Each requires considerable perspective, diligence, objectivity, and grace from the afterpastor, lest he become entangled in the dynamics.

No wonder, then, that many afterpastors report experiencing increased stress. The constant boundary violations and confrontational interactions provoke in the afterpastor a sense of urgency, hypervigilance, and increased anxiety. "I am always on high alert," said one, "always on edge. I used to be able to get away a bit each day and relax, but I can't seem to since I've been here." Another reported that she was fine until church members started using worship announcements to broadcast their positions on controversial issues, including the guilt or innocence of her predecessor, who was accused of "falling in love" with a prominent married congregant. Not until, with the help of a few vestry members, she was able to reestablish appropriate guidelines for announcements and people began to behave less rudely could she relax enough to focus fully on her sermon.

Secrets and Disclosure

In congregations where a predecessor's misconduct is kept secret because of an agreement made with judicatory officials as part of a negotiated resignation, or because the predecessor is still in ministry or considered in good standing pending adjudication, stress is particularly acute. Not knowing the secret keeps a minister in the dark about the real meaning of organizational and individual behaviors and disadvantages him or her in pastoral work. Missing key information, a minister can make decisions that prove ineffective or hurtful.

Knowing and not telling also isolates a minister. One afterpastor reported a church leadership's disappointment with her inability to analyze what exactly was wrong with the church. Her hands had been tied by the bishop, who told her of a predecessor's misconduct, saying, "You should know this," and then instructed her never to speak of it. The energy that goes into keeping silent and keeping others silent is not available for more productive, positive activities. Protecting a secret, a minister must actively if covertly deflect people's attention from activities, conversations, or information that might lead them to the secret. Sometimes, not being able to talk about what happened leads to an afterpastor becoming the object of people's frustration, anger, and criticism.

Even congregations where a previous pastor's misconduct is known may function poorly. Uncomfortable acknowledging past misconduct or incredulous and upset at an afterpastor's suggestion that a previous minister may have engaged in misconduct, a congregation develops a pattern of anticlericalism and organizational upset. Scapegoating a succession of afterpastors, the congregation blames each one for the current difficulties.[3] The lay leaders of one congregation, whose long-tenured, widely influential previous minister had admitted to sexual relationships with women and inappropriate touching of teenage girls, nevertheless berated and vilified their new minister for speaking of the predecessor's misconduct. Only after she resigned was it learned that two previous ministers had been similarly, if more discretely, scapegoated.

Less stress is reported by afterpastors who believe they know as much about the nature of previous misconduct as can be known or certainly as much as is known by the people with whom they serve. When misconduct can be acknowledged publicly and when lay leaders and afterpastors can collaborate on ministering in the aftermath, considerable healing can happen. One congregation that chose to speak about a previous minister's misconduct, despite denominational officials' concern that they might expose themselves to legal action, was able through public and private opportunities for debriefing and counseling to foster widespread healing and to alter long patterns of organizational dysfunction.

Still, the public disclosure or acknowledgment of a predecessor's misconduct—for example, in public meetings with denominational officials, newspaper reports, and legal proceedings—can pose a significant strain on an afterpastor. The preparation for a congregation meeting held for the purpose of disclosing the misconduct to members involves multiple conversations and tasks. Each individual with whom an afterpastor speaks during preparations can require time and pastoral tending around issues of betrayal, loss, and anger. Newspaper reporters often want an interview or a quotable response to a predecessor's actions. Constantly being on the spot to give an appropriate pastoral response or walk a narrow line between being forthcoming and legally prudent is stressful. When afterpastors are responsible for disclosing misconduct, public backlash can occur, and an afterpastor's capacity to serve all people well, especially those who do not believe the allegation, can be damaged.

How Some Afterpastors Respond

Because of congregations' reactivity and stress on the afterpastor, early terminations and shorter tenures are common among afterpastors. Some afterpastors who meet with extreme criticism early in their ministries negotiate an immediate departure. Others, often in congregations where misconduct is a secret, are asked to leave lest the secret be discovered. A few congregations, whose membership or resources have been depleted in the aftermath of misconduct, can no longer afford a full-time minister and may encourage a minister's departure by reducing hours.

More than a few afterpastors have considered changing professions after serving a betrayed congregation. "I never imagined ministry to be like this," said one. "I feel brutalized and defeated, utterly ineffective. I probably should leave or do something else." Some afterpastors acknowledge feeling depressed. "I can't shake how frustrating and demoralizing this experience is. Nothing I do is good enough or makes even a dent of difference to the upset here." A few afterpastors have said that they had found the support of a therapist or coach essential to navigating the interpersonal and organizational chaos of these ministries. A few others report that they had sought treatment for depression or anxiety.

The stress afterpastors experience is frequently expressed somatically. A previously healthy minister serving a congregation where misconduct has occurred can develop physical ailments. Some afterpastors report trouble sleeping, disturbing dreams, and chronic fatigue. One confessed the need for a daily nap "just to make it through the day." Others complain of physical ailments: frequent colds, sinus conditions and headaches, inexplicable rashes, painful joints and muscles, gastrointestinal problems, and chest pains. A few note an increase in or the return of symptoms of previously addressed or chronic conditions: compulsive eating and weight gain, diabetes, high blood pressure, pain from a previously healed back injury. One experienced interim minister, shocked to discover he was an afterpastor, was under pressure to resign after only four months. After suffering a heart attack, he took disability, preempting the pressure to resign. Another, who had known his new congregation was going to be a challenge, was nevertheless unable to continue serving when he experienced a recurrence of serious back pain, requiring surgery and a long rehabilitation. Clearly, good, stable health and access to good medical care help afterpastors serve and survive better.

Afterpastor ministries can be tough on personal relationships. Some afterpastors experience difficulties in their marriage or upset among family members. Ministers often rely on their partners or spouses and family members for support. In the face of increased need for support, relationships may suffer. Families often take second place to the church's demands on a minister's schedule and attention. Afterpastors and their families fare better when a healthy balance between personal and professional life is reflected in their weekly schedule. A minister who has unusual family demands—for example, a chronically ill or disabled family member, an aging parent, or several younger children—would not be a preferred candidate for an afterpastor ministry.

Managing Well

Ministry as a profession is often challenging and stressful. All ministers do well to carefully manage their stress and foster good health, but those serving in afterpastor ministries must give extra attention to stress management and wellness issues. Under extreme stress or situational challenge, some ministers may choose coping strategies that are neither effective nor healthy. Afterpastors who overwork, try to be all things to all people, or substitute professional relationships for personal ones will increase boundary challenges and their risk of ethical violation. Regrettably, afterpastors do appear to have an increased risk for misconduct. Whether this increase exists because of the unique challenges and strain on afterpastors or because betrayed congregations are confused about professional boundaries and do not clearly foster appropriate conduct cannot be known.

Support Groups for Afterpastors

Nancy Myer Hopkins, one of the primary contributors to this volume, was once making a presentation to a group of afterpastors about the dynamics of grief in a congregation where clergy misconduct has occurred. Hopkins reports that as she spoke, she suddenly noticed the faces of the people she was addressing: they themselves were experiencing deep grief about their situations. They were dealing with multiple losses, including lost dreams about "the ministry that might have been" in the congregations they served. As she reflected on this grief, she concluded it is quite possible that the personal grief of the afterpastor is greatly intensified by the phenomenon of countertransference that operates as an unconscious dynamic between cleric and congregant, much as it does between therapist and client. (See chapter 9, "Afterpastors," for a discussion of transference and countertransference.) In other words, clergy experience the grief of others vicariously, and this just adds to the personal burden.

Sometimes congregations will flatly refuse to do anything about their problematic past, and, most disconcertingly, the refusal can be coupled with the assertion that this current pastor is really the problem. Under this circumstance, the afterpastor will need to work with a therapist, pastoral counselor, or spiritual director who is knowledgeable about the dynamics of traumatized congregations. Family members can be supportive, but they are unable to bear this burden, and it is not fair to ask them to. A judicatory staff person might help start an afterpastor support group, or several afterpastors can establish one themselves.

A good model for structuring such a group—as developed by Hopkins, Patricia L. Liberty, and me—includes several elements:

1. Find a professional facilitator who understands the issues. If necessary, ask him or her to learn more about the dynamics of congregations that have been betrayed.
2. Work across faith traditions in your region. This is a great shame-reduction strategy and immensely enriches the sessions.
3. Sign people up for a specific number of sessions and get commitments that they will be at every meeting, barring emergencies. Limit the size of each group.
4. Give participants chances to describe dicey congregational situations and to have access to the group's wisdom for solutions.
5. Help participants determine if and when the messages he or she is getting are "not about me" or "about me."
6. Offer some family of origin work, but be clear that this is not a therapy group. Often the themes prevalent in a pastor's family of origin and the re-

ligious system dovetail. Participants can be invited to answer such questions as: Who is getting under your skin, and why? What family member are you reminded of? Who in your family supported your decision to go into ordained ministry? How is the stress of your position affecting your relationship with your current family, and how are you taking care of yourself? It helps to see the humor in some of these situations. Often they are bizarre in the extreme, and a good laugh helps.

Group members will also want to explore how much of the anger the afterpastor is feeling originates in residual anger still circulating in the congregation from its own grief. Therapists have long been aware of this dynamic; now we know that it is also present in the congregant/pastor relationship, and it is not limited to pastoral counseling sessions. Therapists are trained to welcome and deliberately use transference and countertransference during structured counseling sessions, however, and there are far more boundaries established by the psychotherapy profession. Unlike clergy, therapists are not living day to day with their most troublesome clients. Clients are not harassing therapists at the door on a Sunday morning, calling with endless harangues during the family dinner hour, or threatening to get therapists fired tomorrow.

The afterpastors will also want to help one another take responsibility for setting their own personal boundaries, such as letting people know that the answering machine picks up messages during family time in the evening and that only emergency matters will be dealt with after a certain time of evening. Afterpastors may also need support from denominational officials to establish new boundaries, however. Because boundaries have always been egregiously violated in these congregations, people may test them, to see if this pastor "really means it."

From Surviving to Thriving

Besides participating regularly in a support group, afterpastors can take additional steps to nurture and maintain their own well-being. Regular medical checkups are essential. Regular exercise, meditation, scheduled leisure and family time, and regular sleeping and eating patterns have proven helpful. Healthy and effective professional practices used in the past may need to be rigorously followed. Constantly contending with interpersonal triangulations and mixed messages can be crazy making. As discussed above, having support in sorting out the crazy moments, identifying what is about one's own "stuff" and what is about the unusual challenges of this particular congregation, can greatly enhance the afterpastor's personal well-being and professional practice. Afterpastors appear to serve and survive best when greater attention than usual is given to stress management and health maintenance and when their need for additional support and resources is recognized by denominational officials and congregational leaders. Roles and responsibilities of afterpastors are discussed further in chapter 9 as well as in chapter 25, "Psychological and Spiritual Resources for Afterpastors."

Although the primary contributors to this book have sought to create a "strategic survival manual" for afterpastors, as mentioned above, their hope has been that afterpastors, as well as the congregations and judicatory leaders who work with and support them, will not only survive but, over time, thrive. Congregations are called by God not just to "manage," but to be at work in the world. Congregations led by healthy, well-supported afterpastors can move beyond the betrayal they have experienced and once again open themselves to God's direction and begin to serve as they are called.

PART 1

THE FIRST RESPONSE

When clergy misconduct is discovered, what can and should be done? The best wisdom indicates that, without revealing the identity of victims, the congregation must be told as soon as possible what happened and what the consequences will be for the offending clergyperson. Experience has shown that congregations where such disclosure is not made are negatively affected by the "secret" for perhaps generations, impairing the congregation's ability to carry out its mission. In part 1, Nancy Myer Hopkins provides detailed guidance for a congregation disclosure meeting and follow-up care for members.

1

BEST PRACTICES AFTER BETRAYAL
IS DISCOVERED

Nancy Myer Hopkins

AS SUNDAY SERVICE AT FIRST CONGREGATIONAL BEGINS, Janet is surprised to see that the leader is not her pastor. Her anxiety increases when the stranger announces before the first hymn that he is the conference minister, and there will be a meeting following the service to explain the pastor's absence. Janet sees people turn to each other in confusion as they struggle to absorb the implications of the news.

Bill and Jane have been members of St. John's Episcopal Church for 25 years. For the past six months, they have struggled to maintain their equilibrium while their rector, accused of having been sexually involved with two women, undergoes an evaluation and an investigation as a disciplinary process proceeds. Jane has been a member of the vestry, and she is exhausted. Bill sings in the choir, and he, along with most of the choir, is angry. Next Saturday, they will attend a daylong meeting to hear the result of the disciplinary process, and each of them is looking forward to the event with feelings of both dread and hope.

James is being installed as the new intentional interim at Messiah Lutheran. He begins his ministry following a lengthy process that has helped the congregation through a string of disclosures about a popular youth leader's abuse of three girls in the youth group. The youth leader is now in jail. James knows that many people continue to be in conflict over the meaning of events, and despite his training, he is apprehensive about his ability to provide a steady and helpful ministry in this place.

Irene has been parish secretary and receptionist at St. Jude's Catholic Church for 20 years. She has provided people with a steady and reliable presence in the parish as priests have come and gone. Father Michael was a favorite of hers; his sense of humor always saved the day. However, Father Michael was suddenly removed three weeks ago with little warning and no explanation, and Irene is devastated. She is fielding many phone calls from distraught parishioners, and she doesn't know why this had to happen.

All four of these people experienced being in a congregation in crisis stemming from a leader's betrayal of trust. How can parish clergy, denominational staff, and lay leaders best respond to all the people who are affected by betrayal?

A New Vision for Triage

In medical terms, the word *triage* means the allocation of scarce resources brought to bear when a critical event causes harm to many people. Those who are judged to be the most critically injured but whose situation does not appear to be hopeless are given help first.

How would people respond if a deranged bomber were to succeed in blowing up a building filled with innocent adults and children? And, after a long period of confusion and dithering by officials, who knew the bomber well, a single ambulance appeared to whisk away only the bomber? And, meanwhile, all direct victims, the family members of victims, and those in the wider community who were thoroughly traumatized by the event were left to fend for themselves?

This may seem like a strong analogy to apply to the way faith traditions have historically dealt with clergy misconduct, but I use it to make a point. Victims/survivors and their families experience much damage, which in the most egregious cases can indeed be life-threatening. The harm spills over and affects congregations, as well as those who must manage the cases and administer justice, other clergy, and the wider community. The results are long lasting. They can include loss of trust in all leaders, severely compromised spirituality and sexuality, and diminished emotional and physical health for anyone who is sucked into the vortex of the system's response. Those who serve as pastors in traumatized congregations are themselves at risk, because they are often asked to carry the burden of grief and unresolved anger that frequently continues to lurk just below the surface.

To summarize the old way of handling these cases, the offender was sent to treatment, given financial assistance, and often given a "geographical cure." The victim/survivor received at most a small financial settlement, often in return for silence. Because nothing was revealed about the abuse, all those secondarily affected were ignored. Even if a case became public, no thought was given to the needs of the congregation.

In a more effective practice of triage, the old order is reversed, so that the needs of victims/survivors and all secondary victims take precedence over the needs of the offender. This new practice represents a radical change and can be expected to meet a lot of resistance. Of course, the offender does need assistance from the faith community, yet the others need more—much more. A just response for everyone must prevail if any religious tradition is to survive, even thrive, in good health.

The Congregation's Needs

The focus of this book is primarily the congregation and its leaders, particularly the afterpastor. To ensure a just response for these parties, best practices in the immediate aftermath of the discovery that a clergyperson has betrayed the congregation require the following:

- A system prepared ahead of the need to respond fairly and well to victims/survivors, the accused, and to all who will be affected by hearing that a religious leader has had complaints brought against him or her.
- Ongoing support for:
  — Clergy remaining on staff
  — Professional and support staff
  — Lay leaders, especially if they must be primary decision makers
  — The entire congregation
- One or two full congregational disclosure meetings as information becomes available.
- Disciplinary rules established to ensure as fair a process as possible for all parties, with general principals clearly articulated and understood by all clergy and laity, especially by those who must administer the policies. (See chapter 16, "Judicatory Leaders.")
- Enlightened legal advisors, chosen for their understanding of the conflicting and yet legitimate needs of everyone. (See chapter 19, "Attorneys.")
- Denominational officials who understand the conflicting agendas of the various parties as they manage a difficult case.
- A paid specialist on staff who is trained to respond to leaders' betrayal of trust. This specialist might be shared by several ecumenical partners, to everyone's advantage.
- Trained response teams. These may include investigative teams; legal advisors; advocates, who are not lawyers, for complainants; support people for the accused and their families; and pastoral response teams for congregations. (See chapter 17, "Response Teams.")
- A fair process for the accused. (See chapter 23, "Responding to the Offender and Family.")

Even if all these resources are in place, a case that is blowing up in everyone's face may create chaos in the congregation and even the judicatory or denomination as a whole. At a time when level heads are needed, good sense can be a scarce commodity. For some reason, perhaps because of denial, many church leaders try to do this difficult work without preparation and without asking for outside assistance. If people without training or guidance try to respond, the outcome can be disastrous. One of the entities that will pay dearly for a lack of preparation for dealing with clergy betrayal will be the congregation.

The Crisis Begins

A well-prepared system, however, can respond appropriately as soon as an allegation of clergy misconduct is made, thus decreasing the congregation's burden. The crisis period actually begins when an emotional or sexual boundary is crossed by a clergyperson. Tragically, it is the victim who carries the biggest burden of the trauma until he or she decides to come forward. If the offender is not so badly impaired that he or she still has a conscience, an additional burden will rest on that person. At the time a complaint is made, officials begin to carry their share of the load. If disclosure is made, the burden spreads to all who hear, and the crisis for the entire system begins. The crisis period ends when the results of an investigation and careful disciplinary process are disclosed and processed by the congregation and the wider system. All parties who have a legitimate need to know the outcome of those deliberations then begin to carefully absorb and respond to the news.

An Optional First Disclosure Meeting

If a clergyperson is given a leave of absence, pending an investigation, because of concerns about someone's immediate safety, a two-step disclosure process is helpful. The first step occurs at the time the leave (usually with pay) begins. Officials first notify lay leaders, describe the investigative and disciplinary process, and ask for their help during a meeting to be held with the congregation. Thus, the first disclosure meeting, which will be with the congregation, immediately draws on the strengths of the laity, and this in turn begins the long process of reempowering the laity.

There is no easy way to give people bad news, and the timing is always terrible; however, a church official should do this first disclosure on the first Sunday that the clergyperson is absent. A simple statement that the clergyperson is not present and that an explanation will immediately follow the last service is about all that is necessary at that point. The normal sermon time should not be used for the disclosure, as that may result in ruining the worship experience for people for a long time to come. A follow-up letter can be sent the next day to inform all those who were not in worship that Sunday.

Following the last service of the day, people gather for a two- to three-hour meeting. If the space can be arranged so people can see each other's faces, the meeting may go better, but this is not essential. Local wisdom on this and other similar matters can be your guide. Providing a light meal before the meeting begins, or during a break, may help people maintain their composure and think more clearly. Such common-sense details should be monitored as people embark on what is going to be a painful journey for many. Most of these details can be taken care of by lay leaders, and they will welcome a chance to do something—anything—to nurture their fellow congregants.

The meeting begins with a presentation, preferably by the person who had the most responsibility for deciding that the leader needed to be removed immediately. If legal tangles are anticipated, a lawyer can also help with the disclosure by clarifying legal issues that are often distorted if counsel is not present. Typically, not a lot of information is available at this point, other than that a serious allegation has been made and, as a result, the denomination's disciplinary process has been activated.

The presenter needs to be clear about how much to say and avoid being stampeded into giving more information than is appropriate. The investigative and disciplinary process can be described, and the normal range of responses that congregations experience can also be noted. If the complaints involve sexual exploitation of an adult, the presenter should explain why these complaints must be taken seriously—that a sexual relationship between a pastor and a parishioner is never an affair, because it is always the cleric's responsibility to maintain ethical boundaries. Handouts that further explain the fiduciary responsibilities of clergy and the complex interplay of power between cleric and congregant also help. (See chapter 2, "Theological Reflection," and chapter 4, "Power and Abuse.")

By this time, many people may be in tears or upset in other, perhaps less obvious, ways. Lay leaders who have met earlier with officials will often quietly move to sit beside the people they know will be most devastated by the news. With great sensitivity, they seem to know how to be present for their fellow congregants as the news starts to sink in.

The purpose of this first meeting is pastoral. The intent is to minister to people who may be traumatized and grieving because of their attachment to the person who has betrayed their trust, or who sensed something was wrong but were afraid to say anything. At this point, shock and denial are common responses. It is not unusual for people who were especially fond of the accused person to be in total denial and therefore angry with the messengers or the victim.

Do not muddy the waters at this meeting by asking if there are other victims. Sometimes officials responsible for making the hard disciplinary decisions will be tempted to do just that. However, there are at least two good reasons why this is not recommended. The first is that such an invitation is an inappropriate "fishing expedition" that interferes with due process for the person accused. Such a move can heighten people's anger at church officials, because they begin to fear that the disciplinary process will be unfair to the accused. The second reason is that usually no preparations have been made to assist victims. Most people who have brought complaints would say that even though they are glad they did it, in the end, the process was far more arduous and damaging to them than they ever thought possible.

The Primary Disclosure Meeting

The primary disclosure meeting, perhaps the second of two meetings, takes place soon after the final outcome of the investigative and disciplinary process. There is a fairly narrow window when people will come to a five-hour congregational meeting, but if we hit that window, one to four weeks following the outcome of the disciplinary process, they will come. Together they hear the results and have a chance to ask questions. They will also listen attentively to each other as they share their emotional responses to all that has happened to them. We have learned that an evening is not long enough to do this well. People do much better in such an intense setting if they are not tired, hungry, or rushed. A well-managed meeting can set the congregation on a completely new footing in many different ways.

The disclosure team usually consists of one or more officials coached to be nondefensive; a lawyer who can authoritatively field the thorny legal questions that are often asked; an outside facilitator, skilled in managing the reactivity, who is in charge of timing; and several counselors for anyone who becomes distraught. Members of a judicatory response team, if trained and available, may fill many of these positions. Local lay leaders may arrange logistics and provide hospitality and may also be trained in about one hour to facilitate the small-group listening sessions. Groups of six or eight people are seated at small tables throughout the meeting space and then simply turn in their chairs to face the speaker for the plenary sessions. Larger congregations may need to schedule several identical meetings in order to accommodate everyone.

Consideration for Victims/Survivors

When the disclosure meeting is being planned, leaders must keep in mind that names of victims/survivors are never disclosed by officials. Sometimes victims/survivors will want to attend a meeting and tell their story. This issue is complex, but such participation should be strongly discouraged if the victim does not have an opportunity to work intensively with an advocate both before and after appearing at such a meeting. Most victims are not well along in their own recovery when disclosure is being made, and most congregants are not able to hear a person's story without questioning at least some of it. Many congregants do not yet understand how damaging sexual abuse or exploitation is to direct victims. There is a high probability that some people will overtly blame victims, even child victims or their families. Because victims/survivors are so vulnerable, even a relatively mild question can feel to them like a revictimization. Likewise, an incognito appearance at a congregational meeting can be traumatic for a victim because inevitably, despite facilitators' best efforts, victim blaming will occur.

Very occasionally, a group of victims who have begun working together on their recovery will come forward, and collectively they will be strong enough to participate without risk of revictimization. They can support each other, and if they choose to speak to members of the congregation, they can help the congregation understand the damage done to victims. If they see themselves as witnesses rather than victims, they can indeed provide a powerful witness. However, in my experience, these cases are relatively rare, and they are still very risky.

There may be better ways for victims/survivors to be heard and for congregants to begin to understand the victim's experience. One strategy is to invite survivors to speak to a small group of carefully chosen and prepared representative lay leaders. Another is to make available videos and reading material for congregants. A third is to hear from a victim/survivor who has recovered well from a completely unrelated situation.

Disclosure to the Congregation

The key elements of a five-hour disclosure meeting have been identified through experience with numerous congregations. First, congregants must be given enough information in the disclosure meeting that they are unlikely either to minimize events or to blow them out of proportion. A written statement is read by the highest church official available, preferably the one responsible for making the decisions about the disciplinary outcome. The presence of enlightened legal counsel will help assuage anxiety about legal issues. The statement should be read, not delivered from notes or off the cuff.

Plenty of time should be allowed for questions of clarification. It is not necessary to answer every question, especially if people want more details than is appropriate. If in doubt, leaders should stop and confer with others on the team. A good facilitator can judge when the questions have gone on long enough. There is a point at which further questioning just increases people's frustration, but as long as the conversation remains civil and productive, this process will discharge a lot of negative energy.

Many religious leaders are not comfortable with conflict and would prefer to avoid meetings that have the potential for conflict. They should be coached to expect challenges and anger, and to understand that because this anger and conflict is largely a result of trauma and grief, it is important to remain nondefensive. Sometimes it is appropriate for religious leaders to apologize for their own failure to aggressively investigate or reveal earlier allegations. If so, the leader should apologize.

Sometimes it will be obvious that this segment of the meeting needs to go on longer than the time allotted. Flexibility should be built into the schedule. Lunch can be a "moveable feast," and people should be warned at the beginning of the meeting that the need for flexibility is anticipated. Such an announcement is helpful, so those who are compulsive about schedules will not become any more upset than they already are.

Sacred Listening in Small Groups

Sacred listening is a facilitated sharing of people's emotional responses to all that has happened. The process usually lasts from 45 minutes to an hour. The following guidelines should be provided in writing to each participant:

- You are invited to speak without interruption.
- All who wish to speak will do so before anyone speaks a second time.
- You may pass; you will still give the gift of listening.
- What is shared in the small group does not leave the room.

It takes an hour to train small-group facilitators chosen from the congregation for their "people skills." They are reminded that the purpose of the group is to allow each person who wishes to, to process his or her emotional responses to events, *not* to gather more data on the person who is being investigated or disciplined. However, if people want to tell of their own experiences of his or her previous ministry—positive, negative, or mixed—that is OK, and it usually does happen. In the telling, often the complexities of the situation emerge.

The facilitator's main job is to gently but firmly enforce the "no interruptions" rule. Sometimes using a device, such as passing a Bible or a "talking stick" to the person who is speaking, is helpful, because it clearly identifies who has the floor. It is not advisable to go around the circle in order; rather, each person should be free to choose when to speak. Inviting people to ask for the talking stick and then to offer it to another is a good way to structure the process. The facilitator is also responsible for deciding when she might need to call on a team counselor for assistance, should one of the group members become distraught or out of control. I have learned that there is one forbidden "F" word in congregations—"feelings." So I usually avoid it entirely but talk instead about "emotional responses to events."

There is a predictable flow of energy in the small groups. In the beginning, they may be hesitant to speak, but once someone begins, it gets easier. As trust develops, people will usually open up more, and there may be tears. Toward the end of the process, the mood in the entire room will lift, and it is not unusual to hear laughter.

The response team members will stay in the room where the small groups are working. Periodically, someone will check on each group's progress. This helps to keep long-winded small-group members from using too much time. As the end of the small-group time approaches, twenty-minute and five-minute warnings can be given. Expect that some groups will engage better than others. If some groups move quickly through the process, perhaps tripping lightly over emotional responses, the facilitator can suggest that they use up the time responding to each other, perhaps stating first what they heard another say and checking to see if that was accurate.

This segment of the meeting accomplishes much on many different levels. When clerical power has been abused, the laity have often lost their voices. Sharing in small groups is the beginning of the restoration of trust, opening up communication, learning that it can be safe to reveal one's innermost hopes and fears. The idea that this is sacred listening and not a debate will often help participants start healing the wounds that can lead to trauma-based conflict.

Lunch

Taking the time to have a simple communal meal is an important part of the process. This work is intense, and the afternoon will go better if people take a break. As noted above, it is a good idea to make the schedule flexible, as it is sometimes hard to judge how long the first two segments of the meeting will take. The disclosure and questions may take all morning.

9

Education

The education component of the meeting will be tailored to circumstances and can also address issues that the congregational leaders and staff know need attention. Common themes are the power imbalance inherent in the clerical/congregant relationship, understanding the experiences of direct victims, and naming the congregational dynamics of communal grief when people are grieving different things and on different timetables. Making good reading material available can help immensely. (See appendix A, "Resources.")

Where Do We Go from Here?

Those who plan the disclosure meeting need to think ahead of time about next steps and be prepared to explain them to the group. Participants in a disclosure meeting are always concerned about people who are not present at the meeting. Common questions about next steps include: What will happen to the disciplined cleric and his or her family? How do we interpret and address any split that has occurred in the congregation? When will we get a new pastor? What about the youth and children?

This is a good time to announce scheduled return visits of the pastoral response team. (See chapter 17, "Response Teams.") Some people will feel less anxious if they know that the congregation is not expected to manage alone once this meeting is concluded.

Spiritual Reflection

The disclosure meeting is also a good time to begin empowering people to take back responsibility for the quality of their own spiritual lives. In small groups or the larger group, people can be asked to listen to each other say where and how they know God to be in their midst. Sometimes people find it helpful to reflect on the words of a familiar hymn or scripture passage. People have no hesitation about entering into this task, and it ends the meeting on a very positive note. If arrangements have been made for a replacement pastor to serve the congregation, he or she deliberately keeps a low profile throughout the meeting. At this point, however, this pastor is invited to close the meeting in a way that best fits the congregation's worship style.

Next Steps

Congregational leaders, who may have been immersed for months in the minutiae of managing this situation and who are most likely *very* tired, blanch when told that this meeting represents the beginning, not the end, of the recovery process. Much of their burden can be lifted if they appoint a task force to carry on the work of recovery. The task force should be primarily made up of lay people from the congregation who can assess the needs of members and find resources to address those needs. A time limit on their work, such as six months or one year, is advisable. This strategy also restores power and responsibility to the laity. (See chapter 12, "Lay Leaders.")

Opening Old Cases

The best argument for disclosing clergy misconduct is seen in the dis-ease that occurs in congregations where one or more cases have not been disclosed. Sometimes a pastor enters a new ministry in a congregation knowing that there is a problematic history surrounding former leaders, or even more disconcerting, finding out that such is the case after accepting a call. Unfortunately, many clergy are unwitting afterpastors, serving congregations that have a strong anti-clerical streak or exhibit other symptoms of a troubled relationship with former pastors. Occasionally congregations will seem severely conflicted or depressed with no obvious explanation for the general malaise that seems to permeate even the very building. Whether afterpastors uncover predecessors' misconduct or remain in the dark, they often feel the brunt of the collective, displaced anger generated from unresolved past issues with former leaders. In many cases, even if the precipitating events of long ago are largely forgotten, the shadow images of those events—the ghosts—are still present.

One common scenario when a new pastor arrives is that the people start testing the pastor to determine his or her trustworthiness: "Can we trust you with our secrets?" Little by little, information surfaces that implicates one or more former leaders. In an uncanny way, the information continues to spill out, but it is shrouded in secrecy. Members offer bits of information: "Not many know this, but . . ." or "Old Mr. Pray always used to say that there was a lot going on during that time that we did not know about. . . ." The pastor confronts his or her superiors and learns that either they are clueless, or they knew and covered up. Sometimes, unconscionably, the superiors still refuse to talk with their clergy about what they know.

Old cases may be opened up but only after carefully weighing the risks of disclosure against a congregation's need to know. Because afterpastors who discover misconduct often feel this burden to be a heavy one, they commonly react by seeing everything that happens in the congregation in light of this past and think that if the ghosts can just be dealt once and for all, then the current troubles will magically disappear. Unfortunately, recovery is not quite as simple as this.

Is It Wise to Open Old Cases?

Several steps need to be taken before making the decision to disclose old cases of clergy misconduct. Because opening such cases involves some investigative work and may violate the unwritten "no talk" rules of the congregation, the afterpastor should not try to do this alone. Both denominational staff, beginning with someone in the office of the person responsible for disciplining clergy, and lay leaders should be involved. As much as possible, those investigating want to find information that is a matter of public record. It is not unusual for a case to have been public for just a short time and then repressed. Because people were never given permission to talk about the betrayal in community, it has been "forgotten." Notes of lay leadership meetings going back as far as possible, public information available in local law enforcement archives, and archived press clippings are all good sources of information.

The next step is to ask, "Who will be negatively affected if we open this case now?" The only people who absolutely must be considered are those who were victims. Sometimes their families must also be considered. If they are known by name and still residing in the community, it may be possible to make a face-to-face visit, describe the effect that the secret keeping is having on the congregation, and ask whether they are willing to have the congregation reopen those events. If any victim/survivor says "absolutely not," because if the secrets are told, everyone will immediately know who the victim/survivor is, the case cannot be opened. The needs of direct victims must always be placed ahead of the congregation's need to know.

If careful investigation leads to the conclusion that an old case cannot be opened, those involved should acknowledge that, at least for now, this strategy is not acceptable and move on to another plan. Although opening old cases may be a good way to help a congregation recover, less direct strategies can be employed. (See chapter 10, "Congregations," and chapter 25, "Managing Situations that Might Never Be Good.")

If leaders get a green light because no victim or family member will be revictimized, there are still likely to be others who will resist dealing with the "family" secrets. Unspoken congregational rules will need to be broken, and quite possibly, the same rules pertain in resistant individuals' own families of origin. Some people might also fear losing power if they no longer hold a secret. Some might be holding on to related secrets of their own. If it can be demonstrated to people that keeping such secrets often results in severely skewed relationships and communication, some of the resistance may fade. It will not fade entirely; yet if a majority of lay leaders decide that the risks to be taken are acceptable, and direct victims (and perhaps family members) will not be harmed, the light is still green.

Some of the hardest events to deal with are those that were painful for many in a congregation but, because the behavior did not fit then current definitions of trust betrayal or power abuse, did not result in a formal complaint. Examples are clergy who were tyrants and regularly engaged in severe emotional abuse, or conversely, those who were emotionally or physically absent much of the time, those who were alcoholic or mentally ill, or those who arrived in a congregation with one spouse and left with another who was from the congregation. Other commonly tolerated behaviors may have involved clergy who made women extremely uncomfortable or who abused children or exploited adults—but against whom complaints were never lodged. Laity in these same chaotic systems can also engage in destructive behavior that is still tolerated and hard to confront, thus causing even further damage.

If the decision is made that disclosure can be done safely, without revictimizing any victims/survivors in the process, it is usually helpful to examine the entire history of the congregation, not just the negative and shameful pieces. (See chapter 10, "Congregations.") One way to open things up is to ask leaders and perhaps people from a cross section of selected families in the congregation to meet on retreat for a day or weekend. If the congregation is small, the entire congregation could be invited. It is important that people know what they are being invited to do. The task is to tell each other the story of this particular faith community. Planners may select an organizing device, such as tracing a great faith journey that draws on themes from the Hebrew and Christian Scriptures: What are our Genesis, Exodus, crucifixion, and resurrection stories? The entire life of the congregation can be celebrated by creating a time line and presenting the results to the entire congregation. The format used for the second disclosure meeting, above, can be helpful.

Once the history is laid out for everyone to respond to, members may immediately shut down again. Old cases that are reopened will need to be addressed in the same way current crises are. The congregation will need to relearn how to live together in relationship, creating norms for good behavior and good boundaries (not imposed from outside the congregation or from above). Structural changes may be required, and it would not hurt to examine how the congregation is affected by the wider culture, where much shallowness prevails and civility has, sadly, been lost.

If a congregation chooses to embrace the hard work of recovery when clergy betrayal is disclosed, the results can be astonishingly positive. The work is arduous and sometimes painful, but there are rewards. People agreeing to engage with each other in good faith often embark on a profound spiritual journey, and they do it together. The community can only be stronger as a result.

PART 2

MODELS FOR UNDERSTANDING WHAT HAPPENED

Clergy misconduct can be viewed from a variety of perspectives, each of which will affect how the misconduct is understood. Some perspectives are more helpful than others, although they all have value and limitations, depending on how they are used and in what circumstances. One perspective might be more enlightening when the victim is an adult, another when the victim is a child. One might provide crucial guidance for the days and weeks immediately following disclosure, and another might clarify what strategy will best promote ongoing recovery in the congregation. Those who work with congregations where misconduct has occurred need to understand and carefully select the frame they use at each stage in a congregation's recovery.

2

THEOLOGICAL REFLECTION: NAMING THE PROBLEM

Patricia L. Liberty

THEOLOGICAL REFLECTION PROVIDES A FOUNDATION for assisting congregations in the aftermath of misconduct. A congregation's theology shapes how it names professional misconduct and provides the key to its understanding of the issue. It provides the crucial vantage point for answering the question, "What's wrong with this picture?"

At its best, theological reflection reminds a congregation who it is and what it believes. It grounds a congregation in what is central about its faith, practice, and mission. In short, it reminds the church what it means to be the church when the trauma of abuse is otherwise all encompassing. It also provides the language that a congregation uses to name the abuse.

The strengths and weaknesses of theological reflection as a model for congregational recovery are inherent in the theological concepts considered. Choosing an appropriate theological construct provides the foundation needed for a congregation to do the hard work of recovery. Similarly, choosing too narrow a theological concept or using a theological concept that does not apply to the situation further damages a congregation and undermines recovery. In congregations where there is persistent malaise in the aftermath of abuse, it may be helpful to revisit the theological framework used for understanding the abuse. The theological concepts we most commonly turn to when dealing with clergy misconduct are sin, evil, and, specifically when sexual abuse occurs, adultery.

Sexual Sin and Adultery

Clergy sexual abuse is often referred to as "sexual sin" or "adultery." While these terms may reflect a value of the congregation regarding the importance of sexual purity and fidelity, they are too narrow to name the damage done to the entire congregation. They also fail to describe the level of brokenness and betrayal experienced by victims and congregations. Further, they encourage a privatization of the behavior that keeps the focus on the sexual activity of two individuals rather than on the betrayal of the sacred trust of the office and the pain caused an entire congregation. Clergy sexual abuse is the misuse of power in a sexual way, but focusing on the sexual nature of the behavior is not helpful. Barbara Walsh, a social worker from the Department of Training in Rhode Island, trains counselors, child protective workers, and others in matters relating to sexual abuse and family violence. She illustrates the point well by asking the following: "If I hit you in the head with a frying pan, have I committed a cooking crime?" Similarly, the sexual involvement of clergy with their congregants is not a "sexual sin" but an abuse of the power and authority of the pastoral office that is manifest in a sexual way.

"Adultery" is not only too narrow a theological concept to describe the harm done to the entire congregation, but it is also an inaccurate concept for understanding clergy sexual abuse. Adultery is sexual behavior that happens outside a relational covenant, usually marriage, though it may also include the violation of celibacy vows. In either instance, the focus of adultery is on the violation of the relational covenant and not the betrayal of the office. A second problem with the adultery theology is that it fails to name the power imbalance that exists between a pastor and congregant and errantly assigns equal blame for the behavior to both parties. While it is true that relational covenants are broken in clergy sexual abuse, it is important to note that the adultery is a *consequence* of the abuse, not the foundational construct for understanding it. This distinction is especially difficult for spouses or partners of the victim and the clergyperson to make, because they name the behavior at the point where it affects their life. For them, the behavior is primarily an adulterous affair. While it is important to validate their experience and pain, it cannot become the focus of understanding for the entire congregation.

Sin

Sin can be a more helpful theological construct for congregations. Encouraging reflection about what exactly the sin is and whose sin it is can be empowering to both victims and congregations who are struggling, confused, and misplacing their blame and anger. Congregations will misdirect their anger and, if the misconduct was sexual, blame victims by claiming that the victim "seduced" the pastor. Victims often blame themselves for not being smarter, stronger, purer, and so forth in their own behavior and desires. By identifying the sin as the abuse of power and the betrayal of trust, congregations can hold onto a theological concept that has meaning for them (sin) while accurately naming clergy misconduct, including sexual abuse. Using the language of sin helps avoid misdirected anger and blame and keeps the congregation from overfocusing on the sexual nature of an offense, when that is an element of the misconduct. The sin is the pastor's sin: misusing the power and authority of the office, betraying the trust of the congregation, violating the vulnerabilities of someone who comes to them for help, misusing Scripture and prayer to manipulate victims, and the like.

Evil

Using the language of evil can be helpful, provided that the evil is conceptualized in a way that supports a broad base of reflection. The evil to be named even in clergy sexual abuse is *not* sexual behavior in general, sexual behavior outside of marriage, or homosexual behavior, though all these things may be problematic, given the community's understanding of human sexuality. The evil to be named here, regardless of the nature of the misconduct, is the shattering of the pastoral office, the derailing of the community's mission and ministry, and the deep damage done to victims and their families as a result of the betrayal. Lying, deceit, and deception are necessary to hide clergy misconduct from the larger congregation. Victims are isolated from the community, and the pastor's accountability is nonexistent. Individuals, treasured religious traditions, Scripture, sacrament, and prayer are manipulated. Adult victims of sexual abuse report with chilling frequency that the pastor made comments such as "God knew how much I needed someone and sent me you" and "You are an answer to prayer." The pastor's misrepresentation of God's will and way are among the most profound manifestations of evil we can encounter in ministry. The spiritual damage done to victims is profound. Naming the sin and evil clearly is healing for both victims and congregations. It validates the deep spiritual damage and provides a foundation for sorting out what the pastor said and did from who God truly is.

The Remedy

Finally, the language of sin and evil offers an inherent remedy that can be articulated by the community of faith and expressed in religious rituals that are comforting and challenging—comforting in the sense that these rituals are familiar, challenging in that, when faithfully executed, they will push congregants to clearly articulate their best understanding of sin, confession, repentance, and grace. For example, confession is more than saying one is sorry. It requires openness with those who have been wounded as well as honesty with God. It presupposes an understanding of the behavior that is based on more than embarrassment at being caught doing something wrong. In a similar way, repentance means turning away from the behavior and seeking to live in wholeness. It presupposes a capacity for deep reflection about why the behavior emerged and an ability to articulate how one will live differently in the future. Repentance is more than remorse at being caught.

Further, reconciliation is more than everyone "making up" and forgiving each other. It should never be the goal of a judicial process or pastoral intervention. If reconciliation is to happen, it must be based on a full acknowledgment by the abuser about the damage done and an unwavering acceptance of responsibility for that damage. Any new relationship is then built on the ashes of the old and is guided by the needs of those wounded, congregation and victim or survivor alike. Most congregations want to rush to forgiveness and reconciliation as a way of diminishing their own anxiety and avoiding the deeper work of theological reflection and recovery. It is guaranteed to fail, and it does further damage to victims. Encouraging a congregation's deep reflection on these central theological themes provides a sufficient foundation for its own recovery as well as a framework for understanding the needs of victims and abusers alike. Engaging in purposeful, skillful, and directed theological reflection on the nature of sin, evil, confession, repentance, reconciliation, and grace can specifically move congregations from the tendency to use the language of sexual sin and adultery to a broader foundation that can support the work of recovery and deepen its understanding of deeply held beliefs.

3

JUSTICE-MAKING, ETHICS: DEFINING EXPECTATIONS

Deborah Pope-Lance

CLERGY MISCONDUCT BY SEXUAL ABUSE OR OTHER EXPLOITATION is fundamentally a violation of the ethical standards of ministry. The challenge and disruption that
follow clergy misconduct are evidence of the injury caused by this violation of
standards. Using an ethics model to understand misconduct and its aftermath
suggests strategies for justice making.

Few religious or clergy organizations felt the need to be specific about clergy
misconduct, particularly sexual ethics, until the late 1980s. Before that decade,
the unspoken ethic in ministry was that clergy should not, did not, and would
not sexualize or sexually exploit relationships with people they served. Numerous allegations of misconduct in every denomination, however, were met with
considerable confusion about the nature, adjudication, and consequences of
clergy misconduct. This confusion inspired the development of numerous ethics
codes and resources.

These codes vary in language and in clarity.[1] Some generally state that ministers are not to exploit the intimate bonds of congregants' lives or to take advantage of the access they have to congregants, but some leave out any specific
mention of sexual intimacy or sexualized behavior. A few obfuscate the matter,
indicating that exploitative relationships such as "those with children or other
vulnerable people" are always unethical. But these codes allow that a minister
must always examine his or her motivations and the potential for harm before
pursuing a sexual relationship with a congregant, suggesting that such a relationship might, upon reflection, turn out to be appropriate. To be preferred are the
many ethics codes that are consistent with statutes in 11 states that understand all
sexual conduct and behavior between clergy and those they serve as unlawful
and thus prohibited.[2] The absence of clear written ethical codes renders the

ethics model vulnerable to arguments, by clergy and others, that the particularities of a specific situation makes it an exception to the prohibition against sexual conduct in a ministerial relationship.

Core Ethical Principles

For those writing these codes and procedures, the work of the Rev. Marie Fortune is a well-known and widely utilized resource. Fortune articulates a clear and precise boundary for ministerial relationships, stating that it is always unethical for clergy to sexualize or engage in sexual contact with those they serve and focusing on the reason sexual contact or sexual behavior within a ministerial relationship is unethical.

First, "when a minister engages in sexual contact or sexualized behavior with a congregant client, employee, student or staff member," outlines Fortune, "it is a violation of role and of fiduciary responsibility."[3] Congregants and staff have certain role expectations of ministers. Among these is the expectation that ministers have a fiduciary duty, that is, a responsibility to use their resources, skills, knowledge, and office faithfully in the best interests of those they serve. A further expectation is that clergy, as part of their ministry, will not provide sexual services or pursue the fulfillment of their own or others' sexual needs. Sexual behavior is not part of a minister's job. Indeed, for example, when congregants come to a minister expressing concern about their marriage or their religious beliefs or their involvement as a member, it would be essentially incompetent pastoral practice for a minister to respond by sexualizing the relationship with the congregant. In this way, a minister's substantial violation of fiduciary responsibility is not only unethical but also substandard delivery of service. In the aftermath of clergy misconduct, church leaders often do not recognize the harm that substandard service causes. This harm often leads victims and survivors to pursue legal remedies for their injuries and suffering.[4]

Second, Fortune says, "when a minister engages in sexual contact or sexualized behavior with a congregant, client, employee, student or staff member, it is a misuse of authority and power."[5] Ministers are granted by ordination and call a certain power and authority, and the responsibility to use these in the service of those who come to them for service. A minister's use of this power and authority and accompanying greater resources to initiate or pursue sexual contact with a congregant or others is both a misuse of office and unethical.

Third, Fortune clarifies that "when a minister engages in sexual contact or sexualized behavior with a congregant, client, employee, student or staff member, it is taking advantage of vulnerability."[6] Protecting the vulnerable from harm—that is, protecting those who have less power or fewer resources or who are exposed to possible injury—is a fundamental goal of ministry. When a minister sexualizes or allows the sexualization of a ministerial relationship, he or she is violating this goal. Indeed, a minister who engages in sexual misconduct harms the very people he or she was called to protect.

Fourth, Fortune concludes, "when a minister engages in sexual contact or sexualized behavior with a congregant, client, employee, student or staff member, it is an absence of meaningful consent." (See materials listed under "Ethics for Church Leaders" in appendix A, "Resources.") Because of the inequality inherent in the clergy/congregant relationship, stemming from differences in role, power, and need, the congregant cannot give meaningful consent to a sexual relationship. The absence of meaningful consent renders the minister's behavior coercive and thus abusive as well as unethical. In these four ways, clergy misconduct by sexual abuse or exploitation crosses a boundary in the ministerial relationship, violates the ethics of ministry, and perpetrates an injustice.

Justice Making

Whenever boundaries are crossed, trust betrayed, harm inflicted upon vulnerable individuals, and injustice done, a community of faith is called to bring justice and healing. Justice making—restoring to health and wholeness what has been broken or harmed—is essential to caring for those who are harmed by this breech of ethics and trust, to healing a congregation, and to restoring trust in the office of ministry. In the aftermath of misconduct, when those in positions of authority and responsibility take allegations seriously, formally adjudicate charges, and impose consequences, justice making can begin. More specifically, Fortune identifies seven aspects of justice making:

1. Truth telling: When the silence that has allowed abuse to occur and continue is ended, especially when victims can speak about what happened, justice making can be accomplished.
2. Acknowledging the violation: When the minister's conduct is named as wrong, as something that should not have happened, and when those in positions of authority condemn the behavior and express regret at the harm inflicted by the minister's conduct, healing for individuals and communities becomes possible.
3. Compassion: When victims' suffering and pain is heard and held caringly and empathetically, the isolation that contributed to the abuse is ended, and a new healing connection is made between those who have been injured and those who, through the ministries of the church, are called to mend brokenness.
4. Protecting the vulnerable: When steps are taken to prevent further harm (e.g., when an accused minister is suspended until allegations are adjudicated or when those who have been proven to have engaged in misconduct are removed from ministerial service), then the risk of further harm is greatly reduced.
5. Accountability: When denominations and congregations confront ministers who have engaged in misconduct by sexual abuse or exploitation and impose appropriate and significant consequences, they take essential steps in victims' healing and in restoring a minister—not necessarily to professional ministry but to personal health.

6. MAKING RESTITUTION: While nothing can replace what was lost through misconduct, acknowledgment of the harm done and some concrete means for repairing or healing that harm contribute both materially and symbolically to a sense that the wrong has been righted.

7. VINDICATION: Justice making occurs when victims are set free from the suffering and pain inflicted by the misconduct. Whether justice has been made must always be judged from the perspective of victims.

When these seven aspects of justice making are an integral part of pastoral and strategic responses to misconduct, the justice-making model can help heal individuals and congregations.

Limitations of the Model

As important as justice making is to healing after misconduct, this model is not as useful as others in understanding and responding to the often chaotic behavior of individuals and congregations. Affected individuals experience a variety of disruptions and emotions that justice-making efforts cannot address. Communities, whether confused about ethical standards or in denial about behaviors committed, are often complicit with misconducting ministers, enabling the minister's further abusive behavior during the adjudication process. Refusing to believe that the behavior occurred or that it is wrong, congregations may not allow denomination leaders access to their community, or they may retain an offending cleric despite the removal of ministerial standing. In others, a removed minister may continue to have influence over a congregation or may begin another congregation. All these actions will provoke controversy and conflict.

Those who engage directly in justice making in the aftermath of misconduct will need to be vigilant as they are pushed about by competing constituents with different perspectives on the truth. Supporters of an accused minister are likely to challenge an afterpastor who exclusively employs a justice-making model. They may see an afterpastor who focuses on justice making as an avenger who is unpastorally seeking only to prove an accused minister's guilt and impose harsh, unwarranted consequences. When an afterpastor is seen as biased, ministering to those who believe the cleric is not guilty may be difficult or impossible. Afterpastors who attend to justice-making issues may disappoint those who expect ministers to lower rather than escalate conflict and disagreement. On the other hand, denominational officials, especially those charged with training, certifying, and supervising ministers, will be expected to utilize a justice-making model and may not be directly challenged for doing so.

Justice making is an adversarial model, demanding a righting of wrongs and provoking self-protective stances by parties at odds with one another. While ethical standards are religious in nature, allegations of their violation are often adjudicated under the close watch of attorneys. Rather than attending to the communal and individual upset in congregations betrayed by clergy or to a restoration of the ministerial office and role, attorneys often focus on minimizing a denomination's or congregation's legal exposure and liability. When a justice-making model is used legalistically or exclusively, the church's ministries are diminished. In this way, the fundamental ethical and religious nature of the church is undermined and healing is nearly impossible.

The Value of the Model

Still, the justice-making model can be useful when appropriately applied. In the aftermath of misconduct, use of a justice-making model allows for the clarification and reassertion of the ethical standards and expectations of clergy. An after-pastor by his or her own highly ethical conduct helps restore appropriate expectations to the office of ministry. A denomination official who asserts the standard of competent and ethical ministry and imposes adverse consequences for failure to adhere to those standards vindicates victims and begins the healing process for individuals and a community. Failure to adjudicate allegations of misconduct adversely affects all other efforts to respond to and care for individuals and communities in the aftermath of misconduct. The justice-making model restores an ethical context for all actions.

4

POWER AND ABUSE: ESTABLISHING THE CONTEXT

Patricia L. Liberty

The power and abuse model for understanding clergy misconduct, particularly sexual abuse, is a cornerstone for the recovery of victims and congregations. When sexual abuse is involved, the model is the antidote to the notion that the pastor has had "an affair." It is the basis for understanding how and why a seemingly private act of "sexual indiscretion" has shattered individuals, families, and the congregation. The power and abuse model provides a basis for understanding all misconduct in a context larger than private sexual behavior. It focuses on the professional relationship between the pastor and the congregant and the responsibilities of that relationship. In addition, by acknowledging the congregation as the setting in which the abuse occurred, it validates the feelings of betrayal that emerge in the rest of the congregation. An individual *and* an entire congregation are affected by this behavior.

The premise of the power and abuse model is that the clergy role carries with it legitimate power and authority that is entrusted to the pastor by the congregation and validated by the denominational authority that confers the credential for ministry. The power and authority of that role is to be used in the best interests of those who are served by the role. Pastors are to care for their congregations in their role as preachers, teachers, and pastoral care providers. They are to preside over the sacraments with integrity, lead worship, and work with lay leaders to create an environment that makes possible faithfulness to the purpose of the church.

According to training materials produced by the Faith Trust Institute (formerly the Center for the Prevention of Sexual and Domestic Violence) in Seattle, clergy have a fiduciary relationship and responsibility to their congregations. (This responsibility is also an element of the justice-making, ethics model discussed in the previous chapter.) The term *fiduciary* is borrowed from the banking industry and means "held in trust for another." Clergy have a responsibility to hold the needs of their congregants in sacred trust. When sexual activity occurs between a pastor and congregant, that fiduciary responsibility is breached, and what is held in trust for the entire congregation is destroyed. When sexual activity between a pastor and congregant is framed in this way, it is easier to understand that the one with the fiduciary duty also has the responsibility to set and maintain an appropriate boundary for the pastoral relationship. The question of who pursued whom, how the sexual contact was initiated or continued, becomes irrelevant, because the pastoral role carries the inherent responsibility for maintaining boundaries.

Advantages of the Model

Once the power and authority of the pastoral role and the responsibility for boundary maintenance is established and the focus shifts from the sexual aspect of the relationship to the pastoral context and its wider implications, it is easier to understand the needs of adult victims. Congregations are often confused about adult victims, because of the mistaken notion that equal age (or similar age) means equal responsibility. After all, no one thinks sex between adults and children is a good idea, but it can be difficult to understand the problem with sex between two adults who in many other ways may *appear* equal. The power and abuse model clearly shows how sex between two adults is every bit as abusive as sex between an adult and a child when one of those adults is the pastor and the other is the congregant.

It is important that the principles of the power and abuse model be coupled with a theological base that establishes the sacred nature of the power of the ministerial relationship and its specific purpose in the life of the church and community at large. The ministerial office and the relationships established within it exist to enable the faithful ministry and witness of the church. As mentioned earlier, preaching, presiding over the sacraments, and officiating at rituals that welcome children, unite partners, and recognize death are at the heart of the ministerial role. Those activities establish the church as the place where individuals have myriad human experiences blessed and acknowledged by the divine and by a likeminded community.

As a way of sensitizing lay leaders and clergy to the betrayal victims and congregations feel in the wake of clergy sexual abuse, I often do the following exercise. On a blank piece of paper, participants are asked to list their favorite hymn, scripture, religious holiday, part of worship, and sacred space. Then I say: "Your favorite hymn is the one your abuser hummed to you while you had sex. Cross it off the list. And that scripture is one he quoted to you when you were upset and conflicted about what was happening. It holds little comfort now, so cross it off. Once you talked with him about why that holiday was so special to you, but when that season came last year, the sex became more intense and at times violent. The season now holds only pain, and you dread its return this year. Cross if off your list. During that part of worship, he would make eyes at you from the pulpit. You thought everyone noticed, but apparently they did not. You felt naked during worship. Cross if off your list. That sacred space—you told him about it, and later he asked to have sex there. It doesn't feel so sacred anymore. Cross if off your list." This type of sensitization exercise helps leaders get in touch with the religious and spiritual losses that are at the heart of clergy sexual abuse and clearly illustrates how the power of the role is twisted for abusive purposes.

Another advantage of the power and abuse model is that it minimizes the tendency to borrow the secular definition of sexual harassment and related standards. Churches do have a responsibility to provide a safe work environment for employees and volunteers, as established in the standards of the Equal Employment Opportunity Commission (EEOC) law on sexual harassment. These standards call abusers to accountability by acknowledging that the church is a workplace in the secular sense. Like many other secular notions applied to clergy sexual abuse, however, EEOC standards have their limits, primarily because they fail to address the deep damage to and betrayal of the pastoral role. In addition, the EEOC definition may have unintended and unhelpful outcomes for congregations. It is far too easy for congregants to get caught up in trying to "prove" whether the legal definition of harassment was met (based on criteria of time, duration, power relationships, and so forth) when the only question that needs to be answered is: Was the integrity of the ministerial relationship damaged? Any sexualized behavior, regardless of duration or intensity, will destroy the integrity of the pastoral relationship. This principle, not the EEOC standard, is the appropriate standard for evaluating complaints. The power and abuse model holds the sacred nature of the ministerial relationship and the vulnerability of the victim in clear focus for congregations as they struggle to understand what has happened. By keeping the focus on the professional relationship and its fiduciary responsibilities, congregations are given crucial tools needed to heal the deep betrayal caused by clergy sexual abuse.

5

CONFLICT MANAGEMENT: SELECTING THE RIGHT TOOLS

E. Larraine Frampton

CONFLICT IS PRESENT IN ANY SETTING and is to be expected in congregations where clergy have been removed for sexual misconduct. Conflict may involve relationships, differences in values or beliefs, decision-making procedures, unmet needs, communication processes, disagreement about the congregation's mission, and everyday "life."

Conflicts can occur shortly after clergy misconduct is disclosed to the congregation. These initial conflicts generally arise in two areas:

1. Relationships: the congregation's relationship with the clergy offender and victims
2. Decision-making processes: members' thoughts and feelings about how the decision was made by judicatory leaders to discipline and remove their clergyperson

The intensity of conflicts will vary depending on the degree of anxiety and loss the congregation experiences after the disclosure and removal of its clergyperson.

There are many tools from conflict management models that afterpastors, congregational leaders, and outside consultants may use, but the model or therapeutic process employed in misconduct cases must be carefully selected. The goal of most conflict models is to settle conflicts and to reestablish a relationship between disputing parties, but each has a specific emphasis:

- Mediation: to settle differences through reconciliation
- Negotiation: to reach an agreement through bargaining
- Arbitration: to adopt a settlement determined by an arbitrator (judge)

Clergy misconduct involves many issues, however, including the clergyperson's:

- violation of the professional ethical standards of ministry
- abuse of power
- betrayal of trust and fiduciary responsibility for members
- faith crisis or sin
- psychological breakdown
- breaking of the law (varies according to state law and age of victim)

All of these issues are relevant to clergy misconduct, but some conflict consultants, while addressing one or more of these issues, focus ultimately on maintaining or restoring the clergyperson's ministerial position. For example, some consultants will attend to the offender's sin and work with victims and the congregation to forgive the offender—with the goal of eventually allowing the clergyperson to keep his or her ministerial position. Some experts focus on the offender's faith crisis and recommend spiritual renewal—again, to restore the cleric to his or her position. Or some experts will focus on the psychological condition of the offender and recommend rehabilitation—and subsequently reinstatement to ministry.

I believe, however, that the goal of consultants in initial conflicts should not be maintaining or reestablishing the offender's relationship with victims, the congregation, or the wider church. The goal when addressing the initial conflicts regarding relationships and decision-making procedures in misconduct is the recovery of the congregation and victims. Clergy who violate professional ethics have to be disciplined in order to keep congregations safe from further abuse and give victims justice. In my experience, congregations in which the offender is not removed do not recover well. Victims who do not receive care and justice also have a hard time recovering. I caution consultants not to follow the usual conflict management models in addressing the initial conflicts that often follow the disclosure of misconduct to the congregation. *After* the initial shock of clergy sexual misconduct wears off, however, these conflict models are helpful to reestablish the relationship between the offender, congregation, and victims—if it is appropriate to do so.

My recovery approach is based on the premise that clergy have more power than members. Clergy derive power from the authority of their positions—whether or not members explicitly give them power. Faith communities generally assign clergy the power to interpret Scripture, forgive sins, administer sacraments, provide leadership, care for members, and carry out other responsibilities. The ministerial position in and of itself has tremendous relational power that is intensified by positive psychological and spiritual transference that members give to it, and as a result, to the clergyperson who holds that position. (The power of the clergyperson is discussed further in chapter 4, "Power and Abuse.")

A Trauma-Driven Conflict Model

When judicatory leaders disclose the clergy misconduct to the congregation, members can experience conflicting feelings toward their clergyperson. The more respected and revered the clergyperson is, the harder it is for members to integrate the facts of the misconduct. Members feel overwhelmed as they begin to think back on their relationship with their clergyperson and wonder how to interpret the good ministry they experienced in light of the clergy's misconduct. Questions arise such as:

- Does the misconduct erase the important ministry done by the offender?
- Was the offender constantly betraying them?
- Were the offender's sermons sincere?
- Were significant spiritual experiences led by the offender valid?

I use what I refer to as a trauma-driven conflict model to address conflicts that arise from faith-shaking events such as clergy sexual abuse or other misconduct.

Trauma can be described as any event outside the day-to-day experience that is extremely distressing and evokes reactions of fear, helplessness, and terror. These events usually involve the perceived threat to one's life or the lives of loved ones. Clergy misconduct traumatizes the primary victims, those who were directly abused, who fear disclosure will end their life as they know it. Clergy misconduct also traumatizes members (secondary victims), who wonder how their congregation will survive when their clergyperson is removed. Both primary and secondary victims suffer great loss because of their clergyperson's misconduct.

To address this trauma, I use various tools from conflict management models as well as from the Critical Incident Stress Debriefing (CISD) model (see appendix B, "The Critical Incident Stress Management Method for Debriefing a Trauma"). My goal is recovery, and my task is to provide a therapeutic process, so that members can safely express and discharge their emotions rather than act on them.

Disclosure of clergy misconduct can be so overwhelming to members that it is easier for them to deny the whole situation than integrate the truth into their experience (even if the offender acknowledges the misconduct). Some members immediately want to "forgive" the offender, with the intention that their beloved clergyperson will continue ministry with them. It is at this juncture that relationship conflicts begin. Members of the congregation can become polarized—those who want the offender to remain in the congregation against those who want the offender to leave. Or members can take a stand against judicatory leaders (and victims) and insist on keeping the offender as their minister. Sometimes members leave with the offender and start a new congregation. These initial conflicts need to be processed with a trauma-driven recovery model.

The Process

The entire trauma-driven conflict process needs to be followed. If it is not, recovery will be difficult and more conflicts can occur.

Conflicts have a better chance of being contained and short-lived when judicatory leaders invite the congregation to agree to the following guidelines:

- Believe that the congregation will recover.
- Trust the process.

- Move through the removal of the clergyperson by attending debriefing and recovery meetings.
- Use your spiritual resources to fortify yourself during the recovery process.

In addition, judicatory leaders can also establish communication ground rules for the congregation to follow. The communication ground rules can be presented by the judicatory leaders at every meeting with congregation leaders and members. Ground rules are particularly important at the disclosure meeting, because they provide safe boundaries for expression. Consultants for recovery should be aware of the established ground rules and announce them at every meeting with the congregation. Helpful ground rules include:

- Respect others.
- Do not accuse or judge.
- Speak only from an "I" position.
- Agree to be in different emotional places.
- If you are unable to abide by the ground rules at this time, please do not disrupt other members or the group process. You may make an individual appointment with a consultant.
- Questions or concerns should be directed to consultants or members designated by the judicatory leaders.
- Watch and pray. It is generally better not to make any major decision or take any drastic actions at this time.

With these ground rules in place, judicatory leaders conduct the initial disclosure meeting as described in chapter 1, "Best Practices after Betrayal Is Discovered." That meeting includes a small-group debriefing process, which may draw on a grief model or a critical incident model. While the disclosure immediately elevates members' anxiety, the debriefing begins to de-escalate that anxiety. I generally recommend CISD for cases involving children, multiple victims, or heinous offenses. In cases where the clergyperson has sex with one member and they subsequently marry, the grief model may be more appropriate.

In the months following disclosure, congregation leaders, perhaps working with a judicatory response team or outside consultants, will need to do the following:

- Use rituals, worship services, and other spiritual resources to nurture the congregation.
- Tend to the needs of the victims. (See chapter 11, "Victims/Survivors," chapter 22, "Remembering the Victim," and chapter 28, "What's Ahead for the Victim?")
- Educate the congregation regarding the functioning of the congregation as a system and, when anxiety has lessened, the dynamics of clergy misconduct. (See chapter 6, "Systems.")
- Work to establish safe practices and policies. (See chapter 22, "Creating Safer Congregations.")

Trauma-driven conflicts are not as easily contained as this process may seem to suggest. Initial conflicts surrounding relationships and decision-making procedures may still arise and need to be addressed after debriefing. In my experience, however, the intensity of the conflicts can be lessened and even contained enough that members can work through them. When conflicts cannot be contained and polarities are beyond reason, members will begin to split the congregation. Judicatory leaders will need to convey to congregations the ecclesiastical polity and consequences of the split (see section below on intensity of conflicts).

Tools from Conflict Management Models

Although mediation, negotiation, and arbitration conflict models may not be suitable for dealing with all types of congregational conflict in the aftermath of clergy misconduct, all three models offer tools that can be used to help a congregation recover. Tools that these conflict models have in common are establishing ground rules, separating issues from people, neutralizing issues, assessing the source and intensity of the conflict, and understanding relational systems. Although the tools are similar, the way these tools are used will vary from one model to another. For example, arbitrators have power to dictate the process to be followed, while mediators and negotiators will recommend the process.

Separating Issues from People

One of the tools for relationship conflicts is separating the issues from the people involved; however, this is extremely difficult to do in cases of misconduct. At worst, the issues of misconduct can become personified and twisted in the following ways:

- Victim(s) are the "seducers" who made their clergyperson stray.
- Judicatory leaders are the "offenders" for not treating their clergy with the same forgiveness and love that members receive.
- Offenders are the "victims" of seducers and judicatory leaders.

In situations where the people cannot be separated from the issues involved, especially when offenders are seen as being persecuted, an intense conflict can explode. Members become polarized and begin to choose sides: those for and against the clergyperson, judicatory leaders, and the victims.

At best, the issues are separated from the people, and the situation is understood in the following ways:

- The clergy offender violated the professional ethics of ministry and abused the power of the ministerial position.
- The clergyperson did some good ministry but has to be removed because of the violation.
- Victims have been hurt by the misconduct and will need care.

Neutralizing the Issues

It is not possible to neutralize clergy misconduct. However, consultants and leaders can lessen the emotional intensity by initially focusing on only one issue: the violation of ethical standards of ministry. Members generally understand that professionals such as therapists, lawyers, doctors, nurses, or teachers who violate their professions' ethical standards are removed from their position. Their removal does not mean that people did not get good care from them. It means that in some instances, they violated the professional ethics they agreed to uphold. The focus on the violation of ethics does not negate the fact that there was an abuse of power and that victims were involved. It simply creates a less explosive focus, one that allows members to process their feelings.

When the victims are children, judicatory leaders can focus on the abuse of power. Members generally understand the power differential between children and adults.

The Intensity of Conflicts

Consultants and leaders can assess the intensity of the conflict to determine what conflict model, if any, is appropriate. Alban Institute senior consultant and author Speed Leas, borrowing from models of conflict developed by the military, divides conflict into five levels. Level one is the lowest level, and five, the highest. The lowest two levels can generally be managed with mediation between members, but the highest three are very difficult to process.

In the highest levels of conflict, members become inflexible and self-protective. Secrets are kept, and communication is closed. Members quit communicating with leaders and one another, secrets are kept by small groups, people are more concerned about getting their way and establishing that they are right and others are wrong, and so forth. In general, people are too emotionally distraught to trust others to care for them, and they are unable to listen to reason.

In the higher levels of conflict, triangulation also abounds. Some members will perceive the judicatory leaders as taking sides against the offender and for the victims. Other members will perceive a certain group is against the congregation and supporting the offender. The triangles can be numerous.

When the level of conflict is high, consultants and other leaders need to choose one of the conflict models to use with members. The process *cannot* involve mediation between offenders and victims with the purpose of allowing offenders to remain in the congregation. That absolute aside, consultants and other leaders need to choose the conflict management model appropriate to the situation and will need to stand firm for the conflict model they choose and refuse to take sides, judge or punish members, or threaten members with excommunication. Some members may choose not to abide by the process and may be asked or choose to leave the congregation, but that is their decision.

Consultants and leaders can explain the elements of the selected conflict model: establish ground rules, create open communication, separate people from issues, neutralize the language, practice active listening, hold frequent meetings, and the like. The challenge will likely be getting the faith community to agree to the process. Sometimes resistance can be overcome by focusing on a common need—the recovery and survival of the congregation.

There are intense conflicts in which no conflict model will work. This usually occurs when polarities are fueled by intense emotions and differing beliefs about how the offender should be treated. For example, a group of members is willing to leave the congregation and perhaps the denomination and begins worshiping in a new place—with the offender as pastor of the new congregation. Or a majority of members wants to stay in its place of worship with the offender as pastor and wants the judicatory leaders and any members who disagree with them to leave them alone.

Judicatory leaders and consultants do not have the power to prevent members from leaving their denomination, and congregations do split. At that point, judicatory leaders can rely on ecclesiastical polity, guidelines, and procedures that can offer a measure of predictability. Judicatory leaders can inform members of the denomination's polity and the consequences of their refusal to remove the offender or their departure to start their own congregation. For example, the congregation that remains with the offender will no longer be a part of the larger religious body. As a result, the congregation will lose its property and building, financial assistance from the denomination or judicatory, access to future clergy candidates, and benefits such as pension and health insurance for clergy and staff.

The Afterpastor and High-Level Conflict

If the afterpastor enters the scene when the level of conflict is high, ground rules for communication, behavior, process, and contracts should be in place before that ministry begins. The afterpastor will need as much support and as many resources as the judicatory can provide.

When the afterpastor has been in the community for a relatively short time, factions in the congregation might lift up the "sins" of the afterpastor to judicatory leaders and plead that he or she be removed. The challenge for the judicatory is to resist being triangulated against the afterpastor and for the factions. This is not the moment to conduct a pastoral performance review, even if congregations request it. My experience has been that congregations use pastoral performance reviews at this time to prove that the afterpastor is ineffective and should be removed.

The judicatory leaders may have some power or leverage at this juncture in the congregation's life, because they are the ones who appoint or recommend potential clergy for the congregation. They can use that leverage to encourage members to support outside consultants, who can stabilize the system and provide a process to address the real issues, rather than the personality of the afterpastor. The judicatory may refuse to recommend candidates until the congregation has complied with the process.

Conflicts about Decision Making

The congregation as a whole or a group of members may be angry at the judicatory for disciplining and removing their clergyperson. If the congregation does not respond to debriefing and the conflict intensifies to a high level, the judicatory will need to draw on the arbitration model. The judicatory must stand firm in its decision, although that may mean some members may end up forming a new congregation with the offender as the pastor.

Some members may be angry at the judicatory for disclosing misconduct to the congregation. A common reaction to hearing about clergy abuse is to shoot the messenger. The messenger in this case is the representative of the judicatory who made the disclosure of clergy misconduct to the congregation. This is not an altogether negative reaction. When the judicatory serves as the lightning rod for all the anxiety and anger, it can allow the response team members, consultants, and other leaders to remain neutral and gives them time to debrief intense emotions without being targets.

Symbolic Conflicts

When disclosure is greatly delayed or there is no disclosure, pastors who follow the offender often experience conflict with the congregation for years to come. Unresolved anger or distrust of each successive clergyperson is acted out in indirect and subversive ways. Leaders will find a pattern of short-term clergy with three- to six-year terms.

Types of conflict that can be symptomatic of the ongoing dynamics of clergy sexual misconduct include closed communication system, poor boundaries, dysfunctional decision-making processes, different levels of knowledge about the abuse, and all the other dynamics indicative of clergy abuse. Consultants may be able to use a conflict model to resolve such conflicts, but sometimes conflicts continue regardless of any intervention.

History Taking

When conflicts do not resolve after the presenting issues have been addressed, the conflict is usually a sign that some experience in the congregation's past was never revealed or dealt with. Consultants can use history-taking tools to gather information about previous clergy and their behavior. The history-taking event can function like a delayed debriefing, in that it can expose unresolved feelings about past clergy. When members can identify some of their feelings about past clergy, they can begin to change their behavior with their present clergy. (See Oswald and Friedrich, "An Evening of Historical Reflection," listed in appendix A, "Resources," for a process for conducting a history-taking event.)

Choosing a Conflict Management Model

There are many conflict models available to leaders. The conflict models that I have found helpful are those developed by the Alban Institute (Speed Leas), Bridgebuilders (Peter Steinke), and Lombard Mennonite Peace Center (Richard Blackburn). I have worked with all three of these models and I have found each model to be of value when used in the situations for which it was designed. I find all the tools and skills practiced in these three models to be necessary when working with any conflict. I recommend taking one or all of the workshops these organizations offer—first, to learn the specific skills required, and second, to establish a repertoire of conflict management models that can be drawn on as needed for each specific situation. The flexibility consultants and other leaders will acquire by learning all three models best ensures that congregations will receive the guidance they need.

6

SYSTEMS: IDENTIFYING THE ROOTS

Candace R. Benyei

MOST OFTEN, IF NOT ALWAYS, the roots of the tragedy of clergy sexual misconduct have grown in the soil of the "family history" of the congregation. To look through the lens of this model means to envision the congregation as a family system. A system is an integral unit in which each element, much like those in a hanging mobile, is connected to and influences the movement of the other elements. Therefore, this perspective views the congregation as a network of folks connected by the threads of a common history whose actions, reactions, and unconscious agendas influence the behavior of the entire group.

The threads of common heritage are the historical experiences of the congregation, be they joyful or painful, along with the "family rules"—formal, informal, and tacit—that the group forms in response to its experiences and then passes down from each generation of constituents to the next. Most particularly, the action and reaction of congregants to these family rules often predispose a congregation to a certain vulnerability to clergy misconduct as well as to the perpetuation and cover-up of misconduct.

System Rules

Formal rules, such as constitutions and bylaws, form the exterior structure of the group. For instance, some congregations, by reason of the personalities that founded them, are clergy-centered or authoritarian. These families of faith may be at risk for misconduct, because the members are so used to being led by a strong central figure that they are unable to confront what seems to be unacceptable behavior. Role definition is often poor, so lines of communication regarding the handling of difficulties, particularly regarding the pastor, are muddy.

Informal rules are the "paint and wallpaper" of the sanctuary. They are the unspoken but generally acknowledged behavioral guidelines that the congregants adhere to. Examples of informal rules are: the baptismal font is *always* placed in the back right-hand corner of the sanctuary; we *always* have an eight o'clock and a ten o'clock service; we *always* have Eucharist on the fourth Sunday of the month; we *never* vote with a show of hands but *always* with a secret ballot. This last rule might spell trouble, because it keeps congregants from knowing one another's mind and knowing either where to seek support if it is needed or who is in an adversarial position and needs to be persuaded. Certainly this rule limits the flow of information and helps to maintain secrecy.

This brings us to the third category of rules: tacit rules. Members are not usually aware of these rules, which often would not make rational sense if challenged cognitively and almost always are destructive. Examples of tacit rules are: "Keep the secret"; "Don't rock the boat"; and "The pastor is always right." Needless to say, these rules, which result from earlier trauma either in the corporate life of the congregation or in the personal lives of the leaders, cripple the faith family's ability to act competently in the face of clergy misconduct and predispose it to ignore or cover up unethical behavior. Congregations with these sorts of rules are called "highly defended families." That is, they often look great on the outside, like a castle with solid high stone walls in good repair or the family that is known in the community for its philanthropy or its stellar church attendance. On the inside, however, these congregations are fraught with underground conflict and stagnation, just as castles often stank of human excrement and outwardly "model" families all too frequently conceal incest and physical abuse. These families, and similar families of faith, are too ashamed of themselves to allow outsiders to look in and help but instead steadfastly insist on "taking care of their own problems."

Destructive formal, informal, and tacit rules are formed in several ways. They may be introduced and enforced by outside authority, such as a dysfunctional denominational judicatory. A lay or clergy leader may introduce the rules, because they are familiar rules in that individual's family and the individual is comfortable with the resulting mode of behavior. Or they may result from the reaction of the congregation as a group to a particular trauma, such as the suicide of a beloved pastor who was finally forced to retire, clergy misconduct, or the mass exodus of a large part of the congregation after a particularly awful fight. In each event, and beyond conscious awareness, the group develops a set of rules and behaviors designed to not let that awful thing ever happen again. Unfortunately, the choices about what rules to put in place are often poor ones, such as deciding to deny that anything is wrong so as not to have to deal with it. Congregations that become "ruled" in this way are often a set up for clergy misconduct because they operate in a way that ensures tacit support of unethical behavior or at the very least provides solid denial that bad things are happening.

Advantages and Disadvantages

This model provides an excellent way to understand the problem of clergy betrayal and why things went wrong, as well as guideposts for structural changes to heal the problems. Clearly, one task in such congregations would be to rewrite the bylaws to establish adequate role definition and adequate power checks and balances for important decisions like hiring, firing, and the disposition of funds. The systems model provides ways to uncover and confront tacit rules, so that the members begin to operate in a more conscious, rather than knee-jerk, fashion. The systems model also suggests ways for the members of a system to interact, such as using "I" messages and nontriangular—or direct, party-to-party—forms of communication, and introducing and strengthening boundaries, such as separating thoughts from feelings in interpersonal communication.

However, of itself, the systems model does not help the congregation work through grief or rage, make amends to members it has scapegoated, resolve conflict, or hire a functional pastor. Rather, it is most useful in helping to prevent future misconduct by enabling members to bring into consciousness those rules that make it vulnerable. Then, if the congregation is in a place where it can accept help, members may be coached in ways to change the rules so that it can function more competently. Bylaws can be revised so that roles are better defined. Lines of communication can be opened up and clarified. Permission can be given to talk about uncomfortable things, and grief and rage can be worked through. Ways to get the congregation to this place of healing are the subject of parts 3, 4, and 5 of this book.

7

GRIEF AND LOSS:
DEALING WITH FEELINGS

Patricia L. Liberty

THE PRINCIPLES OF GRIEF AND LOSS THEORY are extremely useful in helping congregations understand and resolve the myriad issues related to professional misconduct. Most people within a congregation have some experience with loss. A pastor with a modicum of skills can interpret the sadness, anger, and confusion experienced by her or his congregation using the language of grief and loss.

The grief and loss models help congregations move to the feeling level at a time when much of their energy is otherwise focused on the disciplinary and denominational issues related to the pastor, potential legal liabilities caused by the misconduct, as well as media issues, rumors, and other concerns. The congregation's move to the feeling level as a way of dealing with some of its pain is an important turning point in dealing with the abuse and moving toward resolution.

In addition, grief and loss models introduce the notion that time is a factor in resolving loss. Few individuals who have been through a loss think those losses are resolved in a short time. Common wisdom suggests that at least a year should pass before major decisions are made after the death of a loved one. Those who have suffered major losses, especially in unexpected or traumatic ways, know that it takes far longer than one year to establish a rhythm of healing and come to a new sense of peace and purpose in one's life. This perspective is helpful in validating the malaise and sadness that permeate a congregation in the aftermath of misconduct. There will always be a segment of the congregation that is ready to rush toward quick (and false) resolution, believing that once the offending pastor is removed, the "problem" is taken care of. Grief and loss models of understanding misconduct validate the need for time, an intentional healing process, and focused attention to complex feelings to heal in the aftermath of loss.

The specific stages of grief are outlined by various practitioners. The hospice movement makes the single largest contribution to the field of knowledge related to loss. Perhaps the most widely recognized of all theories is that of Elisabeth Kübler-Ross, who posits five stages to dying. Her landmark study *On Death and Dying,* published in 1969, revolutionized the way our society approaches terminal illness and loss. The five stages of denial, anger, bargaining, depression, and acceptance form a common vocabulary that most people can acknowledge. The issue of professional misconduct will always engender deep divisiveness and disagreement within a congregation. While members may not be able to agree on what the problem is and how to name it, most people will agree that there is a significant level of pain and confusion at work in their midst, pain and confusion that Kübler-Ross's model effectively names.

Denial

The individual stages described by classic grief theory also provide a context for understanding the different energies at work in a congregation as time goes on. The power of denial cannot be underestimated in the early stages of congregational recovery after misconduct. With or without healthy and intentional disclosure, denial is often a huge factor in congregations. If a structured disclosure has been made (see chapter 1, "Best Practices after Betrayal Is Discovered"), then denial is often expressed in clear and straightforward ways. People in every congregation will make comments such as "The victim is lying," "This can't be true," and "I won't/can't believe our pastor would do this."

If no formal disclosure of the betrayal is made, denial has a stronger advantage and is more difficult to address directly. Comments such as "People are just out to get him (her) because of (some other issue)" or "Sure, I heard that story, and there is no way it can be true" reflect the same level of emotional denial and are typical when the congregation does not have clear information to work with.

The remedy for denial is accurate information given repeatedly over time and combined with an empathetic and caring acknowledgment of the difficulty the information creates for the hearer. Comments such as "I realize this is very difficult to absorb, but it is the information that has come to us, and we are all struggling to accept that it is true" provide a consistent baseline that gradually chips away at members' denial.

There is no value in being confrontational with people in their denial, and it may be psychologically damaging. Denial serves as an emotional firewall, providing protection from information that is too painful and difficult to absorb all at once. The capacity to cognitively receive information and not emotionally absorb it is an important coping mechanism for people who are confronted with information that is potentially spiritually, emotionally, or psychologically overwhelming.

Anger

Those who are responsible for assisting congregations in the aftermath of professional misconduct are no doubt familiar with anger as a response. Denial is difficult to maintain in the face of incontrovertible evidence, which may be manifest in a pastor's loss of credentials, litigation, and additional information that comes from either disclosure or informal networks within the congregation. As the avenues for denial fade, there is often a strong anger response. It is frequently focused on the victim or complainant who may or may not be known to the congregation. In some ways, it is easier for congregations to focus their anger if the complainant is unknown to them, because they can attribute characteristics to the person that allow them to blame him or her. However, there is ample evidence that knowing the complainant's identity changes only the intensity and not the reality of a congregation's ire. Rarely is the anger focused on the offending pastor early in the process, because it is too painful for congregants to believe that their beloved pastor is capable of such behavior.

The line between denial and anger is fluid, and vestiges of denial may remain well into the anger stage. As denial and anger meld, it is common to hear comments such as "It's her own fault . . . she should have known better," "She has been chasing him for months. She is such a flirt; any man would have fallen for her deceitful wiles," as well as more subtle comments that acknowledge the truth of the allegations while drawing inaccurate conclusions. When a congregation focuses on its pastor's "powerlessness" in the face of such behavior, I often make the comment that if the victim was after the pastor's money, he would have been clear about how to respond appropriately.

People may also be angry that the victim is choosing to speak about what is perceived to be "a private matter." Many people in a congregation will see the pastor's misconduct as "an affair" and believe therefore that there is no place for a public or denominational disciplinary process. The privatization of professional misconduct by congregants is an expression of displaced grief that clouds the issue and contributes to denial as well as anger toward victims. (See chapter 4, "Power and Abuse.")

The appropriate response of pastoral, lay, and denominational leader toward anger is to assist in focusing it on the offending behavior and pointing it away from victims. Anger at everyone other than the pastor is a protective mechanism that shields people from the pain of their betrayal by a trusted religious leader. Congregations will not be aided in their recovery, however, if they are allowed to persist in their displaced anger. As time goes on, leaders need consistently and gently to challenge congregants' errant perceptions; however, this must be seen as primarily a pastoral task. Often members' appropriate anger, that is, anger at the offending pastor, comes much later in the process.

Bargaining

Bargaining is a short-lived but important part of a congregation's process. Congregations will often propose that their pastor go through whatever denominational process is demanded (counseling, professional growth, supervision, and so forth) and that they hold the position open so he or she can return later. In more extreme cases, I have seen churches unwilling to fire pastors even when they have been incarcerated for their offenses and had their credentials removed. Intentional, open, and well-communicated judicatory processes assist congregations in moving quickly through the bargaining phase, because they model the accountability required of the pastor. In addition, such clarity provides numerous educational opportunities that help congregations move from their early perceptions of the issue as a "private matter" or an "affair" to an accurate understanding of this as a deep betrayal of the sacred trust of the office. It places recovery on a broad, firm foundation while validating the feelings of loss, sadness, and anger as they appear through time.

Depression

Depression is an important and often lengthy part of congregational recovery, and it may be among the most confusing and distressing. Depression often comes many months into the process and catches congregations by surprise, because they think they should be "feeling better" and "getting on with it" by then. To feel themselves gradually sliding into a deep sense of malaise so many months into their process is discouraging; however, this is often the turning point in recovery. It is here that congregations have the capacity to feel at a deeper and nonreactive level that allows them to see the impact of the misconduct, how their own history as a congregation may have contributed, as well as implications and possibilities for the future. This can be a rich time of recovery and insight. Because depression is so painful, however, there is a tendency to deny it, hurry through it, or move around it without mining its riches. It is common to hear a congregational representative say, "We have been through this; there is no need to dig up ancient history," "Let's move on," "It's time for this to be over; we have a new pastor and there is no value in dwelling on the past," and other such comments.

Because there are those in every congregation who deal with their personal grief by deflecting the deep feelings of sadness and depression, they will believe that response is appropriate to the church's grief as well. While it is important to validate the varying levels of energy and insight that accompany congregational grief, the view that deflection is appropriate needs to be countered by those who have the energy and insight to lead the congregation to a deeper level of resolution. A skilled pastoral leader can provide much needed perspective to help a congregation in its corporate depression and gain the insights that come from it.

Figure 7.1: Dimensions for Congregational Healing

Three Rules
1. People can enter at any point.
2. People can go clockwise or counterclockwise, or can jump across, again and again.
3. This circle tells people that no matter how different from one another they look and feel, they are a unity.

SOURCE: Chilton R. Knudsen, "Dimensions of Congregational Healing." Used by permission.

Renewed theological reflection about who God is and how God interacts with humanity, the seeds of compassion for victims, the meaning of the sacraments, and the nature of worship and the church's ministry are arenas for renewed insight that can emerge during the depression stage.

Acceptance

Acceptance is a nebulous thing. At some level, individuals who have suffered the loss of a loved one are forever changed by their experience. Those who are faithful to their grief work, however, are strong witnesses to the truth that healing is possible. Each person resolves grief in his or her own way and goes on to live out of that understanding. A similar process is at work in a congregation. Individuals will come to their own understanding and peace with the painful events of their history related to the misconduct. Some people will never feel the same about the church, have the same level of involvement, or feel the same level of relationship with those who understood the issue differently than they. Even within families, there can be permanent and painful differences around a congregation's experience of misconduct. Agreement about what happened is *not* the indicator of acceptance. Agreement that the congregation has suffered and a renewed commitment to mission and ministry are more accurate indicators of acceptance and a readiness to move on.

Advantages and Disadvantages

The advantages of the grief loss model are many. Primarily it provides a feeling-based road map through the difficulty and complexity of professional misconduct in the life of a congregation. It introduces and validates the notion that the work takes time and that it is not easily or quickly resolved. The classic grief model as described here does not, however, translate exactly to a congregation's experience following misconduct, and it is important to remember that Kübler-Ross's original work focused on dying patients and not on the grieving survivors left by their passing. The model was developed to show how individuals faced their own death and not how others grieved the loss.

The work of nationally known grief therapist Therese Rando on traumatic loss is especially helpful in dealing with congregations that have been betrayed by clergy. Her book *The Treatment of Complicated Mourning* provides a framework for understanding traumatic loss that broadens and deepens the classic model in ways that are useful for this work. Other helpful models use a "grief wheel." One model, discussed in Trevor Powell, *Free Yourself from Harmful Stress* (DK Publishing, 1997), identifies four phases of grief: shock, protest, disorganization, and reorganization. This model is cited on numerous Web sites, including the Federal Emergency Management Administration site (see www.fema.gov/rrr/bereave .shtm). Another helpful grief wheel has been developed by Chilton R. Knudsen, Episcopal bishop of Maine. (See figure 7.1: "Dimensions for Congregational Healing.") Both grief wheels are helpful for naming the wide range of emotions people feel as they grieve.

⤶

Afterpastors and congregational leaders are wise to explore the literature on grief and loss as a way of assisting their congregations in the aftermath of misconduct. Those who work with congregations during this difficult time have found grief and loss to be one of the most helpful frames for understanding the congregation's own experience and moving toward healing.

8

TRAUMA INTERVENTION: PLANNING STRATEGIES FOR RECOVERY

Deborah Pope-Lance

MINISTERS, RABBIS, AND PRIESTS are not supposed to behave in a hurtful or violent manner. We do not expect to hear allegations that our spiritual leaders have committed immorality and abuse. Upon learning of such allegations, individuals and congregations can be incredulous, angry, even outraged. Later, they and their communities may become disrupted, dysfunctional, and devastated. Individuals may describe losing a sense of God's presence in their lives. In the aftermath of misconduct, congregations may fear the loss of their reputation or their purpose as a faith community. Whether clergy misconduct involves a specific event or a pattern of behaviors, many people experience it as a shocking trauma.

Characteristics of Trauma

A trauma is an event, sometimes a repetitive event, that usually involves threats to a person's life or integrity, or close encounters with violence or death that lead a person to feel threatened. In war, for example, soldiers experience danger and horror. Some react with extreme terror and helplessness. After a tornado, hurricane, or other type of natural disaster in which homes are damaged or destroyed, community residents experience acute stress and loss, and some may react with intense fear, agitation, and hypervigilance. Years after a trauma, some people continue to experience the original traumatic event or encounter.

Trauma and its effects have long been recognized. Military historians discuss "battle fatigue" in the World War II era, "shell shock" during World War I, and "soldier's heart" in Civil War accounts. But not until 1980 did the American Psychiatric Association, in large part because of research compiled from treating Vietnam War veterans, recognize post-traumatic stress disorder (PTSD) as a diagnosis.[1] Numerous armed conflicts, as well as any number of disasters and tragic accidents, acts of violence, bigotry, and oppression have enlarged the understanding of trauma and its aftermath. Some people push aside the trauma at the time it occurs and do not experience any reaction until long after the event. Others have immediate reactions, perhaps seek help, seem to recover, but then experience new symptons long afterwards.

Normal human reactions to danger or crisis include arousal, alertness, intense fear, and anger. These reactions appropriately and predictably incite a person to act to quell the danger or resolve the crisis. Extreme experiences of violence and disaster overwhelm these normal reactions and can render a person's actions futile. In post-traumatic stress disorder, long after the danger has passed or the crisis abated, these normal reactions can persist in an exaggerated form—or reappear after years without symptoms or even recall of the trauma—affecting emotions, thoughts, and memory.

A trauma survivor may display irritability or anger, difficulty concentrating and hypervigilance, and exaggerated or startled responses. A broad array of psychological symptoms may also be present—depression, anxiety, anger, flashbacks, dreams and nightmares, intense reactions to apparently unrelated phenomenon, avoidance, and dissociation. An increase in suicide is also evidenced in trauma survivors. The impact of the traumatic experience can also be somatized. Physical ailments and difficulties can develop. Sleep disturbances and headaches are common. The onset of major medical conditions or illnesses has also been reported.

People react differently to traumatic events. Both people in close proximity as well as those farther away from the geographic center of events can experience traumatic effects. Researchers do not know why some people are more adversely affected than others. Proximity to the event may account for this variance, as may previous experiences of trauma, the extent of material and emotional loss, and disruption of life circumstances. The incidence of PTSD is increased when the trauma involves extreme violence, injury, or gruesome loss of life.

Trauma survivors' ability to function in their daily lives often decreases, and meeting basic needs and demands can become an insurmountable challenge. Treatment for physical and psychological symptoms can interfere with home or work responsibilities and lead to loss of employment and property. Negative thoughts and unstable moods can lead to inaccurate perceptions and upsetting experiences. Low or diminished self-esteem and a mistrust of others can upset relationships. A view of the world as unsafe can discourage usual community engagements. Isolated by a life-altering experience, trauma survivors are sometimes forgotten or rejected by others who incorrectly imagine that enough time has passed and the survivor should be getting on with his or her life. Previously important relationships may be changed or ended by the trauma or its aftermath.

Trauma and Clergy Misconduct

The aftermath of clergy misconduct by sexual abuse or other exploitation resembles the aftermath of trauma. The behaviors and reactions of individuals who have experienced or witnessed clergy misconduct resemble those of victims who have experienced trauma such as tornados, train wrecks, random violence, and rape. In congregations, the chronic, intractable organizational dysfunctions that often follow clergy misconduct are similar to the reactions of communities and organizations that collectively experienced a traumatic event. The trauma of clergy misconduct inflicts significant personal and institutional loss. Clearly, both individuals and congregations lose their pastoral relationship with the offending cleric. Lost as well is any confidence that their minister was a reliable, moral person. Often, individuals lose their relationship with their congregation or with friends and family. Many more report disruptions or losses in their relationship with God.

In the aftermath of misconduct, several layers of trauma are experienced. Trauma is initially inflicted by the unethical, exploitative conduct. This first layer injures individuals who have been immediately involved in the misconduct—direct victims, their families, and friends. A second layer of trauma is experienced in the wake of the misconduct's wider disclosure. Congregation leaders and members are shocked to learn publicly that their spiritual leader engaged in misconduct. People in and out of a congregation often express a loss of trust in clergy and church organizations. Congregations, whose public face is their cleric, experience embarrassment over the media coverage and fear long-term damage to their reputation.

A third layer of trauma is experienced when congregation and denominational leaders respond inadequately. In an ill-advised attempt to limit damage to a congregation's or cleric's reputation, leaders may deny the seriousness of allegations, attempt to cover up or keep secret the misconduct, or fail to acknowledge and address the problem. Sometimes these attempts masquerade as confusion regarding ethical standards. Leaders, for example, may present the possibility that the precise alleged behavior does not appear on a list of unethical actions and therefore cannot be considered misconduct. At other times, misnaming the misconduct, for example, by suggesting that adultery may be a sin but is not specifically unethical, will obfuscate ethical standards and further traumatize.

A fourth layer of trauma is experienced by the absence of adverse consequences or clear accountability. Loss of a beloved cleric after adjudication can constitute trauma, but adjudication that does not lead to adverse consequences or removal of a clergyperson who has betrayed trust can also be traumatic. Confusion regarding appropriate consequences—proposing, for example, "Shouldn't we forgive and forget?"—often obfuscates the harm caused by the misconduct and can result in further trauma.

Advantages and Disadvantages of the Model

Trauma theory provides a useful model for understanding the experience of clergy and denominational leaders in the aftermath of misconduct, providing interventions for recovery and healing. Under this model, for example, individual victims and survivors who attend services but continue to disrupt them with their insistent allegations are understood to be suffering from shock and reactivity after a trauma. In this model's view, congregants who insist that victims' allegations are not credible and that a few "unstable women" should not be allowed to ruin their church are better understood as exhibiting the denial and anxiety common to witnesses of trauma.

Understanding clergy misconduct as a trauma helps identify these and other intense reactive patterns—not as a pathology to be cured, but as a pastoral opportunity to be addressed and tended. Individual survivors, like those traumatized by disaster or violence, need to tell and retell the story of what has happened. They need to hear the traumatic event acknowledged, to report the event to appropriate authorities, in order to make sense of the events. Through this repetitive process, they meaningfully integrate the experience of the trauma into their lives and faith. From this view, their insistence on telling or hearing the truth of the misconduct is not behavior intended to hurt a congregation but the action needed to heal and recover from a trauma.

Understanding the chaotic, reactive aftermath of clergy misconduct as the result of trauma helps afterpastors and others recognize that chronic distress and upset in a congregation are coping strategies initially utilized in response to a trauma. No longer needed, these strategies have become persistent, disruptive, and ineffective patterns of behavior. Once identified as not the fault of poor leadership or mismanaged organization, any efforts to change these patterns become more likely to succeed. In addition, recognizing that traumatic reactions can persist long after a traumatic event will help clergy and lay leaders who serve many years later develop strategies for continued response and recovery.

Understanding clergy misconduct as a trauma helps foster consistent, equitable compassion. Everyone, whether or not they agree that misconduct did occur or consequences are appropriate, is understood as having experienced a significant and terrible loss. Afterpastors and denominational leaders can then plan for the pastoral care of everyone affected, regardless of viewpoint or experience. Some people will be well served with direct contact, others by group programs and services, and others, particularly victims and survivors, by referrals to other helpers outside the congregation.

Understanding clergy misconduct as a trauma helps those who serve in the aftermath of misconduct to cope with the extreme reactions of individual or groups to their presence or actions. Often afterpastors, interim ministers, denominational officials, and response teams are met with distrust, suspicion, undue reverence, or dependence. Some afterpastors report feeling sabotaged or coerced. These reactions reflect individual or communal responses to a traumatic event and are not about the afterpastor, per se. They are not "about them." This distinction helps afterpastors not to take personal offense, exacerbate difficult interactions, or escalate disagreements, and helps them instead to find strategies to serve and survive well.

Understanding clergy misconduct as a trauma is not helpful, however, when the events and circumstances of a clergy offense have not been disclosed or cannot be discussed. Misconduct must be acknowledged in order to identify the occurrence as a trauma and its aftermath as a predictable reaction to a traumatic event. The circumstances of misconduct need to be discussable in order to utilize an understanding of trauma in formulating response and aiding recovery. Specifically, because trauma theory recognizes that recovery depends on fulfilling the fundamental need of trauma survivors—to talk about and make sense of what has happened to them—the inability to do so will diminish the utility of this model.

PART 3

ROLES AND RESPONSIBILITIES

All the players in the drama that unfolds in the aftermath of clergy misconduct have their own perspective on the situation and have different, sometimes conflicting, needs. Each also has unique roles and responsibilities, which are detailed in this section. Contributors describe common experiences and outline best practices for those involved. Although everyone has a different role to play, the healing work of each person or group tends to support the healing of the others, presenting the opportunity for deeper relationships, more mature faith, and a witness of hope to the wider world.

9

AFTERPASTORS: RESTORING PASTORAL TRUST

Deborah Pope-Lance

PASTORS SERVING IN THE AFTERMATH of a predecessor's misconduct often feel like emergency medical responders at an accident. First on the scene, emergency medical responders often feel compelled to attend to everything; however, training and experience teach them that they must not. Emergency medical responders should not be moving debris from damaged automobiles out of the way or directing traffic but should be doing the job of medical responders—tending to accident victims' medical emergencies. In the aftermath of misconduct, afterpastors, taking a cue from emergency medical responders, need to understand that they cannot do everything. Rather, afterpastors must do the job of pastor, restoring trust in the person and office of the minister.

Deciding What *Not* to Do

Beyond the many customary pastoral demands of a congregation—leading worship, teaching, conducting rites of passage, tending to administration, counseling—multiple crises and demands will be presented to afterpastors. Afterpastors may be called upon to interact with the media, minimize poor publicity, stem the flow of departing congregants, reverse financial downturns, restore organizational viability, replace ineffective leaders, and assuage people's disappointment, anger, and grief. An afterpastor may be asked to attend spiritually and pastorally to those who have been injured—direct victims and their families and friends, bystanders, the larger congregation and community, ministerial colleagues, and the family of the offending cleric. An afterpastor may be drawn into judicatory tasks intended to hold an offender accountable—cooperating with investigators, notifying denominational leaders, hosting a disclosure meeting, curtailing the clergyperson's professional activities, supporting victims who want to submit a formal complaint, assisting in complaint and legal proceedings, and responding to the questions and concerns of church members and friends. Any of these tasks may help individuals and congregations in the aftermath of clergy misconduct. But given the essential task of the afterpastor—to restore individual and congregational trust in the person and office of the minister—an afterpastor cannot do them all.

An afterpastor must determine which tasks only he or she can do and which can be done by someone else, whether now or later. Tasks that are the responsibility of others should be left to others to accomplish. For example, legal or investigation work is the responsibility of lawyers or judicatories, and in-depth or long-term counseling is best done by therapists. Meeting with the media, communicating restrictions to an offending predecessor, or conveying the facts of misconduct to congregation members should be delegated to lay leaders or denominational officials.

Regardless of how many other clergy or resource providers are involved, afterpastors are the only ones who serve as a congregation's or individual's pastor, fulfilling the roles of preacher, teacher, celebrant, counselor, and administrator. An afterpastor, no less than any pastor, relates as a religious authority, as a representative of God, as a caretaker of all that is deeply meaningful and spiritual for the congregation. Others may take on aspects of the pastoral perspective, expressing concern for people or supporting them in their faith and spiritual practices, but only the pastor has primary responsibility for those tasks. Others must sometimes temper their words and actions and say or do things a pastor would not. Others may even try to compel afterpastors to act in ways that compromise the afterpastor's role. For example, lawyers may advise afterpastors not to speak about a predecessor's imprisonment, lest the pastor's speaking invite a slander charge. Lay leaders, concerned that fundraising will be adversely impacted if the misconduct is acknowledged, may demand that an afterpastor not discuss the matter. But the afterpastor recognizes that pastoral care to individuals and congregation amid grief and upset is best extended when public facts are acknowledged in a straightforward and caring manner. Afterpastors, primarily charged with ministering to the members and friends of a congregation where misconduct has occurred, should never permit others' perspectives to eclipse their pastoral responsibility. If they do, people's pastoral needs will go unaddressed and opportunities to rebuild trust will be lost. On the other hand, when afterpastors attend to people's pastoral needs, the mission of a congregation is fulfilled, and confidence in both church and its ministry can be restored.

In all clergy misconduct, the trust accorded the position and person of the minister is violated. This betrayal of trust injures the reputation and office of the minister. When misconduct has occurred, a predecessor, whether because of or in addition to the misconduct, has failed to fulfill the roles and responsibilities of minister. In order to repair damage to the office of ministry and to restore pastoral trust, an afterpastor must do an adequate if not better job of fulfilling the position's requirements, showing that a clergyperson can do competent work and be worthy of the trust previously betrayed. Restoring trust cannot be done by simply calling or installing a pastor of impeccable character or reputation. When an afterpastor takes on the particular pastoral role and responsibilities, the specific position or office vacated by the offending predecessor, individuals and congregations must reexperience trustworthiness. Offending predecessors often conducted themselves in ways that were inconsistent and undependable—failing to be on time, complete tasks, keep confidences, or tell the truth. The first step in creating this experience is doing the basic job well, equitably, and dependably.

Challenges to Restoring Trust

The fact that a predecessor failed because he or she engaged in misconduct generates a unique constellation of unusually challenging conditions. Among the most critical conditions is the absence of a consistently positive and appropriately serviceable office of ministry. On a daily, sometimes hourly, basis, an afterpastor who does not have access to this essential resource experiences considerable difficulty in his or her work.

The office of minister includes the good repute, authority, and capacity customarily accorded to ministers by polity, cultural custom, and reputation. Included are the hope-filled expectations people have of ministers; the access people grant pastors to themselves, their families, and the congregation as a whole; and the influence and discretion they permit ministers to exercise. An afterpastor will experience damage to the office of ministry in a variety of ways. Clergy may be frequently tested and countered or may experience odd, disjointed, or unsettling interactions with those they serve. (These interactions are described in the introduction.) An afterpastor may no longer receive consistent trust and respect and may be held in suspicion, silenced, ignored, or sabotaged. In this way, the disappointment, confusion, or anger felt towards the offending cleric is displaced onto the afterpastor. Complaining that the afterpastor does not "deserve" this distrust will have little impact. Instead, an afterpastor must do everything possible to exemplify and foster trust. Simple things like showing up on time to meetings, promptly returning phone calls, and being consistent in word and deed confirm an afterpastor's trustworthiness in a concrete and significant way. Of course, even a well-intentioned afterpastor will sometimes fail to be dependable. Afterpastors need to be certain that such failure is rare and straightforwardly acknowledge it, and then they must apologize for it and assure people it will never happen again—and make sure it doesn't!

Triangulation

Some people in the aftermath of misconduct may be unable or unwilling to relate directly with even the most dependable afterpastor and may interact by triangulation with third parties. Triangulated communication occurs when someone speaks with Person A about matters that are properly part of a relationship with Person B. Instead of speaking with a minister directly about how upset she is with his sermon, a committee chair tells other committee chairs; the minister only hears of her upset after everyone else knows, and the committee chair and everyone else is worked up. When triangulation occurs, upsets cannot be resolved, because the people who could resolve them are not in conversation with one another. An afterpastor needs to interact with others in ways that de-triangulate communication. She or he needs to communicate with all parties, listen openly and nonjudgmentally, raise difficult issues directly and respectfully, and solicit and appreciate both positive and negative feedback.

Transference

Some people will interact with an afterpastor in frustrating, crazy-making, even aggressive ways. Early on, an afterpastor may observe that interactions do not correspond to current events or connect with the afterpastor. Afterpastors may also find they overreact to these interactions or respond ambivalently or aggressively. Clergy, occupying a specific office of ministry, need to remember that they are not a neutral presence in relation to congregants.[1] A clergyperson—before he or she is an individual—is the office of minister. Congregants may relate to clergy first as the office and only secondarily or intermittently as an individual. Consequently, congregants bring needs, impulses, expectations, and disappointments from significant past relationships to their relationship with a pastor.

Transference is the psychoanalytic term used to describe the unconscious process in which material from experiences, people, or feelings in an individual's past is expressed in a present, helping relationship. Transference includes not only the projection of things from past relationships but projections based on idealized images of past relationships and even unmet needs in current relationships. That is, a person might be looking for the opposite of what she experienced in a past relationship. For example, a parishioner who has been abused by her father or husband might see in the pastor an idealized man who is kind, caring, loving—everything not experienced from her father or that she does not receive from her husband. Another person's unconscious response to transferential interactions, in this case the minister's response, is called countertransference. Countertransference in a situation involving a critical congregant, for example, might find the minister reexperiencing through this congregant his judgmental mother and thus choosing to battle with the congregant to prove his innocence. Or a minister who often feels inadequate because of her own growing-up experiences may seek opportunities through interactions with congregants to feel capable and appreciated. In addition, when a pastor believes a parishioner's idealized projections, he is enmeshed in countertransference. Ministers who consciously or unconsciously look for ways to feel good about themselves, whether in response to painful past experiences or because they have bought into a parishioner's idealization of them, are involved in countertransference. They might respond to a parishioner's request, for example, to help out by doing bookkeeping or to acquiesce to her viewpoint by disregarding the inappropriateness of the requests and thanking the congregant for noticing and valuing her capabilities, thus missing entirely the lay leader's own fear of inadequacy and disempowering the leader. In each case, the minister causes further harm to the office of minister by contributing to the adverse impact of the transference/countertransference process and by missing an opportunity to reestablish appropriate role clarity and interpersonal boundaries in pastoral relationships.

Steps to Restoring the Office

An afterpastor must not only fulfill the pastoral role and responsibilities amid uniquely challenging conditions, but must do so while also managing, intervening in, and, if possible, altering these conditions. Afterpastors make reparations to the office of ministry by exercising emotional neutrality, establishing clear boundaries, and rebuilding trust in pastoral relationships. Afterpastors who conduct their business and interact with others in ways that consistently instill confidence, display predictability, connote truthfulness, and evidence authenticity will restore to the office respect and worth, and accord to themselves the support and resources needed for greater effectiveness. Frequently, a predecessor's acts of misconduct as well as his or her many daily interactions were not appropriate to a minister's job. Confusion regarding a minister's responsibilities may be evidenced in oddities in a job description, unusually restrictive personnel policies, or bylaws pertaining to ministers. Patterns of organizational dysfunction involving the minister—chronic conflict, over- and underfunctioning, or controlled or permissive behavior—may occur as well. An afterpastor whose work is appropriate to the role and responsibilities of ministers and who can foster healthy and respectful social norms and interactions will restore to the office appropriate expectations. On a day-to-day, person-to-person basis, an afterpastor heals the office of ministry with every interaction that is truthful, appropriate, competent, healthy, and respectful.

First, afterpastors can heal the office of ministry by providing consistently solid basic ministry, by undertaking the ministry to which they have been called with respect and dedication, grace and humility, and by serving others without need to be revered or loved. Afterpastors do well to remember that competent ministry is intended to serve others, not to impress them. Considerable time may have transpired in a congregation where misconduct has occurred since the congregation has been led by a minister focused more on service to others than himself or herself. Ministers sometimes enjoy being needed, liked, or admired too much. On occasion competent ministry will mean, to a degree, withholding something from or disappointing others. But accomplishing the work of a minister competently and gracefully will go a long way toward reestablishing trust and restoring the office to its appropriate respect, influence, and serviceability.

Dealing with Transference

An afterpastor needs to be clear and cautious about maintaining appropriate boundaries in the role of minister. Violated or poorly navigated boundary challenges may expose a minister to congregant transference. When a predecessor has not clearly maintained the boundaries of the ministerial role or has altered professional relationships to meet personal needs, parishioners and congregants come to expect a degree of intimacy with clergy not appropriate to the role of minister. When boundaries are not maintained, parishioners can be reminded of previous relationships with significant others, may confuse current interactions with these previous ones, or may project onto the pastor their idealized images of significant relationships and may act in ways that reflect these previous or hoped-for interactions, all of which makes the afterpastor's job more challenging.

One of the methods by which offending predecessors may have gotten away with misconduct, at least for a time, was to capitalize on this sort of transferential confusion. The lay leader who invited the pastor to make decisions he or she could (and should) have made wanted to believe that the minister was smarter and exercised better judgment than he or she could. The offending predecessor was often able to have his way or get away with inappropriate behaviors, although he was neither wise nor concerned for others, by masquerading as the minister the lay leader needed him to be. When questioned about whether it was appropriate for him as minister to be making a lay leader's decisions, for example, he might offer, "I'm only doing so because, given my [role, skill, knowledge, reputation, compassion], I was asked to help out." In short, the predecessor indulged in the fantasy that he or she was the perfect minister who, like a fantasized perfect parent, would fulfill the lay leader's every need and wish.

When afterpastors reestablish appropriate role and decision-making boundaries and interact with an emotional neutrality that does not capitalize on transference, parishioners may become disappointed and angry. Because their fantasies are unfulfilled, they may conclude that an afterpastor is not competent and, in extreme cases, they may work toward the afterpastor's dismissal. Afterpastors need to understand that these extreme reactions are not about them, that they have little if anything to do with the *person* of the minister and everything to do with the *office* of minister and the deep needs of the parishioner. Often afterpastors can disarm reactive parishioners with grace and good humor, with a nonanxious presence and unshakeable confidence. Cultivating and using well the support of denominational officials, outside consultants, and influential parishioners can be of significant help in this disarming. Cautiously and strictly maintaining the appropriate boundaries of the pastoral role may initially provoke these reactions but ultimately will help diminish them by restoring trust to the office and person of minister and creating opportunities for real ministry to be experienced.

Doing No Harm

Second, afterpastors can accomplish their unique task by not inflicting further harm on congregations, individuals, or the office of ministry. Guarding the limits of the pastoral role will help lower the risk of inflicting harm. Often when the broader circumstances of a predecessor's ministry are observed, the myriad other ways, great and small, in which the role was violated become apparent. Perhaps individual women with whom a male minister had sexual relations were initially invited to attend elegant private lunches or to linger after a meeting for a personal debriefing over a glass of wine. Perhaps a predecessor who absconded with tens of thousands of dollars in church funds initially asked individual church leaders for small loans that he or she never paid back. Perhaps a predecessor, finally dismissed for berating and yelling at lay leaders, years before began to control from behind the scenes those who voiced disagreement with the minister.

Date-like lunches, late-night debriefings, borrowing money, and silencing discussions are dubious if not rude activities for a minister, poor etiquette, as well as poor ethics that disrespect others and confuse expectations. If an afterpastor, following a male minister who dined with female parishioners, chooses to dine with congregation members, he sends confusing messages about his motivation or worse gives the appearance that he or she is having an intimate or sexual relationship rather than a professional relationship. By doing so, he misrepresents his role, sets up wrong expectations of the office of ministry, and risks causing further harm to individuals, the congregation, and the office of ministry. An afterpastor by strictly exercising both good ethics and good etiquette will lower the risk of causing further harm.

Guarding well one's own limits amid the complicated relationships of ministry can also reduce the risk an afterpastor will cause further harm. In the aftermath of clergy misconduct, interpersonal dynamics can be extremely chaotic and unsettling, especially to afterpastors. Some afterpastors report confusion in nearly every interaction, often getting hooked when they incorrectly imagine or experience the interaction as reflecting something in themselves. As a result, responding effectively and managing stress can be difficult. One way to increase effectiveness and reduce stress is to recognize that this type of interaction is evidence of the afterpastor's countertransference. When odd, confused, or unsettling interactions occur, afterpastors need to reflect on what aspect of themselves may *hook* them into experiencing these interactions in this particular way. Understanding one's family of origin history—relationships and experiences that were part of growing up—can provide some clues. Birth order and sibling relationships, experiences of being parented or being a parent can influence an afterpastor's response to present relationships.[2] An afterpastor's relationship with father or mother (whether they were supportive, abusive, or confusing) can lead an afterpastor to respond to a parishioner in a way not warranted by current circumstances. If an afterpastor, for example, has been raised with love and respect, he or she may have come to expect these responses from others. When this afterpastor does not feel loved or respected, as can happen in ministerial relationships after misconduct, or when the purpose of a pastoral interaction is other than to show love and respect to a clergyperson, an afterpastor who expects or seeks love and respect may respond inappropriately and ineffectively. Unexamined or unresolved family of origin issues may lead a minister to try to satisfy a personal goal (in this example, receiving love and respect) within a professional relationship. When afterpastors understand their own personal history and how this history influences their experience and response, they will make better choices in their interactions with others, regardless of how crazy, irrational, or unsettling those interactions may be.

Fostering Healing

Third, afterpastors can and should foster healing for individuals and for the congregation as long as doing so does not jeopardize the afterpastor's priority, healing the office of ministry. Healing for individuals, especially individuals who were immediately involved in the predecessor's acts of misconduct, can be a long and difficult process. Victims and survivors need to tell the story of their violation, to be heard and understood, in order to heal. Often telling and hearing their stories takes considerable time and requires special skill. Hearing victims'/survivors' stories can be confusing or enraging. Lay leaders and congregation members might see the victim's/survivor's sharing of her story as undesirable and disruptive. An adjudication process, while designed to hear and prove or disprove victim's stories, may out of a culture of ambivalence, encourage or curtail truth telling. Afterpastors who provide significant or primary support to victims/survivors often find the time commitment burdensome. In settings where disclosure is pending or confusion remains about a predecessor's guilt or innocence, afterpastors may be perceived as taking sides and as a result may be estranged or distanced from those they have been called to serve. Afterpastors can avoid these hazards and remain available as pastor to all people by referring victims and survivors to other counseling resources for intensive support. Other individuals with particular perspectives or distinct injuries—for example, the predecessor's spouse, aggrieved partners, affected children, colleagues, or aggressive supporters of the predecessor—might be offered support in a similar manner.

An afterpastor must remain everyone's minister in part by being no one's opposition. In order to safeguard broad pastoral access, an afterpastor does well to foster an image of issue neutrality. Issue neutrality does not mean an afterpastor does not understand that certain behaviors constitute misconduct or consider adjudication efforts optional. But afterpastors must avoid appearing to take an opposing side in a conflicted situation and must not directly oppose or debate the congregant. When afterpastors try to prove that they are right or that they alone know what ought to be done, they risk losing parishioners' support or goodwill. Parishioners may no longer accept an afterpastor as their minister or may begin to publicly deride an afterpastor who engages in argument or oppositional interaction. Given that relationships are the basic tool in the trade of ministry, fostering healing requires at minimum that an afterpastor be in pastoral relationship with individuals and with the congregation.

When a predecessor's misconduct is discovered during an afterpastor's tenure, an afterpastor's pastoral relationships are considerably challenged. Afterpastors should encourage lay leaders to report misconduct allegations to those with proper, expressed authority to adjudicate allegations against clergy. On rare occasions, when lay leaders are unwilling to report a beloved, long-tenured cleric's misconduct, an afterpastor may encourage them with the information that failure to hold an offending cleric accountable will make the recovery and healing of their congregation considerably more difficult, if not impossible. More often, lay leaders do not want allegations of a predecessor's misconduct disclosed to anyone beyond denominational officials, believing that either the allegations are not true or the congregation will be better served by not knowing. In order to safeguard their capacity for good pastoral relationships, afterpastors need to respect this reluctance and remain issue neutral as to the truth or falsehood of the allegations. On the other hand, afterpastors would do well to share with lay leaders the experience of other offended congregations; most allegations are already widely suspected and ultimately are determined to be well founded. Reporting misconduct is the first step in stopping a cleric's abuse, safeguarding other congregations and individuals, and healing those already harmed.

Some lay leaders are reluctant to acknowledge even *proven* allegations or to disclose or discuss these with parishioners in the erroneous belief that keeping the information secret or at least discreet will help the congregation recover more easily or quickly. Regrettably, failure to acknowledge proven misconduct will also slow or postpone healing. Keeping misconduct secret or insisting disclosed misconduct not be discussed will only give the appearance that everything is okay, intensifying distrust while obfuscating the cause. Secrecy discourages healing by inhibiting communication, distorting perceptions, and generally dividing a congregation into those who know and those who do not. In addition secrecy exacerbates every problem great and small by keeping anxiety high.[3] Anecdotal evidence suggests that secrecy about a past misconduct compounds the damage done to a congregation by the misconduct itself.

Frustrated by the ambivalence of lay leaders, some afterpastors may consider reporting alleged misconduct themselves. Before doing so, afterpastors should consider possible adverse consequences to their pastoral relationships. Congregants may see an afterpastor's allegations against a predecessor as fabricated, unbecoming, and self-serving, and react in ways that further encumber an afterpastor's work or lead to an early departure or resignation. Afterpastors must weigh the likelihood that adverse reactions will diminish their capacity to serve in a particular ministry against the likelihood that their report would provoke appropriate responses by authorized denominational bodies. Afterpastors may prefer to report credible information about a predecessor informally or to draw attention to credible information possessed by others rather than present themselves as a primary source of information about a predecessor's misconduct.

In general, an afterpastor should seek out programs designed to help organizations heal that are appropriate to a congregation's level of disclosure and make lay leaders aware of these resources, again, as long as doing so does not adversely jeopardize the afterpastor's priority for maintaining pastoral relationships and restoring the office of ministry. Implementing these without the significant support of lay leaders, however, is not likely to succeed. When lay leaders have not acknowledged a predecessor's misconduct, putting these programs in place could be disastrous. An afterpastor who moves ahead with a program may be considered "ill suited to our congregation's ministry" or "out of step with our way of doing things." Afterpastors can ask denominational leaders to suggest programs to reluctant or oppositional lay leaders. Then the afterpastor, serving as ally rather than an "out of step" pastor, can support lay leaders as they struggle to decide, given the state of the congregation, what is possible and prudent. Then they can work on those programs toward healing to which lay leaders and afterpastor have both committed. Most important, in difficult moments, afterpastors can remind lay leaders of the religious convictions behind these efforts. Lay leaders will come to understand that an essential mission of the church—to companion and comfort those who suffer, to work toward justice—is fostered by the congregation's work toward its own healing and justice.

If a congregation does undertake a program for healing, the afterpastor needs to think specifically about his or her role in that program. Many organizational healing strategies call for congregation-wide meetings facilitated by a trusted leader. An afterpastor may sometimes be asked to serve as facilitator. When a person from outside the congregation serves as facilitator, an afterpastor may be better able to serve as everyone's pastor during the meeting process. A few healing strategies involve making small-group meetings or individual counseling available to congregants. Again, an afterpastor may be asked to facilitate these meetings or provide counseling; finding an outside minister or counselor who can serve in these capacities will help the afterpastor remain neutral and available to all parties.

The Afterpastor's Self-care

Four, afterpastors restore trust and appropriate expectations to the office of ministry by arranging their life and work so that both personal and professional needs are appropriately fulfilled. Serving as an afterpastor is not easy work. Despite the difficulty, afterpastors must strive to serve and survive well. Because through misconduct a predecessor did not survive and serve well, an afterpastor's surviving well is an important aspect of healing. Many ministers are not particularly good at attending to their own or their family's needs. Afterpastors need to learn to take care of themselves and their families, and they need to be especially good at it. Afterpastors who care well for themselves and their family will be well prepared to do their best work. If afterpastors do not feel slightly indulged by their efforts to take care of themselves or their family, then they are probably not allocating enough time or making enough effort at self-care.

Identifying resources for support and using them well is the first step to serving and surviving well. A coach can be helpful in sorting complex dynamics, exploring and choosing strategies, maintaining consistency, and, essentially, fostering patience and keeping anxiety low amid the bumps and bounces that can characterize these ministries. An afterpastor would do well to educate and be in conversation with denominational officials and lay leaders about the unique stresses of afterpastor ministries. Afterpastors may need to cultivate support in managing the stress on themselves and their family. Denominational officials should help afterpastors identify and access additional resources to maintain optimum health and effectiveness. In the absence of financial support for these resources, afterpastors may need to underwrite these themselves, as difficult as that might be, rather than manage these difficult ministries without adequate support. As an alternative, potential afterpastors may need to choose not to serve in these ministries until the resources necessary to serve and survive well are made available. When an afterpastor is unable to serve and survive well, the harm done by the misconduct is exacerbated, and further harm may be inflicted. Serving and surviving well is crucial to healing a congregation.

Among other resources useful in helping afterpastors serve and survive well are education programs on ministerial ethics. When confronted by laity or colleagues, knowing exactly what standards were breached by an offending cleric and what consequences are likely to be imposed by denominations or professional organizations will greatly help an afterpastor. Especially helpful is working knowledge about boundaries and good boundary maintenance. Knowledge about interpersonal abuse and violence and the ways both bystanders and the wider congregation and culture minimize, rationalize, and deny these will also serve afterpastors.

Afterpastor ministries commonly evidence organizational dysfunction and chronic conflict. Knowledge about and experience with these will help an afterpastor manage stress, maintain healthy interactions, and support the resolution of differences. Afterpastors who are provided with as much information as possible about a congregation's history, in particular what is known or can be known about a predecessor's misconduct, will fare better than those from whom this information is withheld.

The Long View

The damage done by clergy misconduct to the office of ministry within an organization or congregation is pervasive and persistent. Healing after misconduct may take as much as a decade if not a generation to accomplish. Some congregations in the aftermath of misconduct may be galvanized by the experience and, after intentional efforts to heal, will be more vital, appearing transformed by the experience. Most congregations, however, will never again be quite themselves. A few will never be healed and will always evidence the damage of misconduct in their relationship with ministers. Certainly all congregations where misconduct has occurred are forever changed. Afterpastors who hope to foster healing in congregations must take a long view. Their immediate job is to focus on restoring trust in pastoral relationships and to the office of ministry amid challenging and difficult conditions. When they do so, they will bring about a unique and essential step in healing congregations and organizations affected by clergy misconduct and thus create the possibility that in the long term, full healing will occur.

10

CONGREGATIONS:
FURTHER STEPS IN HEALING

Nancy Myer Hopkins

WITH NEWLY DISCOVERED CASES OF CLERGY MISCONDUCT, the congregation is past the early crisis phase when the initial disclosure meetings and communal processing of events are complete, as described in chapter 1. Then begins the immediate follow-up period, when an integrated approach featuring cooperation between the clergy, the various programmatic departments, and a task force (discussed below) will go a long way toward helping everyone continue to recover.

During long-term recovery, strategies are dependent on the extent and timing of disclosure. The first and by far the easiest situation is when a disclosure meeting is held immediately after adjudication. A second involves old cases that were never disclosed or were disclosed minimally but never dealt with in the faith community. In these situations, it is necessary to determine if disclosure may now be possible. A third situation involves one or more victims who are not ready to bring complaints. Asking victims to come forward before they are ready is unethical, because the experience of bringing a complaint is fraught with risk for victims.

When a Disclosure Meeting Is Immediately Held

The major strategies employed during the early crisis phase of recovery include those used during congregational meeting(s), as described in chapter 1. They are: disclosure, education, processing individual emotional responses, beginning to look ahead, and spiritual reflection. These same strategies can continue in more depth as people move forward into the next phase of recovery and additional areas needing attention are discovered. This is the time to appoint a group that will be entrusted with the ongoing recovery task. Work that initially addresses the critical event itself will gradually be broadened to include many related topics. While a task force generally does not operate much longer than six months to a year, the work can continue in one form or another for three to five years.

Disclosure

The first question usually asked after a disclosure meeting is: What do we do about the people who did not attend any meetings? It is imperative that everyone have access to the information that was shared at those meetings. Otherwise, the danger is that secrecy and no-talk rules will flood back into a system that may have been too closed for its own good.[1] Those who did not attend the meeting might include several groups:

- Some people wanted to be there but had a legitimate reason for being absent. These folks will welcome a chance to hear about others' experiences and to participate in a miniversion of the congregational disclosure meeting.
- Some peripheral members who tend to gravitate back toward the center whenever something "interesting" happens came to the meeting, but many others did not. The absent congregants will be vulnerable to believing the first scrap of gossip they hear. The intensity of their response may depend on their own experiences of abuse. Many will be receptive to participation in a follow-up miniversion of the congregational meeting, especially if they hear positive reports from those who attended the first meeting.
- A small but vocal group of people were upset at the former pastor's removal, and they may have stayed away because they were in too much inner turmoil. Lay and clerical leaders must try to stay connected to these folks, perhaps spending one-on-one time with them to hear them grieve the loss of a beloved pastor. However, those who remain angry must not be allowed to keep everyone else from doing the recovery work. Allowing those who are protecting their illusions about the former pastor to openly blame victims without being challenged is a justice issue, similar to quietly tolerating expressions of hatred for any other individual or group.

All those who did not go to a disclosure meeting need access to the information that was given then. Sometimes it is possible to put the information in a letter that goes to everyone. Or the information can be distributed in a handout or posted. If no-talk rules have been firmly in place for a long time, expect attempts to repress the dissemination of information, such as the "sudden disappearance" of all books on sexual misconduct from the church library. If intimidation and secrecy have been practiced by the offender, others may perpetuate the intimidation by attempting to shut down the entire process.

Even when disclosure has been made to members, some congregants will want to keep the information from reaching the wider community. Many church leaders particularly fear the press, knowing that press coverage often focuses on salacious details. Often news accounts use unflattering pictures, prominent placement, and screaming headlines to create drama. It is possible to enlist the press to get the story out in a more constructive way and to let people know that this congregation is mending and not covering anything up.

Another good reason to disclose to the wider community is that a fair number of offenders lose their religious credentials, but because of their impairment, they have absolutely no ability to judge the impact of their behavior on others. Therefore, they stick around in the community and go into secular counseling. It often does not seem to occur to offenders that this would be an inappropriate alternate vocation, so the wider community needs to be warned about the offenders' impairment. Disclosure under these circumstances is clearly a justice and a safety issue.

Without disclosure, any attempts to restore justice fall far short of the job religious bodies have to do. As painful as it is to face the truth, if we do not disclose, the malaise often goes underground, only to surface another day in an ever-more-virulent form. The potential exists, however, for churches to help turn around the entire culture. Faith traditions, by looking first to their own houses, can provide a powerful witness by doing careful and responsible disclosure and then providing sensitive pastoral care for all parties affected.

Disclosure issues will be ongoing. Newcomers to the congregation need to hear a frank account of the abuse and the recovery process. Disclosure also needs to be made when the congregation is searching for new leaders or writing histories for inclusion in wider church publications. Any of these communications will be much easier to carry out if the congregation has been engaged in a long-term recovery process. A good test of that recovery will be whether people can collectively arrive at a point where they are neither obsessing about nor burying their past but can comfortably speak about the totality of it without shame.

Education

Education is also an ongoing task. First, people must understand why the behavior of their religious leader is wrong. Leaders can build on the education begun at the congregational meeting, but they should not assume that with one exposure to the concept of power abuse, everyone will suddenly "get it." This is especially true if the misconduct was sexual exploitation of an adult congregant. Often clergy will claim a right to privacy. An offender may try to back people off by saying something like, "We are both adults, and our relationship is just between the two of us." By putting his or her own spin on things, an offender can create confusion and sow terribly destructive seeds of dissension. Describing the relationship as an affair is another common tactic. (See discussion of this issue in chapters 2 and 4.)

People also need to understand what is happening to them. It is possible to soften the impact of clear statements about an offender's culpability if at the same time leaders are able to explain that the congregation is in grief over the loss of a pastor as well as many other losses (see chapter 7). Many people are able to acknowledge their loss of a beloved pastor during the early follow-up phase. Using Chilton Knudsen's grief wheel (page 44) as a visual seems to help, both during the education segment of the congregational meeting and with many other groups later. The pie-shaped wheel illustrates the fact that normal people tend to visit and revisit the stages of grief and are simultaneously holding on to different pieces of the "pie."

The key to getting through this difficult period together is to give people enough space to be wherever they need to be. Both the grief and the denial models illustrate that. It is helpful to unpack the meaning of two stages of anger. Anger I is characterized by blaming, usually anyone but the abuser. Anger II is more productive, as it can lead people to ask, How can we prevent this from happening again? Anger II typically happens later in the grief process and is not likely to surface much during the early stages of recovery.

Another helpful tool is a model of denial developed by psychologist Robert Kearney.[2] He notes that denial is part of our normal psychic defense system that gives us time to absorb bad news or things we temporarily can't acknowledge about ourselves. It is only harmful when it gets entrenched and prevents us from facing the things we must in order to mature into responsible people.

While Kearney developed the model for working with addictions, I have modified the model for understanding how congregations often respond to a leader's betrayal of trust. Picture a person standing in four nested boxes. The outer box wall represents the denial of facts: "It did not happen" or "The victim is making it up." When presented with credible evidence that something serious did happen, and finally believing it, the next wall encountered is denial of the implications: "Well, she asked for it," "They were consenting adults," "The child's parents are to blame," or "The child was seductive." The third layer is the denial of a need to change, which I believe in congregations interchanges with the fourth layer, the denial of feelings. This is where many people will ultimately get caught. Uttered two weeks after the disclosure meeting are statements like: "We've done our work, now it is time to move on," "Time to get on with it," "Time to put it behind us," or "Why can't we just forgive and forget?" This focus on the quick fix means that true feelings are never examined, and nothing really needs to change. The model, however, does not suggest that everyone who does not think the congregation needs to change should be written off as being "in denial." Leaders can instead gently shepherd many people through the walls of denial with carefully chosen strategies designed to produce the desired results relatively painlessly.

Both the grief and the denial models illustrate that recovery is a developmental process; the needs of people will gradually change over time. For instance, at first, music and other elements of worship can be chosen that indirectly acknowledge the fragility and pain that many are still feeling. Singing psalms or litanies may fit the mood and assist grieving better than anything else. Hymns, prayers, and liturgies can gradually be added that are more upbeat and that express communal strength and responsibility. During this time, I would not throw a lot of unfamiliar music or liturgies at people. Music and liturgy tap into our psyches at a deeper level than anything else, and the congregation's natural gifts and worship style can and should be used sensitively and liberally. Unless healing services are already a regular practice in the congregation, it is best to hold off on healing services until people have had a chance to do the work that still needs to be done. When done prematurely, such services may actually shut down the process.

The educational task also broadens with time. People learn from experience as much from sitting and listening to someone else talk at them; the impact on the heart also has an impact on the mind. This is why I put so much emphasis on small-group work throughout recovery. Small groups address educational as well as emotional needs and help to restore trust. Later there can be opportunities to look at the broader cultural context in which our religious systems are embedded. Study groups can examine the results of living in a patriarchal culture, especially where their own faith tradition may still be hierarchal or cleric-centered. They can begin to address questions such as, What is it that gives us "permission" to tolerate abuse and oppression in all its forms? How are racism, classism, heterosexism, and sexism connected to tolerance for abusive behavior? How do we navigate in a world that is simultaneously sex-repressed and sex-obsessed? What are the destructive messages of current media, video games, and advertising? or How do we need to change?

Listening to Individuals

Ideally, there will be many more opportunities for the small-group listening that was introduced during the congregational meeting. The subject matter changes as more and more people get comfortable, but the process for sacred listening does not change. In the next section, which describes the work of the task force, ways to introduce subjects that gradually deepen the listening and therefore the understanding are suggested. Give advance notice about the subject and process, establish and enforce the guidelines, and do not let the process deteriorate into contentious discussion. Ultimately, discussion will be necessary; however, engaging difficult issues will be much easier if people first know each other better because they have been willing to make themselves vulnerable and listen to others.

Spiritual Reflection

Spiritual reflection is the main work of any religious group. However, sometimes we split off spiritual reflection from the issues we face in everyday life, or we hand over this task to our clergy, thinking they are trained to be the experts. The process that was introduced at the congregational disclosure meetings invites the laity to do their own reflection, and this practice, too, needs to be woven throughout the fabric of ongoing congregational life. In addition to the "Where is God?" question, questions of forgiveness, repentance, and a multitude of complex ethical dilemmas are always present.

Sermons are often most effective if they do not directly address the congregation's trauma. When people are able to make their own leaps from sermon content to personal experience, the Word in all its forms may have more impact. Use of metaphor and relevant biblical stories can be powerful. Because there is a great tendency to dispense "cheap grace," encouraging people to forgive long before they have understood how hurt they are, the issue of forgiveness is particularly germane and can be addressed in many different ways.

Organizing a Task Force

Someone has to be responsible for continuing the work already begun, or the congregation can lose momentum and squander the positive energy generated by a successful congregational crisis meeting. Lay leaders may already be exhausted and needing a rest. Usually the crisis meeting will surface new people with energy for the job, and the task force will appropriately be led by and consist of mostly laypeople. Thus the task force also becomes a strategy for reempowerment of the laity.

Members of the task force should be clear that the removal of the offending minister was appropriate but should also be able to both stay connected to any victims/survivors who may be present and known and empathize with those who continue to grieve the loss of the pastor. Being empathetic does not mean, however, agreeing with those who continue to agitate for bringing the offender back or who persist in blaming victims.

It is not advisable to ask for volunteers to serve on the task force, because people with either hidden or overt agendas may volunteer, and they do not make good task force members. Leaders should clearly explain that this is a time-limited but intensive working group that may have to meet quite frequently at first. A six-month evaluation should be built in to assess whether they think the group has completed its work by that time. Most task forces exist for six months to one year. If they go the full year, an anniversary remembrance and a celebration of the life of a congregation that has been intentional about its recovery can make a fitting adieu for the task force.

The listening process that was introduced during the disclosure meeting can be used at the beginning of every meeting, so that people become comfortable with it and each other. The topics can be changed and gradually deepened as trust develops. Here are some possible topics that are best used only one at a time, beginning with relatively easy topics.

- How long have I been a member of this congregation, what attracted me, and what keeps me here?
- What was my experience of the departed pastor's ministry? (Positive, negative, or mixed responses are all acceptable.)
- What are some of the recent losses I/we have experienced in the past several years?
- How do I experience God in our midst?
- How does my participation in this congregation help me with ethical dilemmas I encounter in my life and work?

- What are my hopes for the future of this congregation?
- What is the main mission of our congregation?

These questions are just suggestions for designing a deepening process. Task forces should not be afraid to use their own questions. The planning work of the task force will go much more smoothly if each meeting begins with such a process that leads to discussion only after everyone has had a chance to speak without interruption.

Another advantage of doing this listening process together is that the task force will learn what questions are working well, and what, therefore, might be used later with other groups in the congregation. However, the process should not come as a surprise to anyone. People need to know in advance that a meeting will include a small-group process.

Assess

The task force will assess the further needs of the congregation. (See also chapter 20 for discussion of assessment.) They will survey congregants, research resources, and advise other leaders on strategies for continued recovery, choosing some, but not all, strategies to implement themselves. The group should work closely with those primarily responsible for any programming in the congregation. For example, is the choir or youth group hurting because they had a close relationship with the offending minister? Community helpers, such as police, child psychologists, psychiatrists, and counselors can be immensely helpful. Often parents want to know what information and interventions are age-appropriate. There is always a need to help people understand the experience of all victims of any kind of abuse.

When asking people what they need, remember that trauma victims do not always know what they need. The ambulance crew that arrives at an automobile accident does not take the word of the people sitting at the side of the road in shock from loss of blood that they are okay. Premature expressions that "it is time to move on" may mask an inability to come to grips with the reality of the harm that has been done. Such pressure to move on is especially difficult to manage if it occurs because the experience of direct victims/survivors is not understood. When victims or their families still in the congregation hear such opinions expressed, they rightly read them as indifference to their suffering and are revictimized.

Often, people in traumatized congregations have forgotten how to be in community well. They may need to develop group norms, work on communication skills, help leadership groups function well, or directly address long-standing conflict. It is quite possible that the vision of the congregation has been lost. The complexity of forgiveness always requires attention. Every congregation will be different, and it is impossible to design one plan that fits all.

Gradually the mood of the congregation should lighten. Many of the suggestions for indirect work in part 4, "What Do We Do Now?" can also assist long-term recovery, and some of them can actually be fun.

Evaluate

When the task force is formed, a six-month evaluation should be established to reflect on questions such as: What has been accomplished? What still needs to be done? Are we ready to disband? or Do we need to work for another three to six months? If outside consultants or a pastoral response team (see chapter 18) helped with the congregational disclosure meetings, this would be a good time to ask them to return. Utilizing outside resources from time to time is always a good way to counter isolation and keep any congregation more open to new ideas.

End

The task force will want to design a special process to give themselves closure on their work, and they may involve the congregation in that. Many congregations have come up with wonderful and creative celebrations featuring a homegrown ritual and liturgy to symbolize the journey they have been on and will continue on together.

Recovery after Opening Old Cases

All of the strategies listed above can be used after it has been decided that old cases of betrayal can also be disclosed and some sort of a congregational process has been used to get the word out as completely as possible. Some congregations have used the five-hour congregational meeting described in chapter 1. Others have invited people to gather in small study groups to research various aspects of the congregation's history, creating time lines for which they solicited pictures and artifacts from congregants. Then they gathered, perhaps with a meal, to creatively present the story, putting on historical skits and sketches, or tying the congregation's story to similar stories from Scripture.

Recovery When Disclosure Is Not Possible

In some situations, disclosure is not possible (see chapter 1). Victims may still be unready to bring a complaint. Ethically, it is not possible to push them to do so before they are ready, and they may never be ready. Or people may know that abuse occurred in the past, because it is a part of the public record, but the congregation did not have a chance to process events, or a congregational disclosure meeting was not conducted carefully and ended in a destructive free-for-all. Consequently, no one wants to revisit what is remembered as a terrible time. Or no-talk rules about shadowy and mysterious events have been present in a congregation seemingly forever, and they are still in force.

In these excruciatingly difficult situations, the afterpastor may be feeling the burden of the entire community's pain. People may transfer their mistrust of former clergy to the present clergyperson. (See this book's introduction for more detail about common experiences of afterpastors.) Accordingly, the afterpastor may conclude that all criticisms of him or her can be laid at the door of a predecessor who acted out. This belief may or may not be true. As the primary authors met to develop the outline for this book, one of us observed that in these situations, afterpastors need to remember, "It's not about you—except when it is."

Many congregants may lapse into either intense conflict or depression and hopelessness, because the hurt, if ignored, does not usually go away. It often turns into a need to hurt or blame someone else and then returns to the afterpastor. Denominational leaders should refrain from sending clergy into these congregations without giving them any known history. The afterpastor needs plenty of assistance and support, some of which he or she will probably have to self-generate. The afterpastor, with the blessing and assistance of supervisors, if appropriate, may decide to consult with a group of trusted lay leaders if it is known that they were aware of the abuse but sworn to secrecy, in order to discover some of the causes of the malaise. If the laity know nothing, or if there is a victim who is not ready to come forward, then sometimes the afterpastor must carry the burden of the story alone.

If it is decided that the case cannot be opened up, then it is necessary to proceed to plan B, which involves healing the pastoral office. The strategy includes deciding what elements of the pastoral office have been compromised or lost, and undertaking small, manageable steps to restore them. At the least, the afterpastor will need to help restore trust and be careful not to trigger congregants' abandonment fears. Lay leaders, too, can examine how the congregation operates as a community. Often communal issues such as structure, safety, lines of accountability, and the establishment of healthy group norms need to be addressed. This approach is not ideal, but making healthy, positive choices, even if they are tiny ones, can spell the difference between feeling hopeless and being hopeful. (See chapter 9 for further discussion on restoring the pastoral office.)

In addition to restoring the pastoral office, other indirect methods can be used to further recovery work. Perhaps with the assistance of an outside consultant, congregational leaders can devise strategies for helping congregants discuss specific issues, including grief and loss, lack of trust, skills for effective communication, boundaries and boundary keeping, secrets, power and power abuse, and members' worry about the congregation's survival. Here is one example of a process that can be done even without disclosure to further a congregation's well-being.

A Selective History Taking

Examine the history, going back as far as possible. (See Oswald and Friedrich, *Discerning Your Congregation's Future*, listed under "Family Systems" in appendix A, "Resources," for a guide to such a process.) Identify the positive events as well as the negative. If it has been determined that some things cannot be opened up, so be it. However, there may have been other events—not all sexual in nature or involving the clergy—that also traumatized the congregation and that have never been fully dealt with.

When doing this history taking, new sensitive material may surface that will require an assessment about whether it can be shared. It may be necessary to stop and weigh the risks to all parties in order to make a decision. When sharing the history, it is not good practice to name individuals who have had a particularly bad experience unless they are willing to be identified, but the experience itself is data that helps people understand their history. Like families, people in traumatized congregations do not always know what "normal" is. They think that what they are experiencing is just the way people are, and if they also happen to come from a family that replicates many of the same dynamics, they may *really* not know what normal is.

If the group is working chronologically, each era will also have its positive story. However, a common tendency of people when telling their history is to focus extensively on the positive story, especially if some parts of the history generate so much shame that they have been repressed and consigned to a closet that is fast filling up with skeletons. Sometimes some gentle prodding is necessary to prevent glossing over the painful parts of the story. Always balance the painful story with the hopeful story, as both are always present. Questions that help get out the positive story include:

- Who were the laity who held this congregation together during bad times?
- What, specifically, did they do to accomplish this? How have we built on this?
- Who are the clergy who were steadfast and faithful, even during hard times?
- What traditional events or lay groups have inspired us over the years?
- What positive witness and/or outreach have we provided to the wider community?

It is not unusual for different people to have conflicting perspectives on these questions, and that is all right. An absolutely vital step to this process involves sharing with the entire congregation what has been learned during the history taking. One way to do that is to create a time line and explain it at a supper that also features skits. Ask the rest of the congregation to help fill in the blanks, use drawings, photos, and the like. Invite the children to participate with their own artwork. In other words, have some fun with it.

The Church's Work

Assisting congregations and all others who can be considered secondary victims/survivors of clergy sexual misconduct must be viewed as a vital piece of the work of the church. Failure to address the needs of all victims, primary or secondary, will result in a tragic waste of talented laity and faithful clergy at enormous human cost. Furthermore, the unsupported afterpastor is at risk of burnout, and unfortunately, no matter what form the burnout takes, it is always experienced as another trust betrayal by vulnerable congregants.

There is also the real possibility that the task of recovery, faithfully embraced, will yield positive results that seem unimaginable when the crisis is at its worst. Faith communities can decide to take the risk, open themselves up to the work of the Spirit, and walk together through those walls of denial. When this is done, relationships deepen, faith matures, and congregations present a powerful witness and the face of hope to the wider community.

11

VICTIMS/SURVIVORS:
THE HEALING JOURNEY

Patricia L. Liberty

THE CHURCH, where spiritual growth and development is to be encouraged, is often the last place survivors of clergy abuse, particularly sexual abuse, turn for support in their healing journey. This situation is often due to lack of interest on the church's part, as well as the universal tendency to blame the victim. However, even when churches are open to the needs of the survivors, they do not necessarily know what survivors need. Few church leaders stay with survivors long enough to learn the deep rhythm of healing essential to recovery from clergy sexual abuse. This is due, in part, to the fact that adjudication procedures focus on the outcome for the accused clergyperson and not the victim. Once the complaint is adjudicated, the process is considered complete, and survivors are left on their own to complete their healing work. Even if advocates are appointed to support survivors, it is often only through adjudication of the complaint.

Survivors' issues change as they continue the healing journey and as their life circumstances change. During the acute phase of recovery, immediately following the complaint and adjudication, they may need intense support. As time goes on, issues resurface, and survivors may be actively involved in a variety of healing interventions for 15 years or more as they seek to rebuild what was shattered by the abuse.

Therapy is an important piece of healing work, and most survivors of sexual abuse will spend at least five years in therapy in the aftermath. For some survivors, previous mental health issues are exacerbated to the point where survivors may need hospitalization or medication. For others, new mental health issues such as single-episode depression (the victim/survivor experiences one episode of depression and remains normal thereafter) and post-traumatic stress disorder may emerge. For still others, chemical dependence may be a coping strategy that helps them to survive the immediate pain but leaves them with other issues to attend to later on. Because abuse impacts the entire family system, therapeutic interventions may therefore need to include couples and family therapy as well.

Survivors of clergy abuse come from every walk of life, every socioeconomic status and religious tradition. They are young and not so young, married and single, gay and straight, stay-at-home moms, corporate executives, pastors, educators, healthcare professionals, and laborers. They are Protestant, Catholic, Jewish, and Buddhist. While the abuse may claim a huge part of their energy as they heal, it does not describe their total personhood. Although survivors bear a huge burden of physical, emotional, psychological, spiritual, and financial strain, they often are also among the strongest, most faithful, committed, and insightful men and women we may meet. Often, victims of clergy abuse lose every other identity to the label of "victim," when in truth their victimization is only part of who they are. In the face of enormous pain and suffering, they continue to raise their children, tend to their relationships, and work at their professions and jobs.

Although survivors come from all walks of life and all religious traditions, they have some important traits in common, most notably the profound misfortune of crossing the path of a clergyperson who is unable to set and maintain an appropriate boundary for the ministerial relationship. Survivors often share a deep desire to reconnect with their spiritual selves and rebuild the shattered bedrock of their lives. Survivors also universally request that their churches and religious organizations call their abusers to accountability and stop blaming them for the failures of religious leaders. Having noted their similarities, their healing journeys are as unique as their fingerprints. The particular expression of their pain and healing as they journey is as different as their spiritual journey before the abuse.

Steps Toward Healing

The touchstones for healing spiritually following abuse, especially sexual trauma, include differentiating between spirituality and religion, understanding grief as a model for healing, reshaping the God image, and reclaiming worship and community.

Understanding the difference between religion and spirituality is an important starting point. Often, well-meaning pastors will encourage survivors to come back to church or to participate in religious practices and not realize that the meaning of these traditions and practices has been profoundly distorted by the abuse. Whether survivors were wounded in childhood or adulthood, the church building itself may represent painful memories and trigger flashbacks for survivors. In addition, if there was publicity around the case due to litigation, or if the church failed to make a healthy disclosure of the abuse, survivors will be harshly judged by the church, which makes it impossible for them to return to their community. The loss of church as a safe place is an issue that is not to be minimized or denied in an effort to get her to "come back to church."

However, survivors often want spiritual support. Spirituality is that essential part of our humanness that connects us with the divine, however the divine is understood. Alongside intellect and emotions, it is a core part of one's being. Religion, on the other hand, is the system that springs up around a community's understanding of the divine. At its best, it nurtures an individual's awareness of and connection with the divine, as well as one's connection with self and others. At its worst, it is a structure that serves its own ends, becoming separated from the purpose it claims to serve.

One of the reasons so many survivors have difficulty reconnecting with the church as a place for spiritual healing following abuse is that the church has forgotten why it exists. I consistently hear shock and disbelief from survivors who go to the church in search of justice (accountability for clergy abusers, assistance with costs associated with healing, acknowledgment of the wrong done to them) and discover instead that the church acts like any other secular institution in its approach to and adjudication of complaints. The church, instead of being a place of healing and support, becomes another source of wounding. In addition to dealing with the wounds of the clergy abuse, they now have to heal from wounds inflicted by the church.

Survivors are usually left on their own to seek healing. What they discover is that spiritual healing has its own rhythm and comes in its own time. It is essentially a movement inward, a reconnecting with the deepest places of self and one's understanding of the divine. No one can tell another when or how she should attend to this part of the journey, though many may try. Spiritual healing is, ironically and sadly, the most ignored and misunderstood by those who may successfully companion survivors through other parts of their journey. Few people in the church understand the real work of spiritual healing after trauma, especially trauma caused by its own leaders.

For survivors of clergy sexual abuse, spirituality is the most tender and wounded aspect of self. When clergy, who are entrusted with the sacred responsibility of empowering one's spiritual growth and development, exploit it for their own ends, the God image and one's own sacred interiority are deeply wounded. Roman Catholic priest and psychologist Stephen J. Rossetti contends that clergy are the image bearers for the divine, symbolic representatives of the larger truth and reality.[1] When clergy abuse the power entrusted to them, that abuse is categorically and fundamentally different from abuse by any other professional, lawyer, physician, or therapist. When clergy act in abusive ways, the image of the divine is shattered.

Spiritual healing is about reconstructing the very foundation, the bedrock of one's being, because that is the level at which the damage is done. When the image of God is shattered because of the actions of God's representative, one's most deeply held values and beliefs are also damaged. These wounds are not easily healed. The image of a house illustrates the task. Some helpers encourage survivors to putty the windows and put on a coat of paint, because it will make the house look better. Yet they fail to notice the entire house is perched at a precarious angle because the foundation is shattered.

Authentic spiritual healing grows out of the depths of pain, sadness, confusion, anger, rage, fear, and hopelessness that is the consequence of clergy sexual abuse. The only way out of the pain is through it. The psalmist said, "Out of the depths I cry. . . ." Nothing less expresses the true pain of those who have been abused by clergy and points to the foundation for true healing. Healing begins in the depths. It is the work of saving and sorting, sifting through what has been stolen, what remains, what is salvageable, and what is damaged beyond repair.

Understanding Grief

Much of the work of spiritual recovery is grief work. There are losses to be mourned. The survivor must mourn the loss of faith that can be no more and acknowledge that her or his faith will be permanently affected. Images lose their meaning, rituals are emptied of significance, long-treasured traditions are shattered, and sacraments no longer point to anything beyond themselves. Naming, acknowledging, validating, and sharing these losses are part of the grief process.

Often, the loss of community that comes from not being able to return to one's church compounds the difficulty of grief work, because grief needs to be shared. At the nationally acclaimed "Is Nothing Sacred?" retreats for women survivors of clergy sexual abuse, one of the most valuable aspects of the weekend is the validation participants receive for the enormity of their losses. There is power in naming, and there is healing in receiving affirmation for what has been not just lost but stolen. The integrity of the witness offered by these survivors cannot be ignored.

Honoring the grief process begins with an acknowledgment that what was stolen was of value and cannot be replaced. Personal faith and spirituality are constructed of countless moments in worship, prayer, mindfulness, joy, struggle, tears, laughter, insight, sharing, and loving. They are woven into the fabric of one's life and are as necessary as air and as difficult to describe. To grieve the shattering of such an essential part of one's being is wrenching and painful work. This process takes years—and is a part of the healing process that may take years to get to. In my work with survivors over the past decade, it has become clear that spiritual healing is among the last work done by survivors and the aspect that takes the longest.

Reshaping the God Image

Another aspect of spiritual healing following clergy abuse is reclaiming and reshaping a God image. Survivors of sexual abuse often note that their abuser used God language in the midst of the exploitation. Most survivors report being uncomfortable and confused by the sexual advances of their clergy, knowing they were wrong but listening as that clergyperson used God to "bless" what was happening. Statements such as "God brought us together" or "God knew how much I needed someone and sent me you" are commonly made by abusers to coerce their victims into sexual activity. As a result, survivors are left with confusing and conflicting images of God in the aftermath of their abuse.

When the abusing clergyperson is male, survivors often struggle with patriarchal images of God that are reinforced by the church. Few people who grow up in the Judeo-Christian tradition do not have a male God image. The subtle power of a male clergyperson using God's (male) image to coerce sexual behavior creates deep pain and confusion about who God is and how God interacts in the lives of human beings. Patriarchal images of God help protect clergy privilege and power and reinforce difficult images that survivors have to sort out in the aftermath of abuse. It is important to recognize that there are women clergy abusers as well, though the statistics overwhelmingly indicate that the majority of abusers are male. Regardless of the gender of the abuser, however, the patriarchal system perpetuates clergy privilege and power and affects the God image that many survivors have.

In addition to divine gender issues, survivors also struggle with questions of theodicy, the age-old question of how God can be all good and all loving and all powerful when there is such evil and suffering in the world, and most particularly in their life. For many survivors, the only "answer" is that they themselves are bad, evil, and responsible for what happened. Maybe God loves other people, but not them. While shame is an issue for many survivors of sexual violence and trauma, it is particularly pronounced for those who were abused by a representative of God. Sorting out who God is and who God's representative is (and is not) is a critical part of recovery for survivors. Secular therapy can help address shame and blame, but the spiritual dimensions of these issues are often ignored.

In Judeo-Christian Scriptures, there are over 40 different images of God and a host of qualities attributed to God. Survivors who are reclaiming an image of the divine can discover rich and nurturing images of God within and beyond Scripture. Other religious traditions also offer images of God that may be helpful. Many survivors rediscover nature as a source of comfort from God. Most survivors construct a more eclectic image of God than they had prior to their abuse and, ironically, may develop a richness and depth to their spirituality and God image that they had not known before.

Reclaiming and rebuilding a God image is holy work. It is also painful work. What is most important is that it allows room for all the experiences and feelings, the insights and knowledge, the wounds and growth, the clarity and confusion that are part of a survivor's recovery. Like every other aspect of healing, it cannot be rushed. And those who would companion survivors on this part of their journey would do well to acknowledge the words of Jeremiah, so that we do not heal "the hurt of [God's] people slightly, saying, 'Peace, peace!' when there is no peace" (Jer. 6:14 NKJV).

Reclaiming Worship and Community

Finally, spiritual healing involves reclaiming worship and community. This does not necessarily mean going back to church, but it may. At its deepest level, it is about rebuilding the place of ritual in one's life. Part of the function of worship is to create rituals that mark important places on the human journey. There are religious rituals for birth, coming of age, marriage or partnering, death, and other life transitions. The weekly ritual of worship and the celebration of the sacrament or ordinance of communion are a significant part of what it means to be a person of faith. Religious rituals and worship celebrate and punctuate points on life's journey and mark them as important. They are celebrated in community as a way of grounding the life experience of one individual or family in a group of people with similar values and beliefs.

Beyond that, religious rituals help connect significant movements in human life to the divine. Baptism or dedication acknowledges that a child is God's gift. Confirmation or baptism acknowledges that a child is reaching the age of knowledge, faith, and choice. Weddings and union services acknowledge the divine in the midst of human love and commitment. Funerals remind us that we are created by God and return to God. Attendance at worship and participation in the sacraments are means by which we are connected not only to God but also to others who share similar beliefs. The bonds of community formed in churches are essential elemental parts of life for people of faith. For victims of clergy sexual abuse, that meaning is shattered and the resources of community are ripped away at a time when they are most needed.

Reclaiming the place of religious ritual is the work of an individual survivor that needs to find expression in the life of a community. Unfortunately, the vast majority of survivors are marginalized out of their community by the time they reach this stage of recovery. At the "Is Nothing Sacred?" retreat, participants are invited to create a ritual that expresses where they are in the journey. A small group comes together and plans on behalf of the larger group. The planning group leads the service, and each participant is asked to bring something that she can contribute. If the group is Christian, group members celebrate communion by serving each other using a common loaf and intinction. I learned from the originator of the retreat, Marie Fortune, senior analyst and founder of FaithTrust Institute in Seattle, how important it is to remind survivors that it is their birthright to be at the table. For many, the communion service is the first one in many years. The sadness of that truth is a profound commentary on the church's inability to walk with survivors for the long journey of healing.

The Church's Work of Healing

Some survivors never return to any form of organized religion, and that is their right. It is important to be clear that getting survivors back to church is not and should not be the goal of any support, advocacy, or intervention process. That is an oppressive and abusive expectation, particularly if the church has not done its work. However, it is equally important that the option to return be a viable one, meaning that the church must do its healing work and come to a place where it stops blaming the victim. If it is not safe for a victim/survivor to return to her or his church, then the church has not completed its work. If we believe ministry is a sacred trust and that it is always the responsibility of the clergyperson to set and maintain an appropriate boundary for the ministerial relationship, then the logical outcome of that truth is that victims/survivors not be blamed, marginalized, or excluded from their communities of faith.

It is not coincidental that the healing work of congregations supports the healing journey of survivors. When a congregation does its work, survivors are helped in theirs. What is healing for survivors is healing for churches as well. Honesty, openness, accurate information, just processes, fair disclosure, and vindication of the wrong heal both survivor and congregation. The consequence of churches doing their work is that a place is created where survivors can reclaim religious ritual and community.

Recovery from clergy abuse is a long, painful road. Much of it is traveled alone, but it need not be traveled in isolation. Victims/survivors of clergy abuse are children of God, daughters and sons of the church, heirs to the realm of God as are we all. Understanding the rhythm of healing and the touchstones along the way can help us to partner with them in the work of justice making, restoration, and reconciliation.

12

LAY LEADERS:
TAKING RESPONSIBILITY

Loren D. Mellum

THE DISCLOSURE OF CLERGY MISCONDUCT creates a crisis that disorients a faith community and raises many questions. As the crisis is absorbed over months and even years, the afterpastor lifts before the congregation's leaders the opportunity to live with the questions the crisis stirs and to communally discern together what it means to be church. The crisis provides an opening for the entire faith community to explore its call from God to participate in God's mission for the sake of the world. The afterpastor and lay leaders of a congregation begin to form new ways of being church together that foster shared leadership, power, and ministry. On this courageous journey toward new life, leaders keep in mind that "as we are brought to the truth about ourselves, we are opened to hear the gospel anew."[1] The crisis of clergy misconduct in a congregation offers the opportunity to leave behind what has been in order to embrace the new future God is calling forth.

A congregation on this journey of rebuilding and renewal slowly lets go of the past as it grieves its way into God's future. Leaders need to assure members that it is natural for congregations to experience communal bereavement, and congregational leaders should be encouraged to attend to their own brokenness following clergy misconduct. Particularly those who worked closely with the offending pastor will experience denial and disbelief, sadness and anger, shame as well as feelings of betrayal. The afterpastor can provide a calm pastoral presence amid the unanswered questions and tensions and can assure congregational leaders that grieving is ultimately healthy and a precursor to new life. In fact, occasions and circumstances in every congregation call forth seasons of grieving.

Gerald A. Arbuckle, a Roman Catholic priest and cultural anthropologist, contends that as long as communities and individuals refuse to grieve over what is lost or what is now apostolically irrelevant, they will not let go of the past.[2]

Effectively and thoroughly grieving what has been lost is what eventually opens a vision and path toward the future, so it is imperative in the immediate aftermath of the disclosure that congregational leaders be gentle with themselves and others in the congregation as everyone continues to absorb what has come to light. As time unfolds, congregational leaders will not only attend to their own wounds, but will direct increasing energy and resources toward the health of the congregation as well.

Overfunctioning and Underfunctioning

It is likely that a congregation that goes through the painful loss of a pastoral leader due to clergy misconduct grieves not only the loss of this leader, but the loss of a style of leadership that is excessively pastor-centered. A pastor-centered style of leadership subtly fosters over time an unhealthy focus on the role of clergy in the congregation. Consequently, as a congregation lets go of the past, one of the primary dynamics in the congregation that needs to be addressed has to do with overfunctioning and underfunctioning. Clergy and other religious workers are particularly susceptible to overfunctioning, an insidious illness in a congregation that can go undetected for a significant amount of time. Ronald W. Richardson, pastoral counselor and author of many books on family systems theory, explains, "Overfunctioning happens when one person takes increasing amounts of responsibility for the functioning of one or more other people."[3] Clergy and other religious workers easily take too much responsibility in the congregations they serve. An overfunctioning pastor can be perceived by a congregation as being a very committed and caring leader. However, Richardson continues, "the more people overfunction in the church the more all suffer from the issues of confused responsibility."[4]

When a pastor consistently overfunctions, the faith community begins underfunctioning. People stop taking responsibility for their own spiritual lives and for the mission and health of the congregation, and members' spiritual well-being begins to erode. Frank A. Thomas, a prominent Disciples of Christ pastor, preacher, and speaker, observes:

> Over time the one who overfunctions often becomes angry, hurt, and bitter about congregational dependency and the tremendous weight and load of ministry. At the same time the underfunctioning ones are angry, hurt, and bitter because of their dependency and the fact that they do not get the chance to make a full contribution or have the privilege to participate as equals.[5]

Not only those who underfunction but those who overfunction are harmed by the dance they perform together. People who overfunction attend so excessively to others that they neglect the Holy Spirit's work in their own life through Scripture reading, prayer, Sabbath rest, play, exercise, and other life-giving activities. Edwin Friedman, an expert in family systems, observes, "One of the subtlest and yet most fundamental effects of overfunctioning is spiritual. It destroys the spiritual quality of the overfunctioner."[6] The pastor-centered church can easily go down this road and in the end cause great harm to the pastor, the pastor's family, and the congregation.

In many cases, pastors who violate boundaries are chronic overfunctioners. They are anxiously determined to please everyone and often take on other people's problems as if the problems were their own. Often chronic overfunctioning of this nature causes a pastor to either burn out or act out. Overfunctioning is a leadership flaw that leaves a pastor vulnerable, but what often complicates this scenario is that congregations or other organizations often expect and demand that their leaders overfunction. In this way, a congregation recovering from clergy misconduct bears some responsibility for changing what members expect of their pastor. When overfunctioning occurs, notes Thomas, "the organization places itself in the subordinate role, or what could be called underfunctioning, and forces the leader to be dominant."[7] A congregation that faces the truth about itself reflects on whether the corporate ethos of the congregation requires leaders to overfunction.

A Better Way

The transformation from a pastor-centered church to a Spirit-led, mission-driven, team-based congregation begins with the afterpastor, who places a high value on the gifts of the laity and freely offers them permission and encouragement to be church together. The transformation is not contingent on the pastor doing more, but upon his or her ability to define himself or herself. In the introduction to this book, Deborah Pope-Lance observed that many afterpastors experience manipulation, coercion, and sabotage, as well as distrust and suspicion. Some afterpastors report feeling as if they are in a Twilight Zone, where nothing seems quite "real." Given the sometimes puzzling and even mysterious environment in congregations where misconduct has occurred, the afterpastor needs to be a clear, firm, and public leader. Otherwise, the afterpastor will spend an inordinate amount of time reacting to poor behavior rather than inviting the congregation to focus on what matters and is life giving. When an afterpastor takes responsibility for his or her own health and well-being, the dependency begins to be converted into a healthy mutuality with lay leaders and other members, which fosters shared power, leadership, and ministry.

Pastors who can define themselves and curb their overfunctioning no longer perceive themselves as stuck with the entire responsibility for an organization. The responsibility for the health and mission of the congregation begins to rest on the lay leaders. Leadership systems form in such a way that the whole people of God begins to take responsibility for the congregation and its participation in God's mission. The afterpastor assists the congregation in discovering what health looks like, which includes helping the faith community define itself. Afterpastors and lay leaders who together establish and model healthy self-definition and other sound leadership practices serve as catalysts in freeing the congregation to be all that God has created it to be. Friedman explains:

The basic concept of leadership through self-differentiation is this: If a leader will take primary responsibility for his or her own position as "head" and work to define his or her own goals and self, while staying in touch with the rest of the organism, there is more than a reasonable chance that the body will follow. There may be initial resistance but, if the leader can stay in touch with the resisters, the body will usually go along.[8]

Maintaining appropriate relationships and staying healthy is the pastor's (in this case, the afterpastor's) ethical responsibility. The effective afterpastor moves beyond this core requirement and walks alongside congregational leaders and sometimes out in front of them, articulating and modeling a new vision of leadership in which the pastor does not overfunction and the lay leaders do not underfunction. Ideally, wise afterpastors and lay leaders in a congregation recovering from clergy misconduct together examine the entire congregational system to see if it is healthy. They keep in mind that a healthy congregation does not grant unquestioned authority and sole responsibility to a single leader.[9] Not surprisingly, many congregations where misconduct has occurred find that they have an unhealthy focus on clergy and need to move to a system of governance in which the whole people of God take responsibility for the congregation's mission. A congregation that leaves behind the past and seeks health decisively chooses to raise up leaders who expect and are able to work with others. Roles and responsibilities are clarified and renegotiated as pastor and people partner together.

Spirit-led, mission-driven, and team-based congregations create processes where God's people work together to build shared agendas and collaboratively set goals and initiatives. In fact, meetings freely happen, when appropriate, without the pastor present. Incremental moves into this new way of being church are contingent upon building trust between the afterpastor and congregation leaders. Both the afterpastor and lay leaders invite trust, demonstrate that they are trustworthy, act appropriately and in the best interest of congregation, and speak honestly and forthrightly together when anxiety and tensions arise.

It is in this journey of rebuilding and renewal that a congregation becomes a permission-giving organization that celebrates and experiences the reality that every member of a faith community is a minister and is called to use his or her God-given gifts. E. Dixon Junkin, associate for discipleship and spirituality in the Presbyterian Church (U.S.A.), says that ultimately, "our goal should not be that a few make decisions on behalf of all, even if the decisions are good ones, but rather that all might become reacquainted with gospel, with scripture, with the tradition, and with one another."[10]

Shared agenda building values equality, invites participation, and expects commitment from every member of the body of Christ. Leaders and members of congregations who live intentionally into this new vision of leadership become ministers and partners together in God's mission. They are no longer passive and dependent. They are no longer consumers of religious goods and services. They are disciples of Jesus Christ who are living out their life in Christ. They no longer have church done to them, but they do church themselves as they discover that the Holy Spirit calls, gathers, enlightens, sanctifies, and sends them. Junkin writes:

> All too often, the members of our churches are primarily the objects of ministries of others. Others pray over them. Others tell them what scripture says. Others tell them to what obedience they are called. And others engage in ministry on their behalf. But this means that many of our church members never learn how to pray, never become skilled in using their gifts in the interpretation of scripture or of their own experience. They remain children in faith, dependent upon others, and such dependency breeds voicelessness, powerlessness, apathy, or even anger.[11]

A Spirit-led, mission-driven, and team-based congregation discovers that everyone has something to offer. Underfunctioning is no longer acceptable or appropriate, because all the baptized are invited into the privilege of participation. A congregation that rises from the trauma and losses of clergy misconduct lives out of the conviction that it is a privilege and responsibility to be church. The crisis that occurs when misconduct is disclosed creates an opportunity for afterpastors, lay leaders, and members to step forward and to be church together in a new way.

Leaving Egypt Behind

Leaving behind the pastor-centered style of ministry can be disconcerting to a faith community, but faith communities overwhelmed by change are in good company. We remember the biblical account of the Hebrews two months after leaving slavery in Egypt, when the whole community grumbled about its losses to Moses and Aaron. The people's newly experienced freedom raised their anxiety as they faced the unknown. Overwhelmed by what they faced, they spoke honestly to Moses and Aaron: "If only we had died by the hand of the LORD in the land of Egypt, when we sat by the fleshpots and ate our fill of bread; for you have brought us out into this wilderness to kill this whole assembly with hunger" (Exod. 16:3).

During this wilderness experience, the afterpastor and lay leaders are well served to remember how difficult the transition between the known and the unknown is for a congregation. It is important for a faith community in transition to gather regularly around Word and Sacrament, celebrating that God will provide nourishment throughout this time of change, just as God provided manna from heaven to the Hebrews after they left Egypt behind. The afterpastor and other leaders attend faithfully to this gathering, trusting that this spiritual practice will sustain the community of faith as it copes with change. Arbuckle writes:

> The temptation is to be so overwhelmed by these losses that our communities become numb and our energies drained by the struggle, to either restore that which has been irretrievably lost, or deny that these losses have

occurred at all. Hence, the need for a spirituality to help us both to cope positively with the death of irrelevant structures and pastoral methods and to move forward with risk and hope into the future.[12]

The centrality of worship provides a place of healing that pushes back the overwhelming waves of loss that wash over the congregation. Worship is a spiritual practice that reorients the faith community toward God's future. It is in the context of worship that the afterpastor and other worship planners repeatedly lift up a vision of leadership of the whole people of God in mission together, a vision that places a high value on participation and collaboration.

Rebuilding and renewal take time, unfolding over years rather than months, and the afterpastor and lay leaders will experience twists and turns in this journey. The disorientation that a congregation experiences in the aftermath of clergy misconduct does not end quickly. At times the new life bursting forth in the congregation is exhilarating and deeply satisfying; at other times, exhausting and fraught with challenges. The old way of being church will raise its head repeatedly. Congregational leaders will need to keep looking forward as they glance back to learn from the past.

As the faith community lets go of the past, it envisions a future where the structure as well as the practice of leadership values the whole people of God in mission together. Wise afterpastors invite, encourage, affirm, and challenge lay leaders to step forward at this crucial time, trusting that God will provide what is needed in this journey of rebuilding and renewal. The pastor-centered style of doing church slowly shifts toward a way of being church that is Spirit-led, mission-driven, team-based, permission-giving, and gift-shaped. Lay leaders begin to rise to the challenge of taking responsibility for the congregation as they are given permission to use their gifts in this journey of rebuilding and renewal. Gradually, congregational leaders form a new vision for what it means to be church together and to set in place systems that will serve as a foundation for the new life that is breaking forth.

The good news is that God provides enough nourishment to sustain afterpastors, lay leaders, and the congregation as a whole in this journey toward new life. Over time, both pastor and people begin to see themselves as companions who partner together in God's mission. They see each other as equals, and they believe the efforts of every person in the faith community matter. They leave behind old ways of doing church that, though comfortable and familiar, had so many negative consequences. Pastors and lay leaders now share in a covenantal relationship of mutuality, accountability, interdependence, and interconnectedness with one another and the congregation, which soon becomes a joyful and energetic community of faith.

13

PAID AND VOLUNTEER STAFF:
TENDING THEIR OVERLOOKED NEEDS

Nancy Myer Hopkins

JOE HAS BEEN THE SEXTON for St. Swithin's-in-the-Swamp Episcopal Church for 25 years. During most of that time, he has enjoyed his job. He has taken great pride in keeping the "plant" spotless. He has also been willing to be flexible with his work hours. Fifteen years ago, he was confirmed by the bishop, and he regularly attends services. Many people appreciate Joe's quiet, steady presence, and they tell him so. Others do not seem to notice him at all, unless something displeases them about the building or grounds.

For the previous 10 years, however, Joe's job had become much more difficult under the rector, Father Clueless, who was totally unpredictable. One minute, he was kidding around with Joe; the next, he was viciously putting him down. Occasionally the rector erupted in fits of rage, and if they were directed at Joe, the experience left him shattered and ready to quit. Furthermore, Joe was aware that Father Clueless was seeing several women parishioners for long hours of counseling, each of them three or four times a week. In the course of doing his work, Joe saw and heard unmistakable signs that this "counseling" had progressed to sexual activity.

Joe had taken the training that the diocese required for all church employees on safe boundaries in the church, and he knew that his rector's behavior was wrong. Joe was thrown into a crisis of conscience that he felt powerless to deal with. He was afraid if he reported his suspicions to church authorities, the rector would be able to convince his superiors that Joe was lying. Joe was also very afraid that he would lose his job. His participation in the congregation meant a lot to him, and such a loss would have been catastrophic to the large extended family he was helping to support.

So Joe was very relieved when another person brought a complaint, and the rector was ultimately removed. Joe was still left with his feelings of anger, guilt, and ambivalence, however, especially when everyone else was being invited to work with consultants and response teams. But no one thought to tell him what was going on, ask him how he was doing, or even to invite him to participate in the congregational meeting—except to set up the chairs.

Steps Toward Healing

I am always surprised to find that it seldom occurs to denominational leaders to work with the support staff when a clergyperson is removed for cause. Professional staffs are often considered, but support staff and volunteers can be forgotten. Yet these are the people who are most likely to be answering the phone when it starts to ring off the hook. In fact, congregants may consider support staff more accessible than the professional staff in this setting that suddenly feels unsafe, especially before a good chance to process events has been offered to everyone.

Professional, support, and volunteer staff tend to occupy different levels of responsibility and visibility in congregations. The nature of these roles is largely dependent on class and cultural custom, the size of the congregation, length of tenure on staff, and whether or not staff are also members of the congregation. When a leader is removed for a trust betrayal, staff members are sure to feel the effects acutely. Some may understand that they have been emotionally or sexually abused by the offender. Certain staff who have been abused by the offender, however, because of their deep ambivalence or unwillingness to define what happened to them as abuse, stay loyal well past what most people would consider a rational point.

Whenever a staff person is sexually exploited or harassed by a superior, a pattern of "grooming" will have taken place. Such grooming usually includes focusing on people's vocational vulnerability—the fact that they occupy positions on the lower rungs of the office ladder. If they are made to feel special and absolutely indispensable to the offender and the congregation, then they are more likely to continue to champion the agenda of the offender, long after his removal. Others on staff will have observed this grooming, and seeds of jealousy have been sown that can germinate later into full-scale conflict. Staffs that have been conflicted for any other reason prior to a leader's removal will likely be even more highly conflicted as they respond to the removal of their boss, and often they represent a microcosm of the larger congregational struggle.

Volunteers or seminary interns being mentored by the offending clergy are also vulnerable. In addition to sexual advances, hostility and hazing, especially of women staff, are often reported. Some of this hostility is probably reflective of patriarchal attitudes towards women's "place" in society, which still operate in our culture today. When an impaired cleric is at the helm, the power imbalance inherent in these relationships can quickly edge over into power abuse.

Occasionally, a staff member who is not a member of the congregation will have been a victim of an impaired cleric who was his or her boss. Even though the constitutional separation of church and state means that the religious organization will not be subject to federal or state law regarding sexual harassment of employees, the religious system should, at the very least, honor the principles of federal and state sexual harassment law. It would be unethical to do otherwise.

Whatever the precise roles of church staff members, conflict is likely to result if the staff's needs for healing are not addressed. A conflicted staff can make it much harder for the afterpastor to minister effectively, requiring an inordinate amount of energy that could better be used elsewhere. Small staffs may be able to adequately process their grief along with the congregation, but many staffs will benefit from being worked with separately. Certainly if there is active conflict within any size staff, as much separate time as it takes to reclaim a good working relationship will be absolutely necessary. An outside consultant, *not* the afterpastor, can be helpful. It may be necessary to give individuals clear warnings about behavioral expectations, document significant failures, and as a last resort, let go of staff members who cannot adjust to the new realities. The responsibility for hiring and firing varies with denominational policy, which should be followed carefully and with good legal advice.

In several chapters in part 2 of this book, conflict in "after" congregations was described using the frames of trauma, grief, and power abuse. When addressing conflict among staff members, remember that staffs are also traumatized. Longstanding and unrelated animosity between certain staff members may also be present. Staff turf battles may have been exacerbated by the departed Beloved Former Pastor, who worked deliberately to drive wedges between staff members to further his or her own ends. Those impaired clerics who are manipulative seem to instinctively know how to do this. It takes some probing from a skilled consultant, working with the entire staff, to expose such manipulation and begin to address it. If this work is not done, however, staffs can continue to be conflicted to the point where they cannot successfully serve the congregation.

There is a relationship between a congregation's size and staff issues. Smaller congregations have often had to fend for themselves. They see clergy come and go much more frequently, and if they have strong and relatively healthy lay leaders, they may recover more easily from an isolated offense. However, this advantage seems to be offset if they get a string of inept clergy who either act out in a variety of destructive ways or do not leave well. Therefore, a trust betrayal can be catastrophic to the small congregation, because a critical mass of congregants as well as staff resources are marginal to begin with, and lay leaders can easily burn out while other congregants gradually drift away.

"Tall steeple" congregations may attract clergy who are at risk to offend. Some clergy who are attracted to these "prestigious" settings may have a type of serious personality disorder that on the surface makes them look very attractive to large congregations. A charismatic style of leadership combined with a witty persona and a popular preaching style can grow a congregation, at least in the short run. Many people will "fall in love" with such a cleric, and a clergyperson who is not healthy will encourage the ardor.

Congregants can experience terrible disillusionment later if the attractive style masks destructive behaviors such as emotional manipulation and various abuses of people who are perceived to be either threats or especially vulnerable. For such a cleric, power is intoxicating, and the role itself is seductive. When abuse in this context is finally exposed, we observe extreme and intractable conflict between those who continue to protect their illusions about this pastor and those who understand the extent of the damage. These are also the congregations where afterpastors seem to have the most difficult time, at least in part because of the impossibility of following a cleric who is still "beloved" by many and who may not have even had the grace to leave the wider community.

Support staff may know a lot about the swirl of secrets that has enveloped the congregation for years, yet if support staff are left out of the official information loop and not given a chance to process their own confusion and grief, they will suffer enormously. In their suffering, they will not be able to occupy well that most vital link in the congregation's communication system at a time when clear and truthful information must be carefully disseminated. While they do have a crucial role to play in the congregation's recovery, their first task is to tend to their own healing. Only then will they be able to contribute to the well-being of the congregation as a whole.

14

WHISTLE-BLOWERS: PERSEVERING AGAINST INJUSTICE

Candace R. Benyei

THE ROLE AND RESPONSIBILITY OF THE WHISTLE-BLOWER is difficult to discuss, especially because both currently and historically, blowing the whistle on a clergyperson who engages in misconduct, especially sexual abuse, has been for the most part a sacrificial task. The church—its leadership and membership—has not wanted to know about the problem of clergy misconduct and has most often reacted to the bad news by either denying the reality or shooting the messenger. Given that unfortunate state, however, we can examine the interplay of power, ethical perspectives, and personal development with respect to each possible discloser—victim, afterpastor, lay leaders or lay members, paid and unpaid support staff, clergy colleagues, student ministers, and denominational leaders. Then we may discern different possibilities for each based on her or his role in the religious system and the power afforded the individual by that system.

Denominational leaders and clergy may have the most power and therefore are least vulnerable in a religious system, as long as they are disclosing the unethical conduct of people lower in the hierarchy. In general, from a job security point of view, it is safest to blow the whistle on people who do not have the power to fire you. The risk in such situations then becomes the possibility of being ostracized by colleagues. Afterpastors are particularly at risk of being ostracized or losing their job if they choose to be a whistle-blower, because such individuals are lightning rods for congregational grief and anger in families of faith that have suffered prior clergy misconduct. As such, the jobs of afterpastors are always tenuous. Paid support staff are, of course, at risk of losing at least their job and paycheck, while unpaid support staff who disclose are in danger of losing a meaningful vocation should they blow the whistle on a superior, and especially a clergyperson. Laypeople, while immune to monetary consequences, are at risk for being expelled from their religious community for being "trouble makers," and student ministers are probably the most vulnerable, as they can lose their sponsoring community, their vocation, and a career that has just cost them dearly in educational expenses.

A whistle-blower has usually made a decision to live authentically in a difficult situation. In most Christian denominations, we are enjoined to "persevere in resisting evil" and "strive for justice and peace among all people, and respect the dignity of every human being."[1] Although denominations differ in the way they express such expectations, Christians are generally expected to attempt to live an ethical and responsible life where we do no harm to our neighbor, do not countenance harm done to our neighbor by others, and love our neighbor as ourselves.

Unfortunately, as human beings, consciously and unconsciously we tend to support behaviors and social regulation that are beneficial to us but not necessarily beneficial or just to others. This seems to be a fairly common human trait. Frequently, because we are unwilling to discomfort ourselves, we are not disposed to take even those first steps in understanding our neighbor's situation. Moreover, contact with the pain of another often reminds us of our own personal pain—pain that often we have been trying to deny because we don't know what to do with it. We might suffer the pain of a difficult marriage, hanging on to a meaningless job because it pays well or has insurance benefits, or loneliness. Because we are afraid to confront our own situation, we cannot tolerate being reminded of our personal plight by witnessing the hurt of someone else. God pleads with us to have the courage to touch our own suffering, that we might be willing to touch—and heal—the suffering of others.

Once whistle-blowers or witnesses have accepted the mission, their task is to attempt to make the unethical conduct known in the best way they know how. This disclosure, of course, will vary depending up the whistle-blower's age, role, and power in the religious community, as well as personal resources. There is probably no right way to blow the whistle, and most whistle-blowers will, in hindsight, wish they had done things a bit differently. When a whistle-blower is deciding to disclose information that most folks do not want to hear, it is difficult to be a nonanxious presence. Frequently, religious systems are particularly deaf, so it may take a number of attempts before a whistle-blower is actually heard. Probably the hardest call is deciding if or when to stop trying to penetrate the veil of denial.

After Disclosure

After disclosure, the job of whistle-blowers is to maintain their mental and spiritual integrity in the face of a certain storm. Frequently the congregation or judicatory will react to disclosure by denying not only the allegations, but the personal reality, credibility, and good character of the whistle-blower, and will take action to maintain the secret through intimidation. Messengers of this sort are almost always scapegoated by the community of which they are a part, because they have broken the family rule and told the secret. Family and organizational systems all have tacit rules (see chapter 6) that are enforced by coercive behaviors that always include the threat of abandonment or exclusion should a member dare to breach the agreement. When a community has unconsciously or tacitly agreed to keep shameful, destructive, or unethical behavior secret, it feels betrayed by the secret teller and seeks retribution in order to preserve the public facade of well-being.

Whistle-blowers need to have significant self-knowledge, personal awareness of their own family of origin issues, and the ability to love and accept themselves. These are useful prerequisites to personal survival in situations of this sort. To be effective, such witnesses must stay alive until the message is heard.

Furthermore, to strengthen themselves against the tide of certain reprisal, it is useful for whistle-blowers, before delivering the message, to attempt to identify people they can trust to be emotionally—and often vocationally—supportive. Once the difficult news has been delivered to the religious community, powerful system dynamics will often attempt to deny or distort the reality of the messenger, making whistle-blowers feel more than a little crazy, even to the point of questioning their perceptions. In order to weather this storm and before delivering the message, whistle-blowers want to seek good and supportive counsel to weigh and confirm the evidence of misconduct. If this is not possible, it is useful for whistle-blowers to carefully write out their "case," so that the evidence can be referred to in crazy-feeling moments.

Finally, the largest task of whistle-blowers is to recognize that they are indeed breaking a family rule and that when we break rules, fair or not, we have to accept the consequences. When Jesus turned over the tables of the moneychangers in the temple, he knew that the temple priests' reprisal would not be far behind. It is not useful or kind to oneself to ignore the probable consequences of purposeful actions, especially when retribution is likely. It is important that whistle-blowers not fool themselves about this. To become a whistle-blower without first prayerfully making peace with God—agreeing to step into the unknown, acknowledging the probable consequences, moving in faith that this is what God requires, asking for the strength to endure what is to come, and knowing that somehow, as Julian of Norwich testified, "it will be all right, and it will be all right"—is only to invite an overwhelming sense of betrayal and unrequited anger. Only God gives the whistle-blower a gold star, and that has to be good enough. Although all of us would like to believe that our religious organizations and congregations wish to be healed of the insult of clergy misconduct, the faith community will not likely affirm a whistle-blower for making an uncomfortable subject such as this public.

The Special Case of Victim Whistle-Blowers

Sometimes it is the victim who makes the first disclosure of the unethical behavior of a clergyperson or lay leader. Only very rarely will a child victim disclose, because children are ultimately powerless in an adult system on which they are dependent. A child knows intuitively that to disclose clergy misconduct to people, including the child's parents and siblings, who see the clergyperson or lay leader as "God all good and powerful," will result in rejection, emotional abandonment, and punishment. Therefore, in the service of survival, children usually will not disclose unless they intuit that they have a near and friendly ear.

In a system that adulates and protects clergy, the victim has the least credibility and, therefore, power, due to his or her primary involvement with the offending cleric. The only responsibility a victim whistle-blower has is to attempt to survive well, and this can be a tall order indeed. (See chapter 13 for guidance about victim's/survivor's healing.) Frequently in the case of both child and adult victims, the individual has been groomed to feel as if he or she is special in the eyes of the abuser. As a result, if these individuals disclose the unethical behavior, they feel guilty of the worst kind of betrayal—betrayal of the perpetrator. Adult victims in committed relationships feel doubly guilty of betrayal, as their primary relationship has also been breached. Adult seminarians, student ministers, or associate ministers who are victims almost universally lose their vocation if they disclose, so the fear of the loss of meaning and livelihood is paramount. Victims' primary task is to attempt to survive well by finding appropriate resources to facilitate their own healing as well as the healing of their relationship with their partner, should there be one. In later stages of healing, victims will often make meaning out of their experience by helping other victims.

Victims are most often unaware of any established disclosure process within a religious institution, partly because these processes are frequently not in place, and partly because when in place they are not advertised to the laity. And it is an unfortunate reality that even if such a process is available on paper, most frequently it is poorly—or dangerously—administered with respect to the victim. Victims should never be required to confront the perpetrator as an entry point into the process, and confrontation at any stage may well serve only to revictimize an individual, especially if the perpetrator denies the victim's reality and the abuser's trespass.

Whistle-blowing is a form of witness to a faith that strives to persevere against the evil of social injustice. This is not an easy task, nor did Jesus promise it would be. Nonetheless, we are all called to be prophets; that is, we are all called to stand up and be counted even though we stand against the opinion of what may be the comfortable majority. To do so is to live authentically, and for the Christian, authenticity is the real meaning behind the concept of living one's life in Christ.

Clergy Colleagues: Responding from a Unique Perspective

Deborah Pope-Lance

IN THE AFTERMATH OF MISCONDUCT, the impact of clergy sexual misconduct on clergy colleagues and on the ministerial professions is rarely considered. Focused on the obvious needs of primary victims and the dysfunctional upset in affected organizations, those called upon to deal with clergy misconduct might believe clergy colleagues do not warrant much attention. Nevertheless, as both witnesses to and colleagues of offending clergy, other clergy are adversely affected by the misconduct. Understanding the unique experience and responding to the needs of clergy colleagues will ameliorate this adverse impact and support clergy colleagues in ministering more effectively in the aftermath of misconduct.

The Experience of Colleagues

Clergy colleagues must be counted among the secondary victims of clergy misconduct.[1] Like other secondary victims, clergy colleagues exhibit a range of responses. Some colleagues express shock and disbelief. Members of a trusted and honorable profession themselves, colleagues wonder, How could a person entrusted with the spiritual care of others take advantage of someone like that? How could a person anointed by God, a person called to do God's work, fail so miserably and cruelly? This incredulity can lead to denial that the misconduct did occur.

Other clergy express deep sadness. They recognize the many losses experienced by everyone involved. A congregation has lost its minister. Primary victims have been harmed, as well, having lost church, job, friends, or relationships. An offending cleric's family may lose church, income, home, and a whole network of friends and family. Even the offending cleric loses, suffering at his or her own hand a loss of job, status, reputation, and whatever may have been his or her best aspirations for ministry. Clergy colleagues, recognizing these losses, grieve for others' suffering and their own. Clergy, whether despondent over their own experiences in ministry or already questioning their call or career, may experience these sad recognitions as further evidence of their own tenuous position or lack of suitability for ministry. A cluster of local cases of clergy sexual misconduct by colleagues, as has frequently occurred in recent decades, can provoke noteworthy despair in high-functioning clergy and significant depression among others who were already uneasy.

Those who were close friends or classmates of an offending cleric frequently admit to feeling tricked or duped. Offenders presented themselves as good people, competent ministers, genuine, and trustworthy. In the aftermath of misconduct, colleagues discover that their friend and classmate was not letting them know what was really going on. Beyond being disappointed at their colleague's poor behavior, they feel angry and betrayed: "She knew better. She left this place a chaotic, traumatized mess. What was she thinking?" Clergy support each other's projects and careers: "I helped him get that appointment," one complained furiously, "and he used it to cover his sexual liaison with a district lay leader." Or, "I backed him up when the board questioned him, and now, it turns out their questions were well founded. How could he abuse our friendship like this?"

Experienced as both a personal and professional betrayal, a colleague's misconduct strains clergy relationships. Connections and collaborations within professional organizations, the local and wider church, and denominations are adversely affected. Some colleagues in the aftermath of misconduct report disrupted connection and communion with God. Grieving and uncertain, clergy take sides on issues, sometimes on the basis of loyalty, not reason—creating conflict, animosity, and further public confusion. No longer sure whom they can trust, they may question anyone's motives and honesty. Colleagues in positions of authority such as judicatory staff may become the targets of their uncertainty. "Why did the bishop [or the DS or the association minister] allow him or her to engage in these behaviors?" The adjudication process itself may lose public confidence as some may wonder, How can we know what the truth is when so much is being kept secret? Some clergy may wonder how God could have allowed an ordained person to cause so much harm. In the aftermath of misconduct, some may question whether God is present or acting through this church or these clergy. Clergy may despair of God's presence in their own prayer life, their worship leadership, and the lives of their church members.

Many colleagues do report feeling scandalized and embarrassed. Newspapers cover the stories of offenders, using each new detail or development as an occasion to recap the story. Parishioners, shaking hands after Sunday services, alternatively disparage colleagues by suggesting ministry is "a job with great perks" or "a profession full of charlatans." Nonoffending clergy sense the whole of their profession is painted by the public with the same sordid brush. In order to avoid embarrassment or ridicule, some clergy admit to concealing their profession when in public or removing their collars when not at work.

A Unique Perspective

Unlike other secondary victims in the aftermath of misconduct, colleagues have a particular relationship with and similarity to clergy who engage in misconduct. As colleagues, they are engaged in the same kind of work. While their specific ministry settings or tasks may differ, clergy colleagues understand the nature of each other's labors and identify with each other's experience, both professional and personal. Colleagues appreciate how much of themselves individual clergy give to their work, how often they are defenseless against unwarranted criticism, and how exposed they can feel when helping fragile or needy people. While most clergy serve alone without other ministers as coworkers, as a group, clergy often feel like a team working together for the good of the church. When they hear that one of their own has been accused of misconduct, they can't imagine how it happened. They may think, "I wouldn't have done that" and so "It can't be true." Overidentification with their accused colleague may compel them to over-look evidence, to dismiss charges prematurely, or to rationalize the behavior.

On the other hand, as clergy struggle to make sense of proven allegations against a colleague, they may reason that the misconduct occurred because the colleague is not at all like them. Instead, they assure themselves, in order to have engaged in this behavior, the offending colleague must be sick, needy, sinful, un-suitable, poorly trained, or sociopathic. While some offenders' behavior may be understood to be a consequence of a minister's inadequacies, illnesses, or weak-nesses, not all misconduct can be explained in this way. Ministers who dismiss a colleague's misconduct as something that could never happen in their ministry may not avail themselves of adequate support or training for prevention. They may incorrectly believe that they do not need to consider strategies to prevent unprofessional, boundary-violating, or abusive behavior in their own ministries.

Collegues' Collusion in Misconduct

After a colleague's misconduct has been disclosed, some clergy must face up to the fact that they knew of a colleague's misconduct and did little or nothing to stop it. Others will be reminded of their own misconduct histories—as unidenti-fied perpetrators of misconduct or sometimes as silent victims and survivors. Some will assess the present occurrence of misconduct only through the lens of their own history; others will be compelled to some new assessment and resolu-tion. Two different collegial reactions in the aftermath of misconduct illustrate the difficulty in fulfilling one's collegial responsibility and the confusion that persists about how best to accomplish it.

First, in the aftermath of a colleague's proven misconduct, more than a few clergy, forced to think about their past unethical behavior, now must observe col-leagues being accused and held accountable by adjudication some years after the behaviors ceased. These sometimes reformed colleagues no doubt acknowledge, if only to themselves, that they too may be held accountable. Still others under-stand in a new way that they are currently engaged in unethical behavior that if discovered can lead to removal of standing or litigation. Reasonably fearing disclosure, these clergy colleagues may be inclined to argue that false accusations are common, allegations should be kept secret, statutes of limitations should be imposed, and adverse consequences should be weighed against a colleague's years of otherwise fine service. Regrettably, they appear more concerned with ministers not being accused, found out, or punished than with any effort to prevent unethical behavior and encourage good practices in themselves or others. These colleagues would serve themselves and their profession better by acknowledging their failures to themselves, ceasing their present misconduct, and then with a trusted colleague or well-trained counselor, honestly examining their behavior, assessing their risk, establishing preventive strategies, and agreeing to accountability structures that would ensure they do not repeat the behaviors. Some may need to consider more extensive support and treatment or a switch in careers or career settings.

Second, and stunningly, several surveys indicate that prior to or apart from any disclosure or adjudication of misconduct, most clergy are aware of their colleagues' unethical behavior. In one survey of ministers, 76.5 percent of clergy reported that they knew of a minister who had sexual intercourse with a church member.[2] In another, 70.4 percent reported knowledge of colleagues who had sexual contact with someone in their church.[3] In a recent survey, not a single minister who admitted to knowing of a colleague's misconduct confronted the colleague or reported the misconduct to an appropriate supervisory or adjudicatory body.[4]

Not surprisingly in the aftermath of colleagues' misconduct, many clergy express regret or guilt. They may have suspected a colleague was in trouble, that alcohol or stress was affecting his or her judgment. Perhaps they did not reach out, or when they did, their intervention had little effect. They may have witnessed behaviors that suggested a colleague was engaged in inappropriate behavior with church members but, embarrassed or shocked or incredulous, never said anything to anyone. Or perhaps they confronted the colleague only to be dismissed and belittled. Or perhaps as this clergyperson's associate or intern, there was little they felt they could do without bringing harm on themselves. They may not have known what to do. Any of these clergy may express remorse at not having done something to protect the vulnerable but remain, even years afterwards, confused about what they could or should have done or what they should do now when they know of a colleague's misconduct.

If someone comes to a clergyperson and alleges that a colleague is engaged in sexual misconduct with him or her, the clergyperson should respond first by listening and believing; second, by helping to identify continuing support; and third, by directing the person to those responsible for receiving and following up on allegations. (See chapters 11, 22, and 28 for further discussion of victims/survivors.) A clergyperson who hears an allegation may not be an appropriate source of support for a victim but has a pastoral obligation to make certain that the individual obtains appropriate support and advocacy for reporting a colleague's misconduct.

Clergy who themselves become aware of a colleague's misconduct should report this awareness to appropriate bodies within their denominations or professional organization. Prior to doing so, a colleague would be well served to understand the applicable denominational guidelines, standards of conduct, and policies regarding misconduct. A colleague may wish to understand as well what state statutes may govern a clergyperson's conduct. From this understanding, a colleague should be able to identify the appropriate person to whom to make a report. Before contacting this person, a colleague should choose a trusted friend, minister, or lay leader to advocate on his or her behalf amid any adverse consequences. (See chapter 14, "Whistle-Blowers.") Whenever possible, colleagues should, as a group, report another colleague's suspected misconduct. Colleagues, supervised by or serving in associate or assistant positions to clergy who are suspected of misconduct, should be especially cautious when reporting misconduct to congregation leaders or denominational officials. Individual colleagues who report another's misconduct, perceived as messengers of bad news, have frequently been blamed, isolated, scapegoated, and penalized for alleging misconduct by esteemed elder colleagues. When a clergyperson has reason to believe that a colleague has engaged in misconduct, he or she should not conduct an investigation. A colleague's job is not to determine whether suspicions are true or can be proven. Neither should a clergyperson directly confront a colleague, demanding to know the truth. When confronted prior to any formal report, offending colleagues may attempt to galvanize support, conceal evidence, utilize influence, make contacts to protect themselves, or preempt formal reports to adjudicating bodies.

Ethical Challenges for Colleagues

The ministerial professions possess an inherent ethical challenge. The personal, confidential nature of a minister's work, overlapping roles with parishioners, lack of supervision, and confusion of intimate spiritual experience with sexual feelings generate conditions that can challenge a minister's capacity to maintain ethical practices. Ministers are responsible for managing these inherent ethical risks. When an otherwise healthy, competent minister does not manage them properly or adequately, whether because of his or her own high stress, lack of training, or lack of appropriate support, misconduct is likely to occur. In the aftermath of misconduct, clergy colleagues who recognize that "if it happened to him or her, it could happen to me" will be better prepared to meet the ethical challenges of ministry and less likely to engage in misconducts of all types. Close collegial relationships and a sense of identification with an offending cleric can unwittingly support colleagues' denial or dismissal of misconduct allegations. But when colleagues straightforwardly consider the nature and demands of their profession, awareness of their similarities and camaraderie can foster appropriate concern and lead to good prevention.

In the aftermath of misconduct, some clergy worry that what happened to their colleague—allegations of misconduct—might happen to them. They may wonder whether they are acting as they should or as others think they should. They may ask: Will my behavior be misunderstood as inappropriate? Will church members question the way I conduct myself in ministry? Could false allegations be made against me? Others will realize that they were once close to engaging inappropriate behavior or will fear that they are close to doing so now and will worry, How close am I? Confusion regarding standards of conduct or behavioral expectations for clergy exacerbates these worries.

Honest conversation among colleagues can clarify this confusion and assuage unnecessary worry. First, by talking together about how best to manage interpersonal boundaries, how to work effectively with vulnerable people, or how to ensure adequate self-care, clergy can remain aware of the inherent ethical challenges in ministry and develop successful strategies to meet these. Second, by articulating together an ethical standard of conduct and holding each other accountable to this standard, they can help each other protect against even the appearance of impropriety. Third, colleagues who speak realistically about their professional and personal experience and who can speak honestly about their concerns, acknowledge their missteps, and seek correction from one another will improve their effectiveness and greatly reduce their risk for misconduct or allegations. Clergy are true colleagues when they can take responsibility together for supporting and holding one another to the highest standards of practice in ministry. And fourth, clergy can educate laity about appropriate professional practices in ministry and involve these educated laity in the supervision and support of clergy. Further, clergy can invite laity to participate in the adjudication of allegations of misconduct, generating support—useful resources, understanding and accountability—that will lessen clergy members' worries, minimize their risk of misconduct, and hold to them the highest standard of practice.

Many of the ethical codes that guide ministerial practice speak of a clergyperson's commitment to ethical service and good practices and their responsibility to monitor their own and each other's adherence to these codes. The Ordained Minister's Code of the United Church of Christ (UCC), for example, asks clergy to affirm: "I will not use my position, power, or authority to exploit any person."[5] Some standards of practice are quite specific. For example, guidelines of the Evangelical Lutheran Church in America (ELCA) state, "Ordained ministers are expected to reject sexual promiscuity, the manipulation of others for purposes of sexual gratification, and all attempts of sexual seduction and sexual harassment, including taking physical or emotional advantage of others."[6] Most codes speak of an ordained minister's responsibility to support compliance with these standards, as the UUC code does when it encourages: "I will stand in a supportive relationship with my colleagues in ordained, commissioned, and licensed ministry, offering and receiving counsel and support in times of need."[7] Few codes address exactly how one should stand in "supportive relationship" with a colleague one suspects has failed to adhere to the code. One exception is the Unitarian Universalist Ministers Association (UUMA) Code of Professional Practice, which admonishes, "Should I know that a colleague is engaged in practices that are damaging, as defined in our Code of Professional Practice, I will speak openly and frankly to her/him and endeavor to be of help. If necessary, I will bring such matters to the attention of the UUMA Executive Committee."[8] Unfortunately, the lack of direction offered to most clergy who suspect that a colleague may be engaged in sexual misconduct increases the likelihood that colleagues will not effectively support and counsel one another in times of need.

Colleagues who exercise their responsibility to support one another in meeting ethical standards will hold one other accountable when those standards are not met. Significant education in seminary and continuing education programs help create an environment in which awareness of and intolerance for misdeeds are high. In addition, clear written standards provide a common language and sense of common struggle with which colleagues can support one another in ministering ethically and competently. Consistent application of policies and procedures regarding clergy conduct helps maintain a culture of clarity regarding standards of practice. When clergy colleagues are prominent among those thoroughly investigating concerns, adjudicating allegations, consistently applying standards, and imposing consequences, they send a clear message that they will not tolerate misconduct by their colleagues. Such a message ultimately will reduce the occurrence of misconduct and its demoralizing, harmful aftermath.

16

JUDICATORY LEADERS:
A RESOURCE FOR HEALING

Glenndy Sculley

THE TASKS OF THE JUDICATORY in responding to an incidence of clergy misconduct occur over a long time period—years, not weeks or months—with varying levels of intensity. Judicatory leaders remain committed to the long-term health of the congregation, the victim and his or her family, and the offender and his or her family. Nancy Myer Hopkins has laid out in the first chapter of this book the best first steps when a betrayal has occurred. The health of the postbetrayal relationship between the judicatory and all parties is critical to the long-term well-being of those involved.

Judicatory leaders will usually play important roles in triage and support in the immediate aftermath of clergy misconduct. But anniversaries of the disclosure, anniversaries of events in individuals' lives where the offender played an important role, and important occasions in the church year are all examples of occasions when pain is likely to resurface, and some acknowledgment of the betrayal will be needed.

Judicatory Presence in the Immediate Aftermath

In most mainline denominations, the judicatory plays a crucial role in determining that a pastor must leave a congregation because of misconduct. In most mainline denominations, it is also the role of the judicatory to determine if the pastor is allowed to remain a clergyperson in good standing—sometimes called a licensed or rostered leader—in that denomination. When the judicatory leader meets with the pastor to confront the pastor with the misconduct complaint, it is critical that the pastor be instructed *not* to communicate with the victim, the victim's family, or the victim's friends. Neither should the pastor begin contacting her or his own supporters in the congregation. Often pastors make these contacts to build support before disclosure occurs, but alleged offenders must be clearly informed that any such attempts will only make things worse for them and for the congregation.

When a pastor acknowledges the misconduct, action to remove the pastor from public leadership should be undertaken as quickly as possible. If the pastor denies the allegations, an investigation is conducted according to judicatory rules to discover if grounds for removal exist. Each denomination deals with this process in its own way, and the particulars of each situation will affect how the matter is addressed. For example, the extent and type of misconduct, the age and gender of the victim(s), the relationship of the clergyperson to the victim(s), the clergyperson's denial or admission of misconduct, and many other variables will need to be carefully weighed to determine the proper role of the judicatory office.

When it becomes clear that either (a) the pastor acknowledges the misconduct or (b) the investigation determines that sufficient ground for sustaining the complaint exists, the judicatory official makes an appointment with the church board. The judicatory executive, along with another staff person or some members of the judicatory's response team (see chapter 17, "Response Teams"), should meet as soon as possible with the elected leaders and the staff of the congregation. These are two separate meetings, primarily because the concerns of the two groups will be different. Each meeting should be viewed by judicatory staff as an initial disclosure meeting limited to the particular group. Understanding the meetings in this way will help the judicatory approach the individuals who are hearing the information for the first time with empathy.

Meeting with Elected Officials

Because the judicatory official usually learns of allegations of misconduct from a victim, a member of the victim's family, or a congregational member who has become aware of the misconduct, the initial meeting with the congregation's elected leaders is usually held at the request of the judicatory executive. Sometimes, however, the board will have become aware of misconduct and will call the judicatory office. In some instances, there has already been some initial contact and disclosure to the board president or other congregational leaders. In any case, a meeting with the board should be conducted. At this meeting with the board, the judicatory executive explains to the board the allegation(s) and whether or not the alleged offender has confessed or resigned from the call to the congregation or is denying the allegations.

It is useful at this meeting to provide board members with a draft copy of the letter that will be sent to the congregation or read at a congregational meeting. When possible, congregational leaders should be given the opportunity to have input into the letter. Typically, the identity of the victim is not disclosed, but enough facts are given to indicate the nature of the misconduct (for example, "sexual misconduct with an adult female"). When possible, the victim(s) should be notified of the letter's contents and when it will be sent. When appropriate, it is desirable to also inform the alleged offender.

Time for prayer and time to begin the process of open conversation will be important first steps. Board members should be encouraged to voice their anger, sense of betrayal, pain, and the myriad other emotions this disclosure will bring to the surface. The board should be encouraged to always take time for prayer together throughout the coming months, to disagree with one another while supporting each other in the difficulties they will face, and to make personal use of outside resources (such as therapists, staff consultants, and other professionals).

Judicatory officials and response team members who conduct this meeting should be prepared to answer several questions:

- "Do we really have to tell the whole congregation?" The truth, Christ said, will make us free, and you can honestly say that the church has learned that when congregations keep secrets, they are never healthy.
- "Can't we just forgive him and move on?" The answer to this question is that there is forgiveness in God for all sin, but this disclosure is not about forgiveness. It is about the public practice of ministry, which is not a right but a responsibility to be borne with integrity. Judicatory leaders and response team members can say, again with total care and honesty, that their task is to help the church be a safe place for all people. The church expects that those who have accepted the role of public leader are carrying out their ministries in a way that does not bring reproach to the church.
- "Will we be sued?" Likely at this point, judicatory leaders will not know the answer to this question. It is a good time for the board to be reminded that, for now, that is not the primary concern of the judicatory staff, and it doesn't need to be theirs, either. The judicatory executive needs to demonstrate an attitude of calm around this question, because quite often, this issue is the one about which boards are most anxious. It is *not* the question to worry about now.
- "What do we do next?" The judicatory executive and response team members will help the board begin planning for the congregational disclosure meeting. The disclosure meeting itself is described in some detail in chapter 1.

Meeting with Congregational Staff

Once again, the basic information as it is known by the judicatory staff person is shared with the congregation staff. Staff members will have a range of responses, and the judicatory officials and response team may hear intense surprise and grief, little or no surprise, immediate fear about the future of the congregation or their own positions, or any number of other reactions. Those meeting with the staff will understand that, for the staff, the misconduct feels more like personal betrayal than for some members of the council. It may be helpful to include the congregation's president or other elected leaders in this meeting with the staff. The necessity of working together as staff and board will become even more important in the coming days and weeks.

If the victim is a staff member, it is still important that those meeting with the staff not disclose the identity of the victim unless he or she has given clear permission. Rarely in a disclosure meeting will it be safe for the judicatory to identify the individual(s) who have been victimized. Judicatory leaders may tell the staff (and even the board) that they are secondary and tertiary victims of this pastor's misconduct and that they have every reason to feel wounded by this behavior.

At this meeting with staff, it is important for the judicatory leader to explain as much as possible of the following information:

- What the next steps will be for the judicatory, the board, and the staff
- Which staff members, if any, are to respond to questions from congregational members
- What staff members with communication responsibility, if any, should say
- What communications should be referred to designated congregation leaders

For both elected congregational leaders and staff leaders, the judicatory should, if possible, provide assistance with the following resources, which the congregation will likely need in the immediate future:

- Guidance for dealing with the media
- Copies of the letter the judicatory will be providing in the following days to the congregation
- Copies of the judicatory's prevention policies and practices—for information
- The name of an individual at the judicatory office who will serve as primary contact for the board and staff

As much as possible, the elected leaders and staff members of the congregation who answer questions, whether from congregational members or others, should follow the information in the judicatory executive's letter or in the congregation's own letter, if one has been written. (See also chapter 13, "Paid and Volunteer Staff.")

Meeting with the Congregation

The disclosure meeting with the congregation (described in detail in chapter 1) is critical to beginning the restoration of health in the congregation. The judicatory official(s) and, as appropriate, the response team members will treat this meeting as an opportunity to *begin* a different relationship with a congregation—one now based on a shared wound. Those from outside the congregation who participate in this meeting must be sympathetic, empathetic, and self-differentiated.

The intensity of a congregation's pain in this initial disclosure meeting is palpable. The betrayal cuts to a personal level for many (and usually most) members, and the judicatory official cannot expect to be welcomed. But this meeting is the first of several opportunities to demonstrate the deep care that the judicatory will consistently use when working with a betrayed congregation. Steadiness and compassion must be paramount.

In some instances, the congregation will direct anger toward the victim. It is important as part of the meeting to explain that it is always the pastor's responsibility to maintain boundaries. All steps possible should be taken to diffuse congregational anger directed towards the victim.

As part of the meeting and in written notices, it is important that judicatory and response team leaders invite members of the congregation to contact a named judicatory staff person with further concerns or complaints. Often when disclosure takes place, other victims will come forward. Designating a judicatory staff person to contact will give these victims the opportunity to report their own stories.

The same questions asked by the council and staff will be asked by members of the congregation. Often, the tone of this meeting is antagonistic. Members blame the judicatory for bringing this "problem" to light. Members demand to know the identity of the victim. Members express their grief, which is often layered over sadness that grows out of the fact that this pastor provided wonderful care to them and their families. For these and several other reasons, this meeting is an important time to introduce the response team.

The response team—or other skilled small-group leaders trained by the team or a therapist—can then work with the members in small groups, allowing them the time and the professional resources to begin to process this tragic information. Congregational members and response team members can pray together, in tangible reassurance that the body of Christ is present even through sad times.

What's Next?

The answers to the question "What's next?" depend on a number of factors that the judicatory cannot control. But the judicatory staff and other responders must remain available. Regular check-in with the victim, the offender, and the congregation can aid all in the healing process.

For the Victim

Victims/survivors often describe the anxiety of the initial meeting with the judicatory. Will they be believed? And even if they are, will the judicatory staff person be mad at them for hurting a pastor's career? When the judicatory official conducts the initial meeting well, much of the victim's uncertainty will be put to rest and future meetings will be less anxiety laden.

It takes courage for victims to step into the office of an official who is two or three levels removed, systemically, from them. When the judicatory official, on hearing the complaint, can with good conscience affirm that courage and listen carefully to all that the victim says, it is important that she or he do so. It is important to outline what steps will be taken in response to the complaint. It is crucial to keep the victim well informed about what will be happening throughout the process. To the best of the judicatory officials' ability, power to make decisions should not be taken away from the victim.

Both before and after congregational disclosure, it is critical to provide a victim advocate, if the victim will accept one. *The advocate must not be a judicatory staff member.* The best-case scenario is when several judicatories share advocates, so victims can select an advocate from another judicatory or, if possible, another denomination. The advocate's sole responsibility is to work with, and on behalf of, the victims as they make their way through the process. Additionally, both victim and advocate must understand that though every attempt will be made to protect the victim's identity, judicatory officials cannot guarantee anonymity.

Along with therapy and advocacy, judicatory leaders may offer a victim a pastoral presence. Again, as with offenders, this probably should not be someone from the judicatory staff. Another pastor—if possible, one with experience dealing with victims of sexual misconduct (if the misconduct has been sexual)—can be helpful, *if the victim wishes this help.* It may be desirable for the pastor to be of the same gender as the victim. Geographic proximity is also a concern.

Victim and family will also likely need therapeutic support, especially when the misconduct has been sexual. Many judicatories offer to pay for some (or all) of this support. Some insurance companies may assist in providing counseling payments. Judicatories ought to have available a list of counseling resources that deal especially with victims of clergy sexual abuse. Where such specific counseling is not available, a counselor who works with sexual abuse generally will be helpful. Counselors must also be attuned to the spiritual disruption that occurs in victims, and judicatory officials must share that sensitivity. When such support is offered, it is important at the onset to explain monetary or time limits for counseling.

Judicatory officials will often be presented at this stage with a common request from the offender—to make amends to his or her victim. Offenders often want to make an apology to quell their conscience. It is important to understand and evaluate whether the offender is admitting to all the allegations of misconduct, simply wants to say, "I'm sorry for whatever you allege, true or not," or intends to use such a meeting to intimidate or control the victim. The primary question for the judicatory at this point is, What is best for the victim? Asking the victim, or inviting the victim along with her or his therapist and advocate to discuss this is possible, but judicatory leaders must be careful not to make this sound at all like an expectation. In most cases, the appropriate time for a meeting of apology and possible reconciliation comes much later in the healing process (if ever).

Judicatory officials may respond to a request for a meeting when it comes from victims. By the time they make this request, they are often describing themselves as survivors. The dynamics of such a meeting and apology need to be carefully considered, and advice should be sought from the victim's advocate and therapist.

Survivors will typically not need much more support from judicatory staff. The length of time it takes victims to begin to consider themselves survivors, however, varies from person to person. Until the judicatory leader working with a victim is certain that this stage has been reached, some kind of periodic contact should be made.

Families of victims are also victimized by the misconduct. Pastoral support in the form of another pastor in the judicatory or a pastor from another denomination should be offered to victims' families. If victims have been able to remain anonymous or are determined to stay in the congregation, the judicatory official may help them find a way to do that. If the judicatory official believes they will be in a spiritually safe environment, the support of the judicatory to make that possible may be important. (See also chapter 11, ""Victims/Survivors," chapter 22, "Remembering the Victim," and chapter 28, "What's Ahead for the Victim?")

With the Offender

The role of the judicatory with offenders is at least twofold: first, to be as certain as possible that offenders are removed from any situations where they can do harm to another individual (including themselves), and second, to offer some form of ongoing pastoral care to them.

This role is often difficult for judicatory leaders, because many denominations require that the judicatory official fill the roles of both pastor and judge in these cases. Training pastors to serve on a response team or arranging for clergy who serve in another judicatory or even another denomination to provide pastoral care to offenders are two possible solutions to this problem.

Offenders who resign their denominational standing may need to be directed toward career counseling. It is increasingly possible that offenders will find themselves involved in legal systems as victims/survivors seek recompense. Ongoing therapy, chemical dependency counseling, and other such services may be offered. Some judicatories offer financial assistance for this care, while others do not. Judicatory staff should also advise the offender about the possibility that insurance will cover mental and physical health issues.

Families of offenders are secondary victims to the pastor's actions and ought to be both offered pastoral care and be encouraged to obtain therapeutic care. Spouses of pastors who are sexual offenders must be encouraged, regardless of how painful it is, to leave the congregation where the pastor served. For many clergy spouses, the congregation remains a place of nurture, but usually the continued presence of the spouse prevents the congregation from moving on and, even more importantly, prevents the victim from feeling safe. Every effort should be made to support the spouse of an offending pastor as she or he makes a congregational transition. (See also chapter 23, "Responding to the Offender and Family.")

In the Congregation

With victims/survivors and their families, judicatories are working inside relatively small systems of people. The congregation is another matter. Of course, it would certainly be easiest if, after disclosure, the judicatory could consider its role and responsibilities complete. Closing the file and locking it in the bishop's drawer would be the simplest next step. Unfortunately, congregations are complex systems and, when under a major stress such as clergy misconduct, healthy congregations will teeter on the brink of long-term illness, while congregations that are already teetering will begin to topple. For this reason, the judicatory needs to remain involved in the congregation at one level or another for at least one to two years, and more likely, longer. The judicatory staff should remind congregation leaders that if the hard work of recovery is not done now, even longer-term disease may result.

The first task of the judicatory officials is to find the best possible afterpastor for the congregation. The afterpastor *cannot* be an untrained, inexperienced, on-leave-from-call pastor. Serving as an afterpastor takes tremendous skill and energy, and afterpastors must, therefore, be well differentiated, nonanxious, direct but not aggressive pastors who know their own limits well and are committed to staying healthy for the sake of their own ministry.

If a judicatory must place an inexperienced afterpastor in a congregation, it is critical that the judicatory provide a mentor for that pastor. Afterpastors report needing to check in with a mentor or coach to verify their own intuition and their own experiences. Pastors who serve for the first time in afterpastor settings describe working in church systems that feel "crazy" or secretive. If the judicatory does not have a coaching or mentoring program as a referral resource, then either face-to-face or online support groups should be established for the support of the afterpastor. (See the introduction to this book for more detail about the afterpastor's experience, as well as chapter 24, "Psychological and Spiritual Resources for Afterpastors.")

Under the auspices of the judicatory (or at least with the support of the judicatory), members of the response team should provide opportunities for one-on-one conversations with members and for some large-group gatherings in the congregation within the first two to three months after initial disclosure. The judicatory can be helpful by staying in touch with both the response team and the elected leaders and staff to hear, on an ongoing basis, how the early healing is going. Those who meet with the members, whether individually or in groups, need to exercise care to be responsive, not reactive, especially as some members of the congregation will become reactive.

A congregation that has experienced the betrayal by a pastor of a sexual boundary will usually discover many other kinds of boundaries that have been broken. For that reason, within the first three to six months, boundary training for staff and leadership (even if they've had it before) should be offered. This provides yet another opportunity for the judicatory to affirm for the congregation that there is still new ministry around the corner for them but also to remind them of the work that must be done to get ready for that ministry.

Once the afterpastor has settled in and the congregation is comfortable with him or her, a workshop such as "Healthy Leaders/Healthy Congregations" (created by Peter Steinke) should be held. Many judicatories have staff or clergy trained to lead such a workshop for congregational leaders. Now is the time to help the board learn new ways of working with its pastor, and when members are ready to take the next steps toward health, a workshop like this one can be helpful. Afterpastors, board members, and other congregational leaders can learn to relate to one another in direct, honest, nonconflictual ways. Strengthening the internal communication and health of congregational leaders will aid the congregation in moving through the healing process.

And Finally . . .

The involvement of the judicatory with the elected leaders may last for some time. The aftermath will likely require some assistance with conflict resolution, congregational self-esteem, and especially visioning with boldness for the future.

Once those tasks have been strongly initiated, the judicatory's next role in many mainline churches is to help the congregation find the best possible permanent pastor. (See chapter 27, "Preparing to Call a New Pastor.") One to three years of recovery work may be needed before the congregation is ready to receive a new pastor—to ensure that the permanent pastor actually is permanent. Judicatories may also help congregations in this time by seeking to ensure the health of the pastoral candidates. Many congregations who have experienced clergy sexual misconduct have experienced it with several clergy. For these congregations in particular, the assistance of the judicatory in helping to assess clergy fitness is critical.

Judicatory staff, congregational leaders, call committees, and staffs of congregations all look forward to moving toward renewed mission. Judicatory leaders can be an important resource in congregational healing after an incidence of clergy misconduct. Congregational leaders, staff, members, and the judicatory working together over time can help the betrayed congregation move to a place of health, energized vision, and vital mission.

17

RESPONSE TEAMS:
LAYING A FOUNDATION FOR RECOVERY

E. Larraine Frampton

RESPONSE TEAMS ARE SPECIALLY TRAINED CLERGY AND LAITY recruited by judicatory leaders to help process cases of clergy misconduct in congregations. (See also chapter 29, "What's Ahead for the Wider Church?") Team members generally have special education pertaining to clergy misconduct. Members can also have additional education in other areas, such as conflict management or child protection, so they are active even when there is no clergy abuse case to process.

Why Have Response Teams?

Response teams can be of significant assistance to congregation leaders, ensuring that congregations are participating in the recovery process. They are extremely helpful for afterpastors, too, because they lay the foundation for congregations to recover. Response teams serve a number of important roles:

1. Response teams work with offenders and victims and their families. As a result, afterpastors are able to keep clear boundaries with offenders and victims and avoid triangulation or speculation that they are taking sides. Teams also allow afterpastors to focus on their ministry.
2. Response teams handle congregational disclosure and provide case management, thereby helping to diminish the conflicting dual relationship that arises when judicatory leaders try to serve as both care providers and disciplinarians of clergy offenders.
3. Response teams are able to give congregations the significant amount of time needed for case processing and congregational care, so that judicatory leaders can concentrate on other ministries.

4. Response teams provide stability and continuity of case management during a change of judicatory leaders.

Overall, response teams provide three important functions: receiving allegations from victims, interviewing complainants and the accused, and helping congregations begin their recovery. Teams can also monitor the congregation to ensure they are participating in the recovery process.

Afterpastors become part of the recovery process simply by providing day-to-day ministry to their congregations. It is not recommended that afterpastors lead the recovery process, care for clergy offenders, or provide long-term counseling for the victim(s). Afterpastors can be easily triangulated and lose their focus on their ministries and the mission of their congregations.

Response teams can also be triangulated, becoming targets for intense emotions. Their triangulation can help congregations recover in two ways:

1. Afterpastors are less likely to become targets or "lightning rods" when congregations are venting their emotions to response teams. As a result, afterpastors can focus on their ongoing daily ministry.
2. Response teams use members' focus on them as an opportunity to help the congregation process emotions.

Response teams from several denominations can be invited to go through the response team training together. Denominations are then able to exchange teams, so response teams are seen as neutral consultants rather than as an extension of judicatory leaders.

Creating a Response Team

It is important that the role of response teams be reflected in judicatory policies regarding clergy misconduct. This helps to establish the authority and role of response teams and provides an overview of how cases will generally be processed. It is not possible to follow any policy word for word, so there should be some statement in every policy that variations in procedure will occur. Careful thought should be given to the composition of a team. An effective team typically includes the following:

- Six to twelve people
- Members who are geographically accessible and able to respond quickly
- Cross-section of the faith community
- Lay and clergy
- At least one clergyperson with clinical training
- An equal number of men and women, if possible

Response team members should be trustworthy, possess a high degree of self-differentiation and the capacity to serve as a nonanxious presence, and have conflict management experience, counseling knowledge, leadership skills, teaching ability, and knowledge of systems theory.

Response team members are appointed by judicatory leaders (unless stated otherwise in judicatory policies) after being recommended by people who know them and properly screened. Judicatory leaders can decide which of the three functions of managing cases of clergy sexual abuse, discussed below, would complement their leadership styles and policies. It is recommended that the first function (first contact) and the third function (congregational recovery) involve the assistance of a response team.

Three Functions of Case Management

The response team can have one or all of the following functions:

1. FIRST CONTACT: Response team members receive allegations from victims. The process for reporting allegations should be accessible and safe for victims. Judicatory leaders can send brochures to their congregations that describe clergy sexual abuse and the reporting process. The brochures can list the names and phone numbers of response team members or judicatory leaders whom victims may contact. The primary role of the response team at this stage includes several aspects.

Primary Role

* Listen and respond appropriately to the allegations of complainant.
* Explain the ecclesiastical process.
* Refer the complainant or allegation to the judicatory leaders and civil authorities if necessary.
* If requested by complainant, provide names of an advocate or therapist.

2. CASE MANAGEMENT: Response team members accompany a judicatory leader in interviews of complainant(s) and clergy, investigate allegation(s), make recommendations to the leader and, if the process continues, meet with the congregation's leaders and assist the judicatory leader during the disclosure to the congregation. The team's role varies as a case progresses.

Primary Role for First Week

* Meet with the complainant
* Contact general counsel for judicatory or denomination
* Contact the congregation's insurance company
* Interview the complainant (with judicatory leader present, if possible)
* Request a written allegation or signed affidavit from the complainant
* If requested, give names of advocates, pastors, and therapists to complainant
* Interview the accused (with judicatory leader present, if possible)
* If requested, give names of advocates, pastors, and therapists to accused
* If requested, arrange for pastoral care of the families affected
* Conduct a confidential preliminary investigation to gather information

Some judicatories offer six to twelve therapy sessions to victims out of pastoral concern for them. It can be helpful to have a list of therapists with their contact information. To avoid a conflict of interest, therapists should not be on the judicatory's staff.

In a Timely Manner

- Inform the judicatory leader about information gathered
- Make recommendations on how to proceed

If the Case Is Proceeding to Clergy Removal or Ministry Restrictions

- Meet with the leaders of the congregation
- Plan a disclosure meeting with the congregation in conjunction with the response team members or consultants who will be involved in the recovery process
- Be present at the disclosure to the congregation, which, if possible, is made by the judicatory leader

3. RECOVERY: Response team members are present during the disclosure, so that the judicatory leaders can introduce them and describe their role, which is to provide a therapeutic process for at least one year. The date, time, and place of the first meeting with the recovery team should be announced at the disclosure. Team members can also assist in debriefing the congregation after the disclosure meeting. Afterpastors are reporting that it takes 10 years for congregations to recover. A strong foundation for recovery gives the congregation necessary guidance for the future.

The Response Team's Role in Recovery

The response team's primary role in recovery, providing a therapeutic process of recovery, is extensive. Meetings are scheduled frequently in the beginning and taper off as the emotional anxiety of the congregation lessens. The therapeutic process used for recovery varies but generally addresses five major areas: emotions, communication, information, education, and safe practices and policies.

Emotions need to be addressed first. The congregation will have a better chance of healing without destroying its ministries or becoming involved in conflicts if members deal with their emotions first. There are two models for emotional debriefing that I have found helpful: critical incident stress debriefing (see appendix B) and the grief model (see chapter 7). I have found critical incident stress debriefing a helpful model to use immediately after the disclosure. Most members will be familiar with the grief model, and it also provides an avenue for expressing emotions.

Communication patterns can be as varied and chaotic as emotions; rumors can take on a life of their own. I find that congregations need ground rules for communicating early in the process. For example, congregations might:

- Designate two leaders to answer questions
- Discourage gossip or parking lot meetings
- Encourage attendance at recovery meetings

- Encourage members to speak for one's self, and not generalize or judge what others might be feeling or thinking
- Respect the fact that members will have different feelings and different viewpoints
- Remember the precepts of the faith community
- Pray for all involved

The recovery team assists with communication by maintaining frequent contact with leaders and the congregation during intense emotional periods.

Information gathering is essential for the congregation to gain awareness of the dynamics of clergy misconduct as well as a means for the team to know what steps or recommendations to take for recovery. The congregation can participate in a history-taking event. I often discovered that other boundaries had been violated by previous clergy, predisposing the congregation to misconduct and possibly explaining the poor treatment of clergy who followed them. (See Oswald and Friedrich under "Calling a New Pastor" in appendix A, "Resources," for a group process to create an account of the congregation's history.) The team can gather additional information by working with congregation leaders and youth groups. The congregation leaders can offer information about past behavior and relational interactions of members and clergy. Youth generally know what is happening and need to voice their experiences to the recovery team for healing. The team can also gather information by meeting with individuals who still need to express their feelings or who want to report additional clergy boundary violations. Where there is one boundary violation, there is usually another.

Education about the dynamics of clergy misconduct, especially regarding the clergy's violation of ethics and abuse of power, is important for the recovery process and for the prevention of further abuse. Educational events can be offered in a variety of forums such as women's or men's groups, youth gatherings, leadership meetings, and congregational events. Some congregations have used the *Safe Sanctuaries* materials (listed under "Prevention" in appendix A) as educational guides. Education can take place when members have had the opportunity to express their emotions and have some awareness of their experience and behavior. The treatment of victims can be an indicator of how much the congregation understands the dynamics. For example, if victim(s) are not treated well, that poor treatment indicates members do not understand the dynamics and effect of sexual abuse; in fact, they are continuing the abusive system. Members need to understand how they participate in the abuse; for example, by maintaining weak boundaries (exhibited in behaviors such as not holding the clergy accountable), holding unclear or unrealistic expectations of clergy, treating clergy poorly, or not believing the victim(s). When members understand how they participate, they can change their behavior and make their congregation a safer place to worship.

Safe practices and policies need to be established by the congregation. The response team can ask for volunteers or appoint a small group of leaders to write policies and establish safe practices. The process of discussing and writing guidelines educates leaders, establishes healthy boundaries, and gives the congregation a sense that they can do something to help prevent misconduct. There are many educational resources for this task as well as assistance from some insurance companies. (See chapter 23, "Creating Safer Congregations.")

At the end of one year, the response team members can reassess the readiness of the community to call a permanent clergyperson. (See chapter 21, "Reassessing the Recovery of the Faith Community," and chapter 27, "Preparing to Call a New Pastor.") If appropriate, response teams can encourage the congregation to celebrate the end of this first year of recovery. A special worship service is a wonderful way for the congregation to thank God for the gift of recovery and claim its healing. Some congregations model a portion of this service on a house blessing, beginning in the sanctuary and then moving throughout the building to reclaim the congregation's sacred space. Other congregations collect donations from members to buy a chalice or other artifact that symbolizes their new life with God. Response teams can also encourage congregations to create a ritual to welcome their new clergyperson. However the congregation chooses to mark this anniversary, an emphasis on thanksgiving for healing and openness to God's guidance for the future will help members make the transition to the next phase of the congregation's life together.

18

THE WIDER COMMUNITY: TOWARD RECOVERY FOR ALL

Nancy Myer Hopkins

THE RIPPLES FROM EVEN ONE INCIDENCE of clergy sexual misconduct flow outward to an astounding degree. They travel rapidly beyond the complainant and accused to affect many others. These others include family members of the complainant and accused, the congregation, afterpastors, all denominational leaders who must intervene, and all other clergy in the denomination. But the outward ripples do not stop at the boundaries of the denomination. Anyone who was in a significant relationship with the offender in other systems, such as schools, counseling centers, and a wide variety of civic organizations, can also experience feelings of betrayal. If the offender does not leave the wider community and that community also did not experience full disclosure, other people can become vulnerable to an unrecovering offender still in their midst. The congregation's ability to recover, therefore, is directly related to how well the wider community is also informed and assisted.

Family Members of the Accused and Complainant

Family members of the accused will likely be hurting in a myriad of ways. (See chapter 24, "Responding to the Offender and Family," and chapters 11, 22, and 28, about the victim's/survivor's experience.) A common response of the spouse is an understandable mixture of fear, confusion, pain, and an initial inability to believe that the allegations are true. The spouse stands to lose a great deal and may not be told the truth by the accused. Therefore, the spouse may blame the complainant and become angry at denominational officials, making it difficult for anyone representing the church to be of any help. However, this does not mean that frequent attempts to offer assistance should not be made. Such offers require great sensitivity, as over time, the spouse's mind and needs may change.

Sometimes the family may wish to remain members of the congregation after their clergyperson has been removed. If they can do so without covertly or overtly compromising the recovery process, then they have a right to remain, as long as doing so does not clearly violate denominational policy.

Less commonly, the spouse has no trouble believing that the allegations are true. Occasionally, it is the spouse who is the complainant. In one celebrated case, a clergyman married and divorced three women in succession, each from a different congregation. Ultimately, they found each other and jointly brought a complaint, which finally got him removed from the clergy roster. Under these and similar circumstances, those congregants who have succumbed to the charms of the offender cannot cope with the news and may then turn on the spouse with a vengeance. Of course, the spouse as complainant deserves every bit as much support as any complainant would receive.

Children and parents of the accused also present unique challenges. If this family's relationship with the congregation has been a nurturing one up to the time a complaint is made, they will naturally look to the congregation for support, and they deserve that support. However, if the relationship has never been a supportive one, then their best option may be to leave as things heat up. The appropriate response is very much decided on a case-by-case basis, but the family members need to have a sense of agency about the matter, and congregants as well as church leaders will also need to be sensitive to family members' great vulnerability.

Family members of the complainant will inevitably be extremely upset. Good practice dictates that the identity of the complainant and the family are not known to the congregation, but this may not always be the case. No matter, denominational officials know who they are, and they need to relate to family members of complainants with great patience and sensitivity. It is not unusual for spouses of adult complainants to be angry; sometimes they will be much angrier much sooner than the complainant will. Parents of a minor victim can hold on to their anger for years. The wounds go very deep. Congregants who are protecting their illusions of the beloved pastor may not only scapegoat direct victims, but attack family members as well. "If they had just done [fill in the blank], this would never have happened."

If victims' advocates have been trained and are available, it may be advisable to appoint an advocate to work just with family members, especially if a split develops between the complainant and family members. Just about any combination of dynamics is possible in these complex situations, which involve a variety of interlocking and traumatized systems.

Expect the work of recovery to take a long time and that people will be on different time lines. It is sometimes helpful to remember that it often took years for all the people involved to develop unhealthy patterns of behavior, and it will likely take years of hard work to recover. There really is no "quick fix."

Denominational Leaders

Denominational leaders pay a big personal price every time they must intervene with a colleague who has betrayed their trust. They often feel the betrayal at a deeply personal level and also get caught in the middle of warring parties. Managing a case is extremely stressful. A well-prepared system will anticipate that this stress is inevitable and will provide good support for denominational leaders. Some leaders are good about consulting with experienced people who can help, and others are not. It is a big mistake for a relatively inexperienced denominational leader to "go it alone." Every mistake has the potential to compound the pain and to live on in a troubled system well beyond the initial abuse.

A significant amount of advance training delivered to denominational leaders can help, especially when coupled with the consultant's availability at the other end of the phone. A good team will also include legal advisors who can balance the needs of the congregation against a concern for guarding assets. Instead of working in isolation, a lot can be gained by sharing resources across denominational lines, which is also a great shame-reduction strategy. (See also chapter 16, "Judicatory Leaders.")

Clergy Colleagues

All the denominational clergy colleagues of one who is disciplined will feel vulnerable and be hurting. (See also chapter 15, "Clergy Colleagues.") The atmosphere in even a relatively "normal" congregation can at times feel destructive. We may have in the pews proportionately more people with mental illness than in the general population, and statistically, we know that many people are survivors of some kind of childhood abuse. A traumatized congregation's lowered immune response can give people who are willing to behave destructively more power than they might otherwise have. There has also been a precipitous drop in levels of civility in our culture as a whole.

So when a colleague is disciplined, other clergy may suddenly feel that they have to watch their backs ever more vigilantly, and this feeling interferes greatly with their ability to be effective in ordained ministry. A good disclosure meeting just for neighboring denominational clergy, ideally including their spouses, can go a long way toward calming those fears. Some explanation about why this particular case was judged serious enough to result in a severe penalty is helpful. Leaders should include discussion about healthy boundary maintenance and the need for self-care. A crisis like this gets people's attention and thus presents an opportunity for everyone in the judicatory to do some in-depth self-examination and education.

As with the congregation disclosure meeting, denominational clergy should also be invited to process their feelings together without being rushed. Because of what seems to be an increase in the number of frivolous complaints against clergy, colleagues of the accused might be feeling quite vulnerable about their own position and wonder whether this pastor has even been falsely accused. This is not an idle worry; some laity have discovered that the only thing denominational officials will pay attention to are complaints of sexual misconduct, which often become the weapon of choice in ongoing battles between clergy and laity.

There are at least two explanations for the apparent rise in frivolous complaints. One is that conflicted congregations often, but not always, have experienced an earlier, long forgotten case of clergy trust betrayal that was enough to set people on an endless anti-clerical "tear." This is the hidden afterpastor dynamic. Or some congregations have for no apparent reason adopted a pattern of conflicted relationships among members and with their clergy and just cannot seem to break the pattern. Any cleric serving one of these congregations is going to feel especially vulnerable when a colleague is disciplined. Frivolous allegations sadly mirror our society's increasing penchant for litigation. Even though they are usually quickly adjudicated and the cleric is exonerated, the personal cost to the clergy frivolously accused is still very steep. When a complaint is adjudicated and found to be serious enough to warrant discipline, however, the other clergy in the system need to understand why the relatively severe consequences were appropriate and that the complaint was, indeed, not frivolous.

All other congregations that the offender served will also need attention. A careful assessment can help determine the extent and type of the intervention offered. If a denominational official has offended, the damage is compounded accordingly, and it is imperative that the entire system be offered a timely process to assist with recovery. Such a process can mirror the one used in a congregation, modified for use in the wider and more complex denominational system.

Beyond the Borders of the Faith Tradition

It is not unusual for congregation leaders or others to agree to disclose clergy misconduct to the congregation but to balk at informing the wider community. A number of times, this decision has resulted in further tragedy. Some offenders, astoundingly, seem to think that going into counseling or teaching is a suitable alternate vocation, and because they often do not leave the community, social service agencies get blindsided because of the church's failure to be forthright and open with information.

Church officials should, with the knowledge and blessing of their legal advisors, call all local organizations of which the offender was known to be an active member and tell them that the cleric has been removed from office and why. Ideally, denominational policies include specific disclosure consequences for sexual misconduct, so that denominational leaders are given ironclad protection against litigation when they disclose. Fear of being sued for defamation by the offender needs to be balanced by the recognition that the church is perhaps even more vulnerable to suit from any person who is victimized later because full disclosure did not extend to the wider community. Failure to notify is also an ethical and moral issue.

Which brings us to the press. Many leaders of all faith traditions are leery of letting in the press when cases of clergy misconduct arise. Ideally, congregations have built a mutually beneficial relationship with local press organizations well ahead of a need to deliver any kind of bad news. Then, when a difficult story breaks, an established relationship can be draw on. The religious organization will want to emphasize that these cases are no longer being swept under the rug, explain what they are doing to address the abuse, and, specifically, show how they are providing as fair a process as possible to both complainant and accused. There is certainly bad news, but there is also the good news that these cases are no longer being covered up. Complete press coverage works in favor of continuing safety for everyone.

A reporter will often write a fair and balanced story, but ultimately, the control of the story goes to those who are writing headlines, choosing pictures, and placing the story on the page. Those editorial decisions, while they may sell papers, can be damaging, and the press needs to think about the ethical implications of treating sensitive stories in this way. It may also be possible for leaders of faith traditions to negotiate for fair headline treatment in exchange for transparency; negotiation is certainly worth a try.

A good example of a well-handled case is to be found in the events of the General Convention of the Episcopal Church in the summer of 2003. In the midst of an agonizing but very public debate on ratifying the election of V. Gene Robinson, the first partnered gay man to be bishop of New Hampshire, allegations of sexual misconduct were made against him. The complainant sent a signed letter to all bishops at the convention. Unfortunately, the presence of that letter ensured that the press would also put out the complainant's name, which should not ever happen. All deliberations on the issue were stopped while an investigation proceeded, the process of which was fully explained. The press hovered.

A day later, church leaders announced the exact allegations: touching on the arm or shoulder that made the complainant uncomfortable. The complainant had expressed his dismay that the case had become so public and withdrew his complaint. Church leaders had taken the complaint seriously, kept the gathered community informed, investigated immediately, and refrained from blaming the complainant. This transparency paid off in a multitude of ways, because on the whole, the press was respectful and balanced in its coverage of the entire General Convention.

Summary

The whole task of responding to an accusation of clergy misconduct can feel overwhelming. Because complainants and the accused take up so much of church officials' time and energy on the front end of these cases, others may fall through the cracks. Here again, the trained team approach can go a long way toward helping the entire system recover. Continued congregational recovery hinges, in part, on the ability of everyone who has been affected to recover. We do well to remember the words of Paul to the Corinthians: "If one member suffers, all suffer together with it; if one member is honored, all rejoice together with it" (1 Cor. 12:26).

19

Attorneys:
Finding the Best Advice

Richard B. Couser

The crisis has happened. The church is engaged, however involuntarily, in the aftermath. Every response has the potential of a domino effect. The law of unintended consequences is in full play. Legal pitfalls are everywhere. The church needs a lawyer. This chapter will address why a lawyer representing the church is needed, and how to select, pay for, and deal with one.

Why the Church Needs a Lawyer

A number of parties have an interest in the consequences of clergy misconduct. There are legal ramifications to the church's relationship or dealing with most, if not all, of them. Some of the parties in interest, and the legal issues the relationship to them may raise, include the following.

The Victim

Whether the victim is a minor or an adult, inside the church or out, there will always be possible legal liability of the church as an institution to the victim. Juries have been unsympathetic to churches that failed to prevent abuse or, worse, tolerated it. Verdicts in the hundreds of thousands of dollars or more are not uncommon in such situations. The church should support people who have been victimized by clergy or church personnel, drawing them in rather than circling the wagons and shutting them out. Many lawsuits against churches would have been avoided if the church had responded in a sympathetic and supportive manner.

But the line between support and admission of guilt, or endorsing unproven allegations, is a fine one. How it is walked may determine whether liability is created to someone else, or liability insurance that would have defended the church and covered its obligations is forfeited.

The Accused

The alleged perpetrator has rights, as well, that may be easily violated, especially if the allegations are denied and there is an institutional rush to judgment. There may be employment contract rights. Imprudent statements made to the wrong people at the wrong time may lead to charges of libel or slander, invasion of privacy, or negligent or intentional infliction of emotional distress.

The Insurer

Reports of wrongdoing by clergy or others while engaged in some activity of the church and that injure persons should always be reported to the church's insurer. The church has an obligation under its insurance policy to cooperate with the insurer, provide the company documents and information, and notify it promptly if a claim against the church is asserted or a lawsuit filed. Often there are questions of the scope of the insurance coverage and whether the claim is within the protection afforded by the policy. Insurance issues are almost always best handled in the first instance by an attorney. Congregations should keep in mind that insurance carriers never cover intentional acts or criminal conduct. Although the insurance carrier provides legal counsel, the church usually needs its own counsel, too, because the insurance company's defense attorney is defending the insurer's obligation to the church under the policy, not the church. They are not always the same thing.

The Congregation

While the congregation may not have rights as such in the situation, there are usually issues of what to disclose, to whom, when, and by what means. Because these disclosures necessarily implicate the legal rights of the victim and accused, guidance from an attorney is appropriate in making them. Defamation (libel and slander) can be charged by any party in these cases, so public announcements need to be made carefully. Breach of contract, breach of privacy, and breach of fiduciary duty are other legal issues that congregations need to be aware of and for which they should seek counsel. In addition, congregations should consider calling in a consultant familiar with issues of clergy misconduct to help manage their response, because the attorney's role is to advise about the law and legal risks of specific actions, and an attorney cannot oversee every aspect of a congregation's response to a situation.[1]

The Media

Scandal in churches is a favorite topic for the media. The discovery of sexual or financial misconduct in the very institutions that should embody the highest moral standards of the society makes a good story for public consumption. In any significant church scandal, it is likely that reporters will come inquiring. What is said to them implicates all of the issues of the legal obligations of the church to the victim, the accused, and the insurer. A lawyer's input on what to say to the press, and what not to say, is essential. Again, congregations need to protect themselves against charges of defamation.

The Government

In all cases of abuse of minors, there is an issue of the church's obligation to report to the appropriate child protection or law enforcement agency. State laws, and the reporting obligations of churches and church personnel, vary from state to state. Reporting obligations often mandate prompt notice to authorities by the party with the information that should be reported. In some cases, criminal investigations may follow, and law enforcement personnel may seek evidence from the church. What may, must, or must not be reported to government authorities requires legal advice.

Apart from the need to consider the church's obligations to the various parties in interest, and the pitfalls of dealing with them, any claim or threat of litigation or that might lead to litigation, from any party, should always lead the church to consult counsel.

Finding a Lawyer

The legal profession, like the medical and some others, is diverse. Most lawyers specialize or concentrate their practice in a particular field of law. Lawyers may be litigators, estate planners, business lawyers, real estate specialists, or tax practitioners, or may focus on any number of other fields. Some have specialties within specialties such as the litigator who handles only plaintiff's personal injuries or insurance defense, or the business lawyer who serves only hospitals and health care practices. Few lawyers specialize in working with churches. If the church does not have a lawyer or a law firm that works with it on a regular basis and is familiar with its makeup and needs, however, there are a number of good sources for a suitable lawyer.

- THE CONGREGATION'S DENOMINATION OR JUDICATORY. Chances are, a lawyer has worked with the higher organizational levels of the church's denomination. If that lawyer cannot help the church, she, or denominational personnel who have worked with her, may be able to direct the church to a suitable local attorney who can.

- OTHER SATISFIED CHURCHES. A recommendation by a satisfied client of a similar nature, or with a similar problem, is a good resource. Talk to other churches in the area that have had to deal with the kind of issues you are facing to find out who provided their legal services in the crisis.
- ANOTHER LAWYER. The best judges of the quality of lawyers are other lawyers. Lawyers know the reputation, practice styles, personalities, and field of practice of other lawyers in the area. A lawyer in your congregation or who is friendly to the congregation or its leadership is a good resource for directing the church to the right lawyer to hire.

Most of the issues arising from the kinds of church crises addressed by this book involve the possibility or reality of litigation. For that reason, if the church does not find a lawyer with better qualifications, a lawyer with experience in litigation is likely to be the best guide in dealing with the crisis.

It is also usually best to hire a lawyer whose regular practice includes the area in which the church is located. "Local" does not necessarily mean in the same community—the geographic scope of lawyers' practices varies a great deal, depending on the state and locality as well as the lawyer. Some lawyers practice on a statewide or regional basis, especially in smaller states. Lawyers in communities near state borders often practice across state lines. A lawyer who is familiar with the laws of your state and knows the local court system is better equipped to advise the church, in most cases, than someone who is not.

Churches often ask if it is important that they hire a lawyer who shares their faith, either within their particular denomination or tradition or, at least, within their Christian convictions. Lawyers are generally more effective the better they know their client. Thus, a lawyer who is familiar with the practice and polity of a particular church or tradition does have some advantage over one who is a stranger to it. And a lawyer who shares the church's Christian faith and values will be sensitive to some nonlegal considerations that may be important to the church. Most of the issues on which the church needs advice in these crises, however, do not turn on denominational polity or church tradition. Give preference to an experienced, qualified, and well-recommended lawyer over one who shares your faith, if you can't put the two criteria together.

There are also some sources not to look to in hiring a lawyer. Telephone books or other general advertising is not a good source. The size of the ad or puffery it contains is no guide to the quality of legal advice that lies behind it. Some church-oriented publications, however, may have advertising by lawyers or law firms that do have some specialized knowledge in serving churches. When contacting an attorney for whom the church does not have a strong recommendation from a trusted resource, it would be prudent to ask for names of other churches or religious organizations the lawyer has served that can be contacted as references.

Beware also of using the board or congregation member who is a lawyer and is willing to help the church without a fee. Lawyers who are part of the church are often valuable resources in directing the church to the right lawyer to hire and in identifying when the church needs a lawyer. But unless they are experienced in the matters on which the church needs advice, they are not, just because they are there, necessarily the right person for the job.

Paying the Lawyer

"A lawyer's stock in trade," said Abraham Lincoln, "is his time and advice." Although some legal services are performed on a contingent, fixed, or percentage fee basis, the kind of services the church needs will almost always be performed on the basis of an hourly fee.

Hourly fees for lawyers vary widely depending on the locale, the size of the firm, the experience of the lawyer, and the degree of specialization in the field of interest. In general, larger firms in larger cities have higher fee structures than smaller firms in smaller settings. The church should ask the hourly rate of the lawyer, and others in his firm who might be working on the matter, before hiring him. The church, however, should be more interested in his experience and qualifications than the rate. If the lawyer has the experience and qualifications to do the job, it is "penny wise and pound foolish" to hire a less experienced and qualified lawyer to get a lower rate. In the end, the cost of dealing with a less experienced lawyer may be greater, either because he has to do more work to give the advice that is needed or because the advice is less effective.

Some lawyers ask for retainers for new clients. This is reasonable. Lawyers have to pay their bills, too, and need to be sure their clients are financially responsible and will meet their obligations.

If the scope of services requested is reasonably well defined, it is fair to ask the lawyer for an estimate of the cost up front. Often, however, the services needed are a moving target, and any estimate at the outset is difficult or meaningless. If the church has budget limitations, it should communicate these to the lawyer in advance, so neither party is surprised when the bill comes due: the church, that the services cost as much as they did, and the lawyer, that the church may not be able to pay for them.

Dealing with the Lawyer

The twin hazards of dealing with the lawyer are overreliance and underreliance. Overreliance on the lawyer often results from timidity among church leaders and the desire to have someone else make decisions or tell them what decisions should be made, rather than give them legal guidance for the decisions they themselves need to make. Underreliance may arise from an inappropriate hubris about church leaders' ability to handle problems without advice, a distrust of the legal profession, or a reluctance to incur fees associated with getting sound advice. Both extremes are mistakes.

When a lawyer is hired, the church should define the tasks it is asking the lawyer to perform or the issues on which it seeks her advice. Some dialogue with the lawyer is appropriate in defining what those tasks or issues are. The church may know it needs a lawyer but not know what the right questions are. Whatever the tasks or issues entrusted to the lawyer, the church should provide him with all relevant information it possesses on the issues and withhold nothing. The church will not get the best advice if the lawyer does not know the facts. The "attorney-client privilege" protects communications with the lawyer from disclosure to others. The lawyer has a duty to her client to keep those communications confidential. The church need not fear that by telling the lawyer the bad news as well as the good, it has made information public that it does not wish to disclose. Here are some guidelines for the scope of services that should be entrusted to the lawyers:

- DEALING WITH THE VICTIM, THE ACCUSED, AND THEIR FAMILIES. Unless a claim of legal liability has been asserted or suggested, or a lawsuit has been filed, the church should deal with the victim, the accused, and their families—but after seeking advice from the lawyer to avoid pitfalls in communicating with them. Once a claim has been asserted, however, even if informally, counsel should handle the matter. Lawsuits should always be promptly referred to counsel.
- INVESTIGATING THE FACTS. If there are material disputes about the facts, some action by the church, such as continued employment, may turn on what the facts really are. In such cases, an investigation may be necessary. Lawyers are often good choices to conduct or oversee such an investigation for two reasons. First, it fits their experience and training, especially if they are litigators. Second, an investigation by a lawyer is more likely to be protected from disclosure if it turns up information the church does not want to disclose. Be aware, however, that investigations are time intensive, and the lawyer's fee will reflect this.
- STATEMENTS TO THE MEDIA OR THE CONGREGATION. It is often prudent for the church to formulate written statements that are drafted or reviewed by a lawyer to provide an appropriate level of information without incurring legal liability in doing so. Such statements should be presented to the congregation by the leaders; congregation leaders or the attorney may present them to the media. In either case, it is desirable to designate a single person as a spokesperson, so conflicting information is not given out.
- DEALING WITH THE INSURER. This is best handled by the attorney in the first instance. If there is an issue as to whether or not there is insurance coverage for any liability, the attorney should be in charge. If the insurer acknowledges coverage and wants to investigate or obtain further information, the attorney does not need to be an intermediary.
- REPORTING TO THE GOVERNMENT. If there are issues about whether or not a report should be filed, or the extent of the church's obligation to cooperate with law enforcement authorities, the attorney should be consulted. For example, if disclosures to church personnel were made in a context that may

be within the privilege of nondisclosure of religious confessions, there may be a question of whether the church may, must, or must not, disclose them.

∽

Each particular circumstance will raise a variety of issues that need to be addressed on their particular facts. A qualified lawyer can help to identify them and advise on how they should be addressed.

PART 4

WHAT DO WE DO NOW?

How do we make use of the various models for understanding clergy misconduct and the roles and responsibilities of key players? The chapters in this section help readers develop plans for personal and corporate action that can be
taken after the immediate crisis is dealt with. Over time, congregations will
both change the way they behave and become comfortably able to carry their
total history—the good, the bad, the indifferent—with them. A good recovery
will in turn enable them to respond appropriately to the offender and his or her
family, as well as envision and implement mission and ministry that faithfully
fulfills God's call.

Key to the congregation's recovery is the afterpastor's self-care. This is not
the time to try to "go it alone." The afterpastor needs to tend to his or her psychological and spiritual well-being; consult, collaborate, and connect with others; and exercise the other types of self-nurture discussed in the introduction
to this book. Readers looking for specific guidance for the afterpastor will want
to review that material.

20

INTEGRATING
THE EXPERIENCE

Nancy Myer Hopkins

WHAT ARE THE EARMARKS OF A CONGREGATION that has progressed from an experience of clergy misconduct to the point that it is comfortably able to carry its total history—the good, the bad, the indifferent—with it?

The Laity

Let's start with the laity, the backbone of all congregations, without whom there would be no church. In a recovering congregation, a significant number of people are equipped and ready to take leadership roles, and there is a healthy turnover of leadership in all organizations. The inevitable disagreements are maturely negotiated. People feel free to express differing ideas without putting others down or triangling a third party into tense relationships. People know how to express their own needs in ways that do not put others on the defensive. They listen to each other. Communication is open and direct. If troubled people try to sabotage and make personal attacks, leaders first give them the benefit of the doubt and assume they are capable of being reasonable. If that approach fails, however, troubled folks are either appropriately ignored or confronted on their behavior and not allowed to tie everyone in knots.

If any survivors or families of survivors—known or unknown—who were abused or exploited in the context of the congregation still worship with the congregation, they are fully welcome and made to feel comfortable. Trust levels are strong throughout the system. People are able to laugh and cry together.

The relationships among laity, staff, and clergy are characterized by mutual respect. When problems and disagreements arise among them, they are dealt with forthrightly, using the assistance of outside mediators, if necessary. The laity have realistic expectations of their staff members and clergy, and understand clergy's need for significant time away from the congregation in order to stay spiritually grounded, be in full relationship with their own families, and enjoy time away for rest and relaxation. Laity understand that even when a clergyperson is apparently relaxed and having a good time at parish events, he or she is essentially working, not playing. Congregants are mature enough to realize that Sunday morning is not a good time to overwhelm their pastor with complaints, complicated suggestions, or bad news. Everyone in the congregation knows healthy boundaries are essential and that ensuring healthy boundaries requires that as many people as possible understand the issues and "buy into" the concept.

Laity are willing to be stretched to grow their faith and examine how their faith affects their relationship to the world. The congregation is open to new ideas, new experiences, and new people.

Clergy and Staff

The painful parts of a congregation's history, as well as the positive parts, are fully shared by all search committees with candidates for new staff or clerical positions. Any written histories incorporate a full accounting of the painful times, including a specific acknowledgment of sorrow for the suffering of survivors, as well as a description of the steps taken to recover. Newcomers are also told what happened. Framing the full story as a faith journey and relating it to similar biblical stories of other faith journeys can be a very effective way to do this.

Clergy who follow are comfortable advocating for themselves in matters of fair housing, benefits, and salary. Beginning with the search process, there are clear expectations for all parties, and all agreements are in writing, thus avoiding starting a new ministry with either party feeling resentful. Clergy entering the system understand that a pitfall to be avoided is that even in relatively healthy congregations, some laity may try to play "capture the rector." Members' overattentiveness may lead to relatively minor boundary crossings, such as offering personal loans or temporary housing in their home. There is a greater risk of this happening if the entering cleric is feeling lonely and vulnerable. He or she may inadvertently encourage a relationship to become too emotionally close, and then later, when the cleric tries to get some distance, the parishioner may suddenly turn into an enemy. Many denominations now provide very helpful start-up conferences for clergy moving to a new call, such as the Fresh Start program offered by the Episcopal Church. Families of clergy should be included in any program that involves a transition for the family.

Reestablishing appropriate boundaries—neither too rigid nor too loose—in all areas of congregational life is always necessary when sexual boundaries have been violated. This is much more easily done if the clergy have the full backing of their denominational superiors. If changes are made too abruptly and without explanation, feelings of abandonment can be triggered in some congregants, resulting in yet more conflict. I hear stories from afterpastors all the time that their superiors are working extremely long hours, and these judicatory staff members have no idea they are setting a poor example. When one afterpastor told her district superintendent that she was working a 50-hour week, the response from the district superintendent was, "You should be working 60 hours a week." When self-care and consideration for the cleric's family disappear, clergy are set up for yet more boundary violations.

In a congregation that is recovering well from clergy misconduct, clergy take responsibility for their own mental, emotional, and spiritual health, and are sensitive to the needs of their own family members to have significant time available for nurturing relationships. Just as laity understand the pressures clergy are under, so clergy are sensitive to the needs of laity. Today's families are often time-starved and running on empty. Many families are overextended and exhausted, even sleep deprived. To the extent that we are applying a nineteenth-century model of congregational ministry to the twenty-first century, we cannot survive in any recognizable form for long, and radical reworking of what constitutes "church" may need to happen. There are some exciting models out there for ways to be church today.

Communication

Careful thought is given to ensuring that newer means of communication, such as the Internet, phone answering devices, and videos are appropriately used. By now, we have enough experience with modern technology to understand that these tools all represent a very mixed blessing.

Answering machines or voice mail do free up time and sometimes the expense of full-time secretarial help, but if overused, they can also make people feel alienated. Elderly people who may be hard of hearing often feel frustrated with even simple messages, let alone a multitude of voice mail options that require immediate response. Messages are kept simple, refraining from pious add-ons (which maddeningly drive up long-distance charges) and giving clear instructions about how to leave messages. Messages are responded to in a timely manner. Clergy families set boundaries around their home life by appropriately explaining that the answering machine will pick up calls during dinner hour, after a reasonable evening hour, and on days off. A back-up number that can be called in the event of a real emergency is always provided. Congregants understand the need for such boundaries and what constitutes a real emergency.

The Internet presents yet another set of communication challenges. Many people use e-mail as their major means of communication. The ease of getting business out of the way quickly and relatively cheaply is attractive, and the ability to copy a note to everyone in a particular group generally saves a lot of time, provided our spam filters are working. When anything controversial is sent by e-mail, however, the potential for misunderstanding is great. Careless words written in the heat of the moment, without the interpretation provided by voice inflection or facial expression, have the potential to wound far more than they would if expressed in a face-to-face encounter. Some people seem to become much less careful about what they say by e-mail than they would be if they were communicating face to face. Hapless pastors have sent blistering notes to a few people they thought were allies in the congregation, only to have the notes quickly copied to everyone on the parish list, with disastrous results. Again, boundaries around e-mail access are set. Many clergy have one inbox for church business that is only accessed on their computer at the office, and another unlisted inbox for their personal use. Otherwise, they can get into compulsively reading church business e-mail at home late at night, and then have difficulty unhooking from the parish and end up losing sleep. A well-recovered congregation will have ongoing discussions about the uses and misuses of e-mail as a means of communication.

Even videos can trip us up. In one situation, a pastor who was experiencing a lot of flak in his congregation went to a workshop at which he was taped role-playing an encounter with his most difficult parishioner. He brought the video home and stashed it in the church office on the shelf with all the other educational videos. His Christian education director came looking for a particular educational tape and, you guessed it, grabbed the wrong tape. She proved herself not trustworthy, because she chose to use the tape as a weapon, and it quickly went the rounds of the disaffected group. Of course, the pastor did not last long after that episode. Here again, a recovering congregation has the conversation about the ethical use of all recently developed communication aids. While we might think twice before we spread around the contents of a handwritten letter we found, we have not caught up with the novelty of new technology and its ability to both enhance and destroy relationships.

Getting On with Business

This description of a recovering congregation may sound like some kind of an unreachable nirvana, but it is possible to have a vital, healthy congregational life. Size does not have much to do with the basic criteria for human decency to be observed, though demographic factors such as size, financial depth of members, and location can present unique challenges. A major positive outcome of doing the hard work of recovery is that a congregation is truly presented with opportunities to grow spiritually and deepen its inner life. That inner growth can in turn free up the congregation to revisit its concept of mission and to look outward toward needs in the town, city, country, and world. In the best sense, a congregation that has well integrated its total history, including its experience with clergy misconduct, will be far stronger and can then go about the business of being the church.

21

REASSESSING THE RECOVERY OF THE FAITH COMMUNITY

E. Larraine Frampton

The faith community will need to be reassessed periodically to determine how it is recovering and what issues still need to be addressed. It will be easier to assess the congregation if a response team or consultant began working with the congregation soon after the misconduct was discovered and disclosed, evaluated the congregation's status at that point, and provided a process for recovery for one to two years after the disclosure. (See chapter 17, "Response Teams," and chapter 29, "What's Ahead for the Wider Church?") The recovery consultants will have observed the dynamics of the congregation and will be able to establish a baseline for the health of the congregation and recommendations for continuing recovery.

The recovery process usually includes debriefing the congregation, providing spiritual guidance and nurturing, gathering historical information, examining communication patterns and decision-making styles, educating leaders about the dynamics of clergy misconduct, and establishing safe practices and policies to help prevent further abuse. The recovery process is based on a therapeutic model that promotes expressing feelings, self-examination, understanding behavioral dynamics, effecting healthy behavioral changes, and establishing appropriate boundaries.

Factors that Affect Recovery

Several factors affect how congregations recover from clergy misconduct. Healing will be affected by the relationship between clergy and congregation, the duration and severity of the abuse, the number of victims, the offender's leadership style, the congregation's day-to-day decision-making processes, the degree of secret keeping, whether the congregation has an open or closed system of communication, and whether the abuse was disclosed and the congregation debriefed after the disclosure. The four factors that appear to have the most impact on recovery are the following:

1. THE CONGREGATION'S RELATIONSHIP WITH THE CLERGYPERSON. If the clergyperson is well loved and has been idolized by members, they will need to be debriefed more than once and in different settings to deal with the traumatic news and engage in a grief process to separate from the clergyperson. In my experience, those who were either closest to or most distant from the abuser leave after some form of in-house fighting has occurred.

2. THE IMPACT OF THE CLERGYPERSON'S BEHAVIOR. If the abuse included several victims over a long period, the clergyperson would have established a pattern of unhealthy communication that encouraged secret keeping and discouraged clergy accountability. In addition, clergy might have used their power to dictate decisions instead of including the congregation's input. After a few years, such unhealthy dynamics become accepted as normal. In one extreme case of such ill health, several female members were jealous of the victims, because they had not been chosen by the offender. When the congregation adopts unhealthy behavioral patterns over a period of years, the impact on the congregation is tremendous. The afterpastor cannot be expected in one or two years to change behaviors that have been in place for ten years.

   On the other hand, when the clergyperson has one victim and the abuse is disclosed shortly after it takes place, and if unhealthy patterns of behavior have not been established, the congregation may be able to recover in a short time. Certainly, the congregation will have to be debriefed and engage in a recovery process, but it may take only two years instead of ten.

   Regardless of the degree of impact the offender's unhealthy behavior has had on the congregation as a whole, some individual members may have difficulty recovering from the abuse. Clergy misconduct is traumatic; some members never fully recover. The recovery of the congregation does not depend on the recovery of every member, however, but on establishing a healthy system of communication and behavior that is reflective of its faith.

3. THE CONGREGATION'S TREATMENT OF VICTIMS. When a congregation responds to victims with empathy and compassion, there seems to be a better chance that both the members themselves and the victims will recover. Positive treatment of victims can also indicate the community has the ability to view the offender as separate from its identity and faith.

4. THE DEBRIEFING OF THE CONGREGATION. Debriefing is a therapeutic process to be used shortly after misconduct has been disclosed to congregations. (See chapter 1 on disclosure and appendix B on critical incident stress debriefing.) When congregations are not debriefed in a timely manner, within two weeks after disclosure, it can take longer for them to recover. Members

tend to become anxious, often resulting in some other crisis or conflict that inhibits recovery. When a congregation establishes a process for emotional expression and creates guidelines for behavior, anxiety is reduced, and conflict and crisis are easier to contain.

Behavioral Signs of Recovery

Some afterpastors have reported that it takes at least 10 years before a congregation's behavior really changes. This is particularly true in cases where the offender had a tremendous impact on the congregation's patterns of relating, as discussed above. What the afterpastor and judicatory leaders are reassessing is whether the congregation is showing signs of abusive or healthy ways of relating. There are two questions to ask to gauge the church's progress toward developing a holistic and healthy response to the crisis of clergy misconduct.

The first: Is the church reenergized for mission and ministry? Every church has a mission, and it is not to self-destruct over the misconduct of a religious leader. When a church begins to reinvest its energy in the mission it defines as its reason for being, it is well along in the healing process. Educational opportunities, mission projects, building campaigns, and reenergized music programs are all indicators that a church is moving away from its preoccupation with the issues related to the misconduct. In my experience, churches that have good disclosure and support for their healing work through time are able to reclaim their mission with renewed energy and enthusiasm. They also bear witness to a deeper understanding of ministry and a healthier approach to community life. An honesty born of much pain and struggle adds a measure of authenticity to the witness of the church and the integrity of its ministry. Like individuals who work through personal crisis and tragedy and come to a renewed, wiser, and deeper faith, churches that attend to their healing work embody a similar spirituality that grounds them in mission and ministry.

A second question should be asked: Is it safe for survivors to return to the church? Whether the survivor actually returns to the church is not the point. The question is asked as a way of gauging how well the church understands what has happened. If members are still blaming the survivor, they have more healing work to do. If it is safe for a survivor to return and be welcomed into the life and ministry of the church, then the church "gets it" and has shifted its paradigm from blaming the victim to holding the offending clergyperson accountable. The ability to answer yes to that simple question reflects a long, difficult journey through grief, sadness, and anger as well as theological reflection and organizational review. When churches are faithful to their healing journey, everyone benefits. Survivors are restored to their community, the church's mission is reclaimed, the vulnerable are protected, the denomination's integrity is restored, and offending clergy get both the help and accountability they need.

Behavioral signs are a fast way to reassess the congregation's recovery progress, but the progression of recovery is not linear. Traumatic events, internal or external, can cause the faith community to quickly regress. National or international political catastrophes, natural disasters, or prominent media coverage of accused offenders' court trials can cause anxiety in the faith community. It is not unusual for judicatory leaders to receive complaints about their afterpastor's behavior when such events occur.

A variety of complaints may be made against afterpastors during traumatic times. One afterpastor was reported to be preaching only about the abuse. Another afterpastor was said to pray too long during the service. Yet another reportedly spent too much time with a select group of members. When the complaints were investigated, none of them was found to be true (although it can be difficult to determine whether someone is praying too long). See table 21.1 for a list of signs of both abuse and health.

Information Gathering

Response team members and consultants can use several tools to help congregation leaders gather information about the congregation's behavior and the relational dynamics that perpetuate that behavior. When these outside observers help congregations become aware of and understand their behavior, leaders and members can then begin to purposefully change unhealthy behavior. Three primary tools are used for information gathering: history taking, evaluating normative behavior, and listening and observing.

History Taking

With history taking, members gather for a history-taking event during which they describe their past joys and sorrows, and their relationship with previous clergy. One design for this process is described in *Discerning Your Congregation's Future: A Strategic and Spiritual Approach* by Roy M. Oswald and Robert E. Friedrich Jr. (See appendix A, "Resources.") Your judicatory leaders may have a design for you. (See also chapter 10, "Congregations.")

History taking can begin by creating a time line of major congregational events, including names of clergy and length of their ministry. At one history-taking event, members reported inappropriate clergy behavior that took place 25 years before. This clergyman wanted to date high-school girls in his congregation; he also expected his house to be cleaned and meals to be cooked by his members. Six other clergy followed him but did not stay very long. The seventh clergyperson became an offender. It was helpful for the congregation to note how their boundaries had been eroded years before and never restored to prevent misconduct.

Evaluating Normative Behavior

By evaluating normative behavior, leaders describe how members and clergy normally relate to each other. They discuss, for example, how a concern about their clergyperson gets processed or how leaders make decisions. Participants might

Table 21.1

Signs That a System Is Abusive	Behavioral Signs of a Healthy System
• Low participation in recovery meetings	• High participation in recovery meetings
• Denial of abuse	• Admission of abuse
• Keeping the secret	• Open system of communication
• Blaming the victims	• Empathy towards the victims
• Poor relational boundaries	• Good relational boundaries
• Formation of small groups or cliques based on level of knowledge of abuse	• New small groups
• Inability to form new small groups with diverse membership	• Ability to invite nonmembers to worship
• Unwillingness to invite nonmembers to worship	• Celebrating traditional events
• Avoidance of traditional events such as an annual potluck dinner	• Holding the offender responsible for the abuse
• Blaming the afterpastor, judicatory leaders, and victims	• Trusting afterpastor and judicatory leaders
• Distrust of afterpastor and judicatory leaders	• Generous offerings of money, time, or talent
• Reenactment of abusive behavior by members (e.g., leaders yelling at women's groups or having extramarital affairs)	• Stable membership (although membership may not increase for several years)
• Decreased offerings of money, time, or talent	• Active prayer life
• Membership changes, decline	• Ability to make decisions and follow through
• Loyalty to the offending clergyperson; members following the abusive clergyperson to new settings	
• Objection to length and content of prayers	
• Inability to make or follow through with decisions	

discover unhealthy patterns. For example, when a member is angry, other members might tend to do what the angry person wants. The goal of this process is to help leaders become aware of the congregation's behavior patterns, because self-awareness allows the leaders to make decisions about the congregation's behavior. *Discerning Your Congregation's Future,* mentioned above, also includes a group process for identifying congregational norms.

Listening and Observing

When judicatory staff, recovery consultants, or other outside observers meet with groups of members, they can both listen to and observe the relational dynamics. They can record these dynamics for use in future meetings or describe the dynamics when they happen. This kind of exercise can help raise awareness of how certain behaviors are perpetuated.

Listening is an important tool for gathering information about a congregation. Consultants can set up specified times when members may talk with them, or they can simply stay after a meeting to listen to members. It is helpful to establish both formal and informal times for listening. As consultants or others listen, they need to be sure they understand how members want the information that is shared used or not used in the recovery process.

Periodically reassessing a congregation's recovery process ensures that the congregation is progressing towards a healthy ministry. A congregation that is not healing can evaluate how and why it is stuck and take steps to move forward. A congregation that is recovering well will receive tangible evidence that its hard work is paying off, a great reward and motivation to continue its recovery.

22

REMEMBERING THE VICTIM

Nancy Myer Hopkins

CONGREGATIONAL MEMBERS—themselves hurting following clergy misconduct—can revictimize direct victims. In order to help prevent such revictimization, congregants must first fully understand the power imbalance between congregant and pastor. (See chapter 4, "Power and Abuse Model.") It is also helpful if congregants understand the experience of victims as fully as possible.

For some congregants, however, no amount of understanding can repair their own shattered selves, damaged by their illusions about their pastor whom they loved so much. These strong bonds, which sometimes develop between congregant and pastor, seem to develop mutually and operate at a deep level. The offending pastor, himself "damaged," emotionally seduces congregants who are willing to give up pieces of themselves in the process. At its most extreme, the attachment approaches the dynamics of traumatic bonding, where people who are in captivity or in thrall to a dictator or an abusive religious leader fall in love with their oppressors.

Given the complexity of the many interconnected relationships in a congregation, including the family systems every member and staff person brings into the faith community, responding to victims with justice and compassion can be difficult for a congregation. However, the challenge cannot be avoided.

Predators and Victims

"Predator" is a strong word to use, but it does fit those clergy who are multiple offenders. If we think about animal predators, they choose their victims carefully to ensure success. They identify their prey by drawing close and watching the herd for signs of weakness—age, illness, or injury.

Vulnerability and Grooming

What are some common vulnerabilities of congregants, and how do they contribute to the likelihood that a person will be exploited by a predatory pastor? Often the way misconduct actually plays out can be quite involved. The normal, complex boundary issues present between any congregant and clergyperson are further complicated by the personal attributes of the two individuals.

Fixed variables that contribute to vulnerability include characteristics that augment the imbalance between the clergyperson and congregant, such as race, class, gender, age, income, ethnic background, sexual orientation, and a history of having been abused, neglected, abandoned, and the like. Situational variables that contribute to vulnerability include current marriage or family problems, relationship problems, major illness in family, recent death of family member or beloved pet, recent financial reverses, loss of job, and so forth.

Although we generally assume that clergy have more power than laity, the circumstances of the individuals might tip the balance. For instance, it is one thing for an older, wealthier, and well-educated male cleric to use the sacred power of his office to exploit a young, poor, and poorly educated female congregant. It is quite another matter for a younger female cleric, just out of seminary, swamped by debt because she took hefty school loans, to be sexually harassed by an older, wealthy male lay leader. Ultimately, every case is unique.

Still, predatory behavior has certain characteristics. As they take advantage of their power in relationships, human predators often engage in grooming, targeting a person's vulnerability. Grooming of children is the most obvious; more than anything, a child craves attention. Children are susceptible to the attentions of an adult who shows an interest in them, who will take them places, feed them, and give them things, especially if the children are escaping a chaotic home environment. Children are easily set up to tolerate sexual advances from a trusted person, especially if the advances build gradually. Often what begins as "kindness" eventually turns to coercion backed up by threats and alternating with abject pleas for continued and more depraved forms of abuse. A person experiencing such abuse as a child will likely have tremendously confused feelings about sexuality, intimacy, trust, and all adult caregivers throughout life. Responses can range from the relatively mild to exceedingly severe, and there appears to be as yet no way to predict or quantify the severity of such long-term responses.

Grooming of adults is somewhat more subtle than with children but observable when one knows what to look for. Adults also crave respectful attention. Women want to be appreciated for who they are and what they can do in addition to being someone's "arm candy" and meeting the nurturing needs of others. "Hooks" in a congregational setting might include a paid job, an attractive office, private lunches, promises to help the woman develop professionally, "consultation" about confidential aspects of congregational life or other members, in addition to pleas for nurturing. Many women have never really experienced being taken seriously, so they can be exceedingly vulnerable to this kind of grooming.

Do clergy who groom consciously know they are setting someone up to be violated? Maybe, maybe not. Often, they have emotionally "split off" their destructive behavior, or they are in full-blown denial, or they justify their own behavior out of a deep, damaged sense of entitlement. Many simply do not understand the impact of their behavior on others. It takes a good psychiatric evaluation and a lifetime of hard work in therapy to get to the bottom of things for those who so egregiously harm others.

Responding to Predators and Victims

What betrayed congregants need to hear and understand is that whether a predator is consciously aware that he has abused his power in a relationship, an offender does not begin to face his or her own responsibility until appropriate consequences are experienced. The very common impulse of congregants to immediately offer forgiveness, often referred to as "cheap grace," does an offender much more harm than good. When victims/survivors hear such ready forgiveness offered to the person who violated them, they perceive the offer as yet one more slap in the face. As mentioned above, congregants who continue to be in thrall to an offender often have been emotionally seduced, and they may be protecting their illusions when they offer ready forgiveness to the predator and at the same time blame victims for their victimization.

Unfortunately, victim blaming has become elevated to a fine art in North American culture. We tend to believe that the world guarantees safety and success as long as we believe and behave the right way. We get what we deserve. If we are operating out of this view, we believe victims of any misfortune have somehow brought the misfortune on themselves and that we do not bear any real responsibility for changing the basic conditions that create, for example, poverty, exploitation, oppression, or sexual violence. We use rational and nonrational ways to avoid having to change anything. Rational ways to avoid change in secular institutions include "band-aid" approaches such as soup kitchens, food pantries, and sexual assault hotlines.

In religious institutions, a major avoidance strategy includes taking preventive measures aimed at risk reduction. Nonrational responses when we are faced with actual victims are to shun contact with them, avoid learning anything about their experience, reframe sexual exploitation or assault as an "affair," say the victim was the seducer, and most damaging of all, reinterpret the character of the victim so that she becomes in people's minds dangerous, vindictive, and manipulative. Victim blaming should be no more tolerated than racist or sexist jokes and comments, however. The members of the congregation will need to be reminded that the chaos and pain they are experiencing stems from the behavior of the offending pastor, not from the point at which the victim(s) came forward.

A More Just Way

Making structural changes in our religious institutions can decrease the likelihood of congregations and others blaming victims and can lead to a more just response from all involved. Such structural changes first require being ready ahead of the need, disseminating in all congregations descriptions of exploitation and abuse along with published phone numbers for victim's advocates and a safe place where complaints can be brought. At the beginning of a case, it is vital to take the complainant seriously. It is not necessary to *believe* the victim's story, as there is still a presumption of the innocence of the accused, but taking the complaint seriously will usually suffice as long as the distinction can be explained to a person bringing a complaint. Complainants' names are always confidential, and complainants must never be asked to tell their story to anyone in the church other than the official investigators. Investigators, if church people, as they usually are, should receive training before they undertake the task. Untrained investigators tend to be naive, to want to gloss over uncomfortable details, and not to ask the hard questions that will yield good information.

A complainant will benefit greatly from having an advocate or support person, also trained in advance. This person is not a lawyer, but it is made clear to the complainant that there is no reason why a complainant should not also have a lawyer, unless it is specifically prevented by written policy. An advocate who can also relate to the congregation can help congregants understand the needs of any victims/survivors and act as a liaison.

Denominational policies differ widely in the thoroughness of their written policies and procedures. Whatever is officially written to flesh out the legalese of most traditions' disciplinary laws must be followed to the letter. This is another area where prior training will pay off in a more just outcome for all parties involved.

In recent years, some legal advisors have begun to recommend that policies should be less detailed in order to avoid a suit if they are not followed exactly. The danger of following only general principles may be that important steps will not be taken to ensure fairness for all parties. This whole area is somewhat in flux at this writing. At any rate, church officials should continuously keep the complainant in the information loop and make frequent contact, even though there may be nothing new to report.

When the complainant is interviewed, he or she will appreciate being asked what a just outcome would look like to him or her. Bear in mind, however, that this response may change over time, as the complainant moves further along in his or her own recovery. It is not unusual for a complainant at the beginning of the process to say things like, "I just want this to stop," "I want him to get help," or "I want to be sure no one else will be hurt like I was." This type of statement is indicative of victims' own understanding of themselves and the situation when they first find the courage to come forward. Often long accustomed to putting themselves last in relationships, they can think only of others. However, as the rage kicks in—and it almost always does—a shift is usually observed, and requests may expand. This is actually a sign of emerging recovery for complainants, who, perhaps for the first time, are exercising a healthy self-interest.

As the process unfolds, adult female complainants who have begun to enter their "rage stage" often stop being good girls. This is the point when everyone involved suddenly wants to be somewhere else to avoid the complainant's rage. However, this is precisely the point when a steady and supportive presence is absolutely necessary, and a well-trained advocate can be helpful. In addition, church officials, pastors, and lay leaders in the congregation will need to be understanding and try to stay well connected to the complainant, no matter how difficult that is or how long the process takes. Because a person's trust has been profoundly betrayed, it will take a long time to learn to trust again, and the burden is on the church to make it happen.

Sometimes insurance companies get involved and essentially tell victims that they must sue if they want to get a fair settlement. This is unfortunate, because the relationship between victim and congregation becomes adversarial. A better way has to be found to provide a fair settlement in these cases. The restorative justice model is being explored by some denominations as an alternative approach. (See chapter 5, "Conflict Management.")

Sometimes victims seem to get stuck in perpetual victimhood, and this is painful to watch. I believe that in may of these cases, had people been able to stay supportive of victims throughout the process, much of this out-of-control rage would eventually fade into a manageable anger that is always going to be present but that can be appropriately expressed.

A Call for Wider Change

When people are wounded and in pain—any kind of pain—it is, of course, necessary to put on bandages, both large and small. But bandages are not enough. A radical cultural paradigm shift will ultimately include addressing all the root causes of oppression. We often hear weary religious leaders say they resent having to put so much time and energy into "cleaning up these messes," and they would like to get back to the real "work of the church." They should look closer. There can be no more important work than this.

The practical implications that determine the actual "work of the church " in the broadest sense entail bringing about structural change in the status of women, children, and all people who historically have been marginalized or oppressed by both the institution and the culture. Structural change includes ensuring more than just a token number of historically marginalized people are in positions of leadership and receive equal pay for equal work. It also includes changing attitudes at all levels of the culture that enable racism and sexism to exist. Study groups in congregations can use resources available from the Center for Media Literacy or the Media Education Foundation (see "Organizations" in appendix A, "Resources") to raise awareness about the steady drumbeat of pernicious material we are subjected to throughout our society to the point that we have stopped noticing.

Having worked on mending much of the internal, emotional, and structural damage, continuation of congregation recovery would entail looking outward. Helpful questions include:

- How do we need to change in order to better address sexual and domestic violence in our own community?
- How do we help bring about structural change that will address the spiritual, emotional, and physical needs of all people in our community?
- How do we need to change in order to make a difference in our global village?
- What negative influences of this culture have crept into our common life together?
- What have we learned from taking a good, long look at ourselves?

When the recovery is fully embraced, a major trust betrayal can be viewed as an opportunity to grow and change in every way—individually, communally, and globally—with justice and compassion at our core.

23

CREATING SAFER CONGREGATIONS

Nancy Biele

"**TELL US WHAT WE CAN DO SO THIS WILL NEVER HAPPEN AGAIN.**" Every denominational leader, afterpastor, or consultant who enters a congregation in the aftermath of misconduct hears this. Whether a pastor has been removed for sexual misconduct, embezzlement has been discovered, or there has been malfeasance of some kind, people want the magic answer that will prevent "this" from happening again.

Obviously, a congregation that is surviving misconduct wants to know about prevention. Prevention will be seen from a unique perspective, however. Everything is filtered through the veil of emotions and experience. Members may feel a sense of shame about what they "should" have done or known. There may be anger at offending clergy or anger at denominational leaders over their "interference" in removing a pastor or calling for consultation. Congregations may overestimate their ability to control behavior and respond with hypervigilance and rules-based restrictions. Or congregations may surrender any control or power and become even more vulnerable.

Congregations where there has been no misconduct are often reluctant to embrace the idea of prevention—for example, to review administrative policies or provide boundary training—without the impetus of an actual violation. Church leaders commonly claim, "Nothing like that could happen here, not in my church." Besides, prevention work takes time and energy and, sometimes, money—resources in short supply in most congregations.

While this chapter is titled "Creating Safer Congregations," it is not so much about safety as about good ministry and healthy congregations—good practices of congregational care. Even if a congregation implements prevention policies and follows them to the letter, there is no guarantee that misconduct or crime or misfortune will not occur. But prevention measures may help. Remember, no one can prove that an event did *not* happen as a result of prevention. However, congregations can be role models of recovery and preventive action. Recovering congregations will ask these questions:

- Knowing what we know now, what could have helped prevent this?
- What do we think the congregation needs to do to move on in safety?
- Are there lessons from our congregation that could be shared with others?

The Congregational Milieu

When we join a congregation, we come with our whole being. We bring with us our families of origin and their complexities. We bring with us our current relationships and those needs. We bring our professional lives and skills. We bring our religions of origin with their tenets and traditions, and our current spiritual longing. And we join hundreds of people with different histories and lives in worship and prayer. Congregations are complex structures with constantly changing needs and roles. We need to respect those complexities while creating common ground. A clear mission, well-trained leaders and appropriate leadership structures, and healthy communication patterns are helpful tools for establishing that ground.

A Clear Mission

One aspect of a congregation's common ground is its mission. What is a congregation's reason for being? Some congregations began long ago and never thought about their reasons for beginning; others have worked hard on developing a mission statement to reflect the times and their changing needs. A mission statement sets out the philosophy of a congregation and the values that will guide it. Clarity of purpose that has been lost or been subverted by time, apathy, or the dictates of an all-powerful authority—often a problem in congregations where misconduct has occurred—need to regain or develop that clarity. Many mission statements clearly say that the congregation is a welcoming and safe place. A congregation cannot be a welcoming and safe place and at the same time abet misconduct.

Reviewing or rewriting a mission statement in the aftermath of misconduct can be an important tool for reclaiming values and lessening shame for the congregation. A mission statement also serves as a prevention tool, because congregations that are clear about their purpose are less likely to foster conditions that may lead to misconduct. The mission should not only be understood; the congregation should embrace it. If staff or board members' personal goals supersede their commitment to the mission, those people may be at risk of misusing their power and authority in the congregation.

Well-Trained Leaders

As a congregation clarifies its mission, it should also attend to leadership in the congregation. The weeks after a misconduct case is discovered are absolutely the worst time for a church board to be apprised of the fact that board members have a fiduciary responsibility to the congregation and legally authorized duties to perform. But this is the time members most commonly learn of these responsibilities. No church board member ever signs on thinking that she will be spending all of her time at church dealing with a misconduct case. By the time a consultant had been called into one congregation, however, most of the committees had been disbanded through lack of use. There had been no elections to committees in years. The minister had handpicked the governing board. The lone independent voice left was trying to chair a personnel committee where no one wanted to hear complaints by the congregation that the minister was abusing power (and engaging in sexual misconduct with a leader in the congregation). A board member reflected that board work had all sounded so easy when a nominating committee came to her and said it was her turn to serve. Going over financial statements, developing budgets, and planning stewardship campaigns are hard work, but they are simple in comparison with civil lawsuits, insurance settlements, and congregational trauma!

Part of regaining normalcy is recalling a former, healthy structure or creating a new one that provides for clear committee roles and descriptions, tenures, election procedures, and meeting structures. It is up to the governing body to provide direction, especially in a time of crisis, and a well-informed, appropriately structured board will carry out these responsibilities more effectively than one that is caught by surprise and already in chaos.

Healthy Communication

To support its mission, congregations also need to tend to their communication patterns and strategies. What are the key communication tools in the congregation? Who has control over the newsletter, bulletin announcements, and Web site updates? Increasingly, the speed at which news can be transmitted makes for communication that is not well thought out, and communication via e-mail that was meant for one can be forwarded to hundreds at the touch of a button. There is absolutely no control over who might read the item or how something might be interpreted. When one can write a "stream of consciousness" e-mail, reflection and judgment are sometimes missing. In healthy congregations, the cultural atmosphere is one of sharing information in a direct and honest manner. Information is not distorted for political reasons or to serve the vested personal interests of a few members or the clergy. Principles of healthy communication can be expressed through management practices that provide open communication, shared work, and consistent messages to help ensure a safe congregation.

Policies and Procedures

At the same time as congregations work on broad issues related to mission, leadership, and communication, they need to think about specific policies and procedures. Most congregations that belong to major denominations have in a drawer somewhere policies and procedures governing the administration of their congregational life. They were mandated, written, argued over, passed, and left to wither. Now things are done "because that's the way the pastor wants it" or "because that's the way the treasurer has always done it."

Some congregation leaders think establishing administrative policies and procedures is too secular—that belongs in business, not a house of God, and besides, God will always point us in the right direction—so the congregation has no such guidelines in place. While I respect the concern, congregations are businesses to the extent they must deal with personnel, assets, liabilities, and income and expenses. Good administration is as much a service to the congregation as good sermons or good pastoral counseling.

Congregations that have no policies and procedures can look to denominational offices or other congregations for samples. If these documents are already in place, a review of current policies and operating procedures should be conducted. Have the systems of the congregation changed since the policies were created? Have laws or denominational mandates changed? Once congregations have developed clear policies and procedures, of course, they must be used. Any policy or procedure is only as good as the person or group implementing it. It is not enough to assume that everyone will act in the best interests of the congregation. Clearly, that is not always the case.

Financial Policies

Each congregation should have a written policy regarding financial management. Who handles the cash? Who signs the checks? Who has authority over financial decisions? Policies must be created or reviewed that answer those questions. In addition, the time to check about liability insurance coverage for the congregation is before a congregation must file a claim or contact the insurance company to defend against a misconduct claim. Each year, the congregation should review all policies, procedures, and insurance coverage for needed changes and updates. Assumptions about honesty and ethics cannot be made.

One congregation's policy was to have the treasurer count both worship attendance and the offerings for every service. The church had an evening service every Wednesday that was difficult for the treasurer to attend, so the minister said he would be happy to count attendance and money on Wednesdays. Within a few months, there seemed to be less money coming in from that service. When the treasurer asked the minister about it, he was told that there were fewer people attending. The numbers seemed to dwindle over time. The worship committee, hoping to revitalize attendance, addressed the issue. None of their suggestions seemed to work. It was not until the minister's gambling habit was discovered that the treasurer realized that the number of attendees on Wednesday night was being "fudged," so that the lower offerings being reported could be justified. The money was being spent at a nearby casino.

In another congregation, a consultant had been hired in a case of sexual misconduct. The offending minister was no longer present. One night, a very upset administrator called the consultant, saying that she had been part of a cover-up without even being aware of it. The pastor had come to her some months prior and told her that one of the part-time staff members was having both money and health difficulties. Even though, according to personnel policies, the staff member did not qualify for the group health insurance benefit, the pastor told the administrator to add the staff member to the policy. He also said the staff member would be embarrassed if anyone else knew. The church was large and had many staff, so it was not difficult for the administrator to add the few hundred dollars a month to that line item without it being noticed. It was not until the pastor's sexual abuse was uncovered that the administrator guessed who the victim might be and realized she was part of the collusion. She had thought the pastor was simply being his usual helpful self.

I have also seen cases where an endowment or bequest (not part of the monthly financial statements) was not regularly monitored and the corpus was ransacked to provide for a pastor's hidden second life or cyberporn accounts. Whenever a case of misconduct is discovered, the best advice is to get an audit done. The misconduct may have been sexual or spiritual, but it may also include financial misconduct. Or it may be all about the money.

Personnel Policies

Personnel policies should include a complete set of job descriptions and a system of supervision to ensure that the work of all staff members is regularly evaluated in order to address any problems that may arise and to promote professional growth. Such policies are needed whether a congregation's paid staff consists of a pastor, a part-time secretary, and a custodian, or a multilayered megachurch with a school. All staff should know by whom they are supervised and when and how they are evaluated.

In a number of congregations where misconduct has occurred, staff said neither the minister nor the personnel committee had paid attention to them for a very long time. Or staff said that job descriptions, pay rates, and lines of supervision changed arbitrarily at the hands of a punitive minister or a committee that was trying to fix something without knowing what was really wrong.

Vacation and sick-time policies should be spelled out with the clear understanding that sick time is to be used when needed and vacations are meant to be taken. Two issues often arise here for ministers, both resulting in overextended and therefore vulnerable clergy. Some ministers say there is a difference between the policies and the practice. So, for example, when they try to take time off, something else (not always of great importance) always takes precedence. Other pastors who have committed boundary violations will proudly say that they have not had a vacation in 10 years—that the congregation always comes first. Pastors who are not getting their personal needs met outside the congregation are likely to look for fulfillment in the wrong place—within the congregation.

Many personnel policies now have a chemical health clause that delineates generally accepted behavior around chemical use. It should also provide for consequences for use of illegal drugs. Many cases of misconduct could have been prevented or detected earlier if an intervention had been called for. Years ago, people assumed one of the reasons for sexual misconduct was chemical dependency because, upon investigation, it was found that the minister had always been drinking before, during, or after an incident of misconduct. So an offending clergy was sent to treatment, thus creating a sober offender. What was not taken into account was that the drinking before an offense may have been to instill courage, drinking during may have been the vehicle to lessen a victim's resistance, and drinking after may have been to assuage guilt.

Cybersex and pornography must also be addressed in personnel policies. Increasingly, denominational officials are intervening when pornography is found on a congregation's computer, often to the shock of the church secretary or youth leader using the same computer. If there are no policies addressing the issue, it is difficult to discipline or get help for someone who is having a problem. Obviously, cases in which child pornography sites have been accessed or where there has been solicitation of a child via the Internet are illegal and need immediate intervention by authorities.

Congregations should also establish continuing education practices for all staff. Congregations that believe all ideas and information should come from within are most likely to develop an environment where misconduct can occur. Exposure of staff to new ideas that stimulate professional growth helps to ensure an open environment.

Hiring Staff and Using Volunteers

Great care must be taken about who is allowed to hold responsible positions in our congregations, whether they are paid staff or volunteers. While much of the discussion has centered around misconduct by pastors, dealing with sexual abuse of a child by a church custodian, embezzlement by a church secretary, or sexual harassment by a counselor at the church camp is certainly traumatic for a congregation. Anyone applying for any kind of position should complete an employment or volunteer application that asks for current and past residences, current and previous employment, qualifications for the position, and references (and permission to contact references). A statement that the information the applicant is providing is true and that false or omitted information will be grounds for dismissal should be included. Congregations should review the statements, check references, and conduct interviews thoroughly.

Careful congregations conduct criminal background checks. The congregation can do them, or congregations can contract with private companies or the denomination to aid them. (See "Calling a New Pastor" in appendix A, "Resources," for names of two companies that conduct such checks.) Some insurance companies recommend fingerprinting of staff with the belief that someone with a criminal background might back out of the employment process.

Every congregation needs guidelines for working with children and vulnerable adults. In the case of those who work with children, a set of operational rules governing the ratio of adults to children, transportation issues, overnights, and the like should be developed and adhered to. Volunteers who engage in helping ministries such as care teams and Stephen Ministry or Befrienders programs should have parameters regarding their behavior with those they are helping. For all groups, supervision and evaluation are important prevention tools.

Sexual Misconduct and Sexual Harassment

All major denominations now have policies and procedures that govern identification of and intervention in sexual misconduct and sexual harassment. An independent association or congregation that does not have policies is well advised to develop them. The main differences among denominational procedures have to do with polity and which entity intervenes. Regardless of differences in structure and definitions, a checklist of policies and procedures should be included. If a review of denominational policy or an initial congregational policy is needed, the following should be considered:

1. Is there a policy statement clearly indicating the conduct considered unethical by the congregation or the judicatory?
2. Does the procedure address:
   - procedures for reporting allegations of misconduct, including reporting to authorities in cases involving children and vulnerable adults?
   - a process of impartial investigation and adjudication?
   - support and advocacy for the complainant and the complainant's family?
   - information and support provided to the accused and family?
   - assistance provided for the congregation, including notification of the entire congregation?
   - systematic training for the congregational or denominational staff appointed to implement the policies?

Physical Plant

I have been with many victims as they walked through a church building attempting to reclaim the sacred space denied them by pastoral abuse, particularly sexual abuse. We have gone to the choir loft, the church school classrooms, the fellowship hall, the bathrooms, the boiler rooms, and sometimes in front of or behind the altar. If an offender is sufficiently adept and the victim has been properly groomed, there is no space where abuse cannot occur. Off-church sites have included the minister's home, the victim's home, cars, and local motels.

Carpenters are busy cutting holes and placing windows in the doors of pastors' studies and classrooms. Many church insurance companies list this as a prevention technique. Anyone passing by a room can see that nothing untoward is happening inside. Unfortunately, putting a window in the door of a pastor's office might also mean that anyone who would like to see the pastor in confidence could be denied that privilege (unless the room is arranged so the pastor, but not the counselee, is visible through the window). There is no one way to be sure that a space is 100 percent safe. But smart congregation leaders weigh the alternatives and use their best judgment about ensuring their building is as safe as possible.

Education for Everyone

How many acts of misconduct could have been prevented if every member of every congregation had been told that it was wrong for a pastor to ever engage in sexual behavior with a member of the congregation, adult or child? If there were brochures in the pews and other gathering spaces that outlined warning signs and specified where to go for help? Many cases have been brought forward not by a victim of misconduct but by an astute family member or close friend who had seen the warning signs. Congregational meetings, adult education classes, newsletter articles, and brochures in the pews could go a long way toward preventing the next generation of victims. Sunday school, children's time during services, confirmation class, and youth gatherings are also prime opportunities for education about abuse prevention. Also, since a significant percentage of the population will have been victimized outside of the church realm, making available general information about all types of abuse and sources of help in a congregational setting could empower those who have been victimized to get help.

All those who work with youth and vulnerable adults should participate in mandatory training sessions about recognition, intervention, and reporting of abuse—including mandatory reporting laws, policies, and procedures for responding to complaints and prevention issues. Lay leaders need education about their responsibilities and the congregation's and denomination's policies and procedures regarding intervention in misconduct cases.

Clergy themselves need training on boundaries and how to reduce their risks of engaging in exploitive behavior. Guidelines need to be established for pastoral care. Reasonable expectations regarding workload and counseling responsibilities should be openly stated. Clergy need to be encouraged in self-care; those who are getting personal and family needs met are less likely to engage in misconduct. Vacations, study time, and sabbaticals should be encouraged. Clergy should be encouraged to consult with professional counselors when needed, to participate in a peer support group, and to work with a spiritual director. Funding and support for these activities could be offered as part of pastors' salary and benefits package.

The discussion here has been mainly about primary prevention—prevention of any occurrence of misconduct. Creating safer congregations also requires secondary prevention—paying attention to "minor" offenses and slight boundary violations, rather than accepting rationalizations or excuses. Minor offenses may turn into major issues and require careful review. (Most congregations are not engaged in tertiary prevention—the issue of reoffending by someone who has been treated, in large part because experience indicates that the risk of reoffending is high, so most congregations are reluctant to work with clergy, other staff, or volunteers who have offended.)

Congregations need to encourage prevention at all levels. Putting policies and procedures in place and educating staff and congregation members about keeping the congregation safe are duties as sacred as providing theologically sound sermons or good pastoral care. Congregations need to be safe for everyone.

24

RESPONDING TO THE OFFENDER AND FAMILY

E. Larraine Frampton

I KNOW A PASTOR WHO WAS A GREAT PREACHER, wonderful counselor, and inspiring visionary. I had great respect for him. Then I was told by our judicatory leader that this pastor had confessed to sexually abusing a member. How do I respond to him and his family? Others in the faith community ask the same question. In addition, how does the judicatory respond? How does the congregation respond? How do these responses affect victims?

Some concerns—the need to care for victims, provide safety for anyone exposed to offenders, and establish justice—take precedence over the care of offenders. When these concerns are not taken care of first, recovery can be difficult for victims and congregations. The need to care for victims/survivors and congregations does not mean that the offender and family are to be ignored, however. In my experience, it is easier for congregations to let go of pastors who have violated professional ethics when members know that someone is caring for their pastor. If pastors are not cared for, members may take over that role, usually with some anger toward judicatory leaders and victims/survivors.

Judicatory Leaders' Response to the Offender

Judicatory leaders can offer some guidance in responding to the offender and the offender's family without causing harm to victims. (See chapter 16, "Judicatory Leaders," and chapter 29, "What's Ahead for the Wider Church?") Judicatories generally do not have legal obligations to care for offenders if they are removed from the clergy roster. Still, they may provide care to removed offenders out of pastoral concern for them and their families. Judicatories can clarify that the care is time limited, around three to six months, as the offender transitions to a different setting.

Dual Conflicting Roles

Judicatory leaders can have dual, conflicting roles in relation to offending clergy—as both disciplinarians and caregivers of offenders. They can alleviate the conflict by designating a clergyperson to serve the role of caregiver for the offender, or by having offenders ask someone they trust to support them. Ensuring that the offending cleric is receiving pastoral care allows the judicatory to properly discipline clergy offenders without giving mixed messages.

In addition, there are times when judicatory leaders believe that they cannot be impartial in a case or it would be so emotionally draining for them that they would be unable to tend to their other ministries. In these situations, the leaders could delegate a case manager and only intervene when absolutely necessary. (See chapter 17, "Response Teams.")

Restriction of Ministerial Duties

Every case of misconduct is different. Throughout this book, you may assume that the offender has been removed from the congregation and the clergy roster; however, this is not always the case. Many variables affect clergy removal, such as the following:

- If there is no allegation or the victim does not want to file an allegation, judicatory leaders cannot discipline and remove the offender. Sometimes victims feel responsible for the misconduct or have mixed feelings of love and hate toward their offenders. Sometimes victims continue to have a relationship with the offender, perhaps even marrying the person.
- Sometimes the allegation is not deemed credible, making removal impossible. For example, the investigation does not turn up any evidence that the misconduct occurred, the alleged offender denies the allegation, or the victim has psychotic episodes.
- The victim(s) might request that the offender not be removed from the congregation, because the victim(s) would be easily identified and, as a result, suffer from the reactions of the congregation and loved ones
- In some denominations, ecclesiastical polity does not require that the clergy be removed from the roster, only from congregational ministry.
- Sometimes denominations do not remove offenders from the roster, because they could lose health benefits or pensions.
- In cases of lesser offenses (e.g., when there has been no sexual genital contact, only inappropriate sexualized behavior such as sexual jokes or sexual innuendos), the offending cleric might not be removed from clerical roster.

When judicatory leaders are unable to remove offenders from congregations, they can use their power to place limitations on them. Such limitations can include:

- Establishing a two-adult rule (The clergyperson is never allowed to meet alone with a member for counseling, home visits, and the like.)
- Enforcing no contact with youth

- Reporting to an assigned supervisor on a regular basis
- Undergoing an annual performance review
- Entering therapy (See section below.)

These limitations provide some accountability for clergy and help make the congregation safe. The congregation can also institute safe practices and policies to add further accountability. (For further guidance, see chapter 23, "Creating Safer Congregations," and the "Prevention" section in appendix A, "Resources.")

Surrender of Ministerial Privileges and Relationships

If a clergyperson is removed from a congregation as a result of discipline or resignation, it is helpful to clarify the clergyperson's relationship with congregations. The key expectation is that the offender will not assume any ministerial functions in any congregation and will not participate in any event in a congregation where he or she has abused members or where the offender's victims worship. The following list includes some of the expectations:

- The offender may not participate in ministerial acts such as weddings, funerals, baptisms, house calls, or hospital visitations in any congregation.
- The offender may not worship or participate in any other way in congregations where misconduct occurred or where victims worship.
- The offender may have no contact with members of congregations in which misconduct occurred.
- If members contact the offender, the offender is instructed to say that he or she is unavailable for any ministerial duties or social events.
- The offender may have no contact with the victim(s), and victims should be instructed to contact judicatory leaders if this happens.

It has been reported by some afterpastors that offenders' participation in congregations where misconduct occurred impedes congregational recovery and prevents bonding with new pastors. Some offenders keep relationships with former members outside of the congregational setting and may even continue to deny their offenses. This further prevents members from coming to terms with the abuse and letting go of the offender, so that new pastoral relationships can be formed. Members need closure with offenders to facilitate congregational recovery. In order to ensure that the above listed expectations are met, judicatories can request offenders and congregations to sign a covenant to abide by them. Legally, judicatory leaders may not be able to force offenders to abide by them. We can hope, however, that members will abide by them for the good of their congregations and victims/survivors.

Independent Psychological Evaluation

Generally, offenders should have a psychological evaluation by a professional who has expertise in the area of sexual deviation. The professional should be independent—not the offending cleric's therapist or someone who is employed by the judicatory. The evaluation can assist in determining the clergyperson's mental state. Some offenders contemplate suicide, and a psychological evaluation could be a preventive step. It can also provide guidance for offenders seeking employment by highlighting their abilities and interests. In addition, if a denomination has a reinstatement policy, the initial psychological evaluation can establish a psychological baseline. If an offender later seeks reinstatement, another psychological evaluation can be done by the initial evaluators to help determine personal growth and assist in supporting or discouraging reinstatement.

Therapeutic Treatment

Clergy who are removed from the roster may decide whether they want therapy separate from independent psychological evaluation. Some will enter therapy in hopes that they can be reinstated. Clergy who are not removed from the roster but who are on restrictions can also be requested by the judicatory leaders to enter therapy. Judicatories need to clarify whether offenders could ever be reinstated, as well as who is paying for the therapy. If there is a chance for reinstatement and the offender is interested, judicatories can establish goals the offender must attain in therapy, such as the following:

- Understand the abuse of power
- Understand behavior, use of touch, manipulation
- Be able to confess offense
- Have a sense of remorse and understand the magnitude of offense
- Provide restitution to the victim(s)
- Examine intimacy needs and self-care
- Establish healthy boundaries, both professional and personal
- Address current family or marital issues
- Explore issues related to family of origin
- Attend addiction treatment when appropriate

Judicatory leaders can encourage clergy to choose a therapeutic model relevant to their personality and behavior. Depending on the issues to be dealt with, individual or group therapy, inpatient or outpatient treatment, psychotherapy, behavior modification, vocational or addiction counseling—or several of these models—may be most appropriate. If addiction is involved, a therapist who specializes in the offender's specific addiction could be chosen.

When offenders are in therapy, judicatory leaders can ask offenders to sign two separate release forms. One release form gives judicatory leaders permission to share information with their therapists, and another release form gives offenders' therapists permission to share information with the judicatory leaders. This sharing of information assists judicatory leaders in determining the mental state of offenders, establishing therapeutic goals, measuring therapeutic progress, and estimating prognosis for future ministry. In addition, this information helps judicatory leaders monitor the behavior of offenders who are on restricted ministry to determine when or if they can be restored to ministry.

Reinstatement

I discuss therapy for offenders because some offenders are not predators and have not engaged in sexual genital contact but show signs of inappropriate sexualized behavior. These offenders might be able to remain in ministry with therapy and accountability to members and judicatory leaders. Another reason to discuss therapy for offenders is that some denominations have reinstatement policies, and guidelines need to be in place to ensure the safety of victims and the accountability of offenders. Reinstatement is rare and is generally not recommended, for several reasons.

- Victims need justice and safety to facilitate their recovery. Their safety and feelings should be considered first.
- Offenders can repeat sexual abuse, and no amount of therapy or evaluation can guarantee that they will not sexually abuse again.
- If offenders are reinstated and other offenses are committed, the employer (congregation or judicatory) could be held legally responsible for endangering members.

If your denomination has a reinstatement policy, the following guidelines could be included in your policy:

- Follow the therapeutic treatment process as described above (especially independent psychological evaluation by a professional who specializes in the unethical behavior, particularly sexual deviant behavior).
- Permit no reinstatement for at least five years after removal from roster.
- Consult victim(s) to see if they approve reinstatement. (I do not recommend reinstatement when victims object.)
- Require an interview and examination process similar to the one used for certifying candidates for ordination.
- If reinstated, judicatory leaders should give a disclosure of the clergyperson's offense to congregations that are considering the candidate for their minister.
- Require ongoing supervision of clergy's ministry by a professional therapist.

A Note of Caution

I have interviewed offenders who were in therapy for years and wanted to be reinstated, and it was difficult for me to know whether they were sincere or manipulating me. I also found it difficult to accept the recommendations of offenders' therapists, because they had a vested interest in the therapeutic outcome. For that reason, I believe that it is important to have additional sources of information. I recommend obtaining a recent psychological evaluation report from a professional who specializes in the type of behavior the offending cleric engaged in and an evaluation from the group that certifies candidates for ordination in your judicatory. In addition, I would have conversations with the offender's family and people in the community who have observed the individual's behavior over a long period before I would consider lifting restrictions or reinstating offenders.

Clergy misconduct is a violation of professional ethics that has severe consequences. One of the consequences can be removal from the ministerial position. The misconduct is not a private, psychological, or religious matter. There are victims involved. I caution judicatory leaders not to view misconduct as a psychological disorder that can be remedied or a sin that can be forgiven with no consequences for the offender. It is a violation with victims. Truth, justice, and restitution to victims are the ethical and religious precepts to be upheld.

Care of the Offender's Family

Clergy misconduct, particularly sexual abuse, is devastating to the offender's family. The offender's family is directly impacted by the clergyperson's losses, which can include income, parsonage, health benefits, pension, status, and relationships. The family's losses can be so comprehensive that they can feel overwhelmed by the enormity of it, and they can experience a wide range of emotions, including disbelief, grief, anger, and shame. Feelings can be complicated by the offender's denial of the misconduct or blaming the spouse for not taking care of sexual needs. Unfortunately, there are times when the faith community blames the spouse for the abuse and treats her or him poorly. The offender's family needs both pastoral care and financial direction.

When the abuse is initially disclosed, the judicatory leaders can meet with the family and pray for them, as well as assign a clergyperson for them. The clergyperson should probably not be the same one assigned to the offender. Some denominations have trained advocates who can befriend the family in their time of distress and provide emotional and spiritual support.

There are short-term financial issues to be considered when an offender is removed from ministry. The family will probably need short-term assistance in paying for their health insurance, housing, various daily expenses, and counseling. Judicatory leaders often discover when it is too late that they do not have the financial or staff resources to address the needs of the family. It is strongly recommended that leaders create a budget line for such incidents, so that proper care can be given to the family.

The family's role in the faith community can pose challenges, depending on the response of the faith community. The family can decide to continue to worship with the congregation where the misconduct occurred. Sometimes when the family stays in the faith community, relationships are challenging because of the trauma of the abuse. It is important for all involved to work through their feelings and come to realize that the family and the faith community are both victims of the abuse. In the end, it may still be best for the family to worship with another faith community.

The Congregation's Response to the Offender

Members are dealing with two intense issues: the clergy misconduct and the loss of their clergyperson. In most cases, clergy are immediately removed from the congregation, and members are not allowed the opportunity to say good-bye. As a result, members lack closure with their clergyperson and continue to think about him or her. They often ask consultants and judicatory leaders how the clergyperson is doing and what they can do to care for their former pastor. Judicatory leaders and consultants can provide a process that will provide some closure for the congregation, including:

- Frequently update the congregation about the offender's status
- Allow members to write a farewell letter to the offender (with the offender's consent)
- Role-play a dialogue between the offender and members (consultants can play the role of the offender)
- Listen to how members would like to say farewell to the clergyperson (without actually making contact)

Structuring a farewell for the offender is important in moving members to recovery. The farewell follows the debriefing of members.

Congregation's Response to the Offender's Family

Congregations are also experiencing a change in their relationship with the offender's family. Family members may have been active in the congregation and have many friends who are still members of the congregation. When the offender is removed, members can be confused about how they can relate to the family. If family members remain in the congregation, they can be easy targets for the congregation's anxiety or anger. Or, the family can provide easy access to the offender and thwart closure. Judicatory leaders often recommend that the offender's family find a different place to worship to protect them or to provide closure for the congregation.

Family members are victims too. They are not responsible for the misconduct, but they will suffer great loss and humiliation as a result of it. They are in need of care from their fellow members. Members can care for the family in the following ways:

- Pray for them
- Establish a fund to defray expenses that result from the offender's misconduct
- Say farewell (if they leave)
- Avoid communicating with the offender through the family

Family members need care from their congregation during this difficult time in their lives. Clergy misconduct elicits a variety of responses from congregations that can be destructive or healing; however, thoughtful judicatory leaders can help create a process that helps promote recovery.

25

PSYCHOLOGICAL AND SPIRITUAL RESOURCES FOR AFTERPASTORS

Candace R. Benyei

STAYING WHOLE AND GROUNDED, and maintaining an intact faith are serious projects for a victim/survivor, whistle-blower, lay leader, afterpastor, or judicatory official whose task it is to deal with issues of clergy misconduct. The pain, betrayal, abandonment, outright attack, twisted communication patterns, and crazy-making behavior in this sort of conflicted system are more than even a healthy individual can withstand without serious support strategies. Of course, in order to use these strategies, individuals must first give themselves permission to be taken care of, be open to trying something different, and have the courage to walk into the uncharted realms of the unconscious.

Essential Strategies

There are many historic practices and disciplines coming out of traditions not associated with Christian faith that are increasingly being seen as helpful resources for those who might never have considered them before. Eastern thought has embraced many spiritual and physical approaches that can be seen as ways to support traditional spiritual healing without abandoning one's own belief system. We all know God can work in multiple and surprising ways if we open ourselves to them. In my experience, psychotherapy, noncognitive bodywork, and physical/emotional grounding are necessary to withstand and repair the damage caused by systemic reaction to a breached secret. Employing all three can help a person involved in some aspect of clergy misconduct maintain mental and physical integrity in the face of severe stress.

Psychotherapy

It is important to remember that psychotherapy is not for "sick" people, but rather for people who want to grow, integrate, and individuate. Any individual involved in an abusive system similar to that resulting from clergy misconduct will benefit from psychotherapy, be it systems therapy, psychodrama, or one of many other approaches. Systems therapy and psychodrama will help the individual become aware of his or her family of origin issues, family rules, and destructive messages, so that he or she is better able to take charge of self, not act in a knee-jerk manner, and have a better chance of not only surviving, but staying out of trouble. Systems therapy also provides coaching in how to avoid triangles, understand double-binds, analyze behavior patterns, confront situations directly, define boundaries, and even become a nonanxious presence.

Psychodynamic psychotherapy such as gestalt, object relations, and cognitive behavioral therapy will enable an individual to identify and make aware unconscious processes and personal agendas, and serves to provide additional opportunity for a conscious choice of behavior, especially in interpersonal interactions. These therapies will also surface existential binds—especially those around the issues of values, vocation, meaning, and authenticity—and provide an arena for working through them.

Often one of these "heady" therapies, combined with one of the various body-oriented psychotherapies, such as rebirthing or bioenergetics and its precursor, Reichian therapy, helps bring up issues more efficiently, so that they can be worked through faster. This is because we stuff the emotions that result from psychological—and physical—trauma into our musculature, producing the chronic tensions we experience as stiff necks, tight shoulders, and bad backs. Our experiential memories are written on each cell, much like a hologram, and once released through some form of body therapy, these emotions and memories are once again available for the cognitive work needed to heal the trauma.

Noncognitive Body Work

Stress causes all sorts of physiological and energetic imbalances in the body. The various forms of massage therapy, including Shiatsu, deep tissue, Feldenkrais, and Rolfing, help reduce acute and chronic muscle spasms that inhibit nerve function and block the energetic pathways of the body impeding healthy physical performance. Chiropractic medicine helps reduce these spasms by realigning the spine, so that the function of important spinal nerves that serve the organs as well as the musculature are not compromised.

Eastern therapies work on the principle that the body has recognized energetic pathways, or meridians, that course through the body. There are 12 paired acupuncture meridians, replicated on the right and left sides, that from an Eastern standpoint affect our physiologic and psychological functioning.

Acupuncture techniques clear the blockages in these pathways that have produced symptoms, returning the organism to healthy energetic functioning. Acupuncture can produce anesthesia, alter blood pressure, release muscle tension, enable organ healing, facilitate excretion, and stimulate or modulate the immune system, among a host of other things. (It can also help people stop smoking!)

Eastern thought also recognizes eight energetic centers, or shakra, that, although they are related to levels of spiritual functioning, can be impeded by, or produce, physical and psychological phenomena. From an Eastern perspective we are energy, rather than merely a biochemical and physical entity, and to function well the current has to be balanced and running. Additional Eastern body therapies that might be considered are the Chinese art of Qigong, and the Japanese practices of Reiki and Jin Shin Jyutsu, among others.

All of these noncognitive therapies may bring up the emotion of past events and serve a cathartic function as emotions are released along with the muscle tensions that have contained them. However, their practitioners are not generally trained to aid in the working through of the trauma, as do practitioners of the psychologically oriented body therapies.

Physical/Emotional Grounding

Physical/emotional grounding is important to good functioning. We can compare the body to an electrical machine. Often a machine, such as a car, will not turn on if the battery is not grounded. Or, if a power tool or appliance is not grounded with an appropriate three-prong plug, faulty electrical circuits or wiring could give the individual holding or using the equipment an electrical shock. Since we are energetic beings and, due to various environmental and chemical insults, our circuits can become faulty, it is important to ground ourselves so that we suffer the least shock and can keep on running.

Daily grounding in order to accommodate all the short circuits in our lives, our work, and our relationships can be accomplished by activities such as gardening, physical exercise, active rather than passive sports, and good old-fashioned manual labor such as chopping wood, raking leaves, or peeling potatoes. Grounding is a physical thing and requires a physical activity. Meditators call it a "work practice." When we say about someone, "She has her feet on the ground," we are referring to our intuitive sense that the individual is grounded and therefore not impulsive but able to stay straight to the task and withstand the push and sway of life.

Faith, Meditation, Prayer, Spiritual Guidance, and Journaling

Discovering God's will is a constant endeavor. Only by having a sense that God is indeed guiding us do we find the courage to enter into a thoughtful struggle against injustice, knowing the almost certain cost.

Faith and the Search for Meaning

One of the most important tasks in life is to make meaning out of it, to find the thread that strings all the pearls of our experience together. Often our religious beliefs help us do this. However, when our religious institutions fail, betray, or abandon us, we are often left wondering what life is really about and what God wants of us—if there is a God. Our beliefs fall short of true and sustaining faith. This is because faith is not something magically given to us at our baptism or religious initiation. Instead, faith is a process and a becoming.

As a starting point, I often ask seekers what it is they want to give the world. That is, what gifts of self or service do they wish to offer the world in order to make it a better place now and after they have moved on to an other-worldly life? Ultimately, meaning is not about accumulating toys or wealth. Rather, as Carl Jung recognized, to be fully satisfying for the mature individual, meaning must stretch between persons or be *transpersonal.* Knowing who you want to be as a person and what you want to do helps provide necessary direction for the journey ahead.

When we lose our congregational family, a paid or unpaid position, or a vocation to ministry because of an institutional dynamic surrounding an issue of clergy misconduct, we frequently lose our sense of meaning. We lose our sense of who and why we are on this planet and what we want to become and do, and begin to struggle with our crumbling belief system. Inherent in this crisis is the opportunity to take apart what is often a childish theology and build a real faith now established on a firm foundation. If we are successful, we will have a structure that helps order our lives and helps us think about and relate to God in a new and nurturing way.

Clergy are particularly at risk for what is called a loss of faith but is really a loss of belief—a theology based on church doctrine that is frequently founded on mythology and bound together with religious jargon. Clergy, like the rest of us, often fail to examine their religious belief systems and are therefore frequently unaware that the pieces do not make an integrated whole. Seminaries are not very intentional about or good at developing the spiritual life of prospective clergy. As a result, clergy are expected to proclaim something they often have never really come to understand, and to live by a resource—faith—that they have frequently never developed.

We acquire the faith of our childhood from family members, Sunday school teachers, literature, and our social milieu. It is obtained in bits and pieces, many of which do not fit together. We often swallow it without chewing on it intellectually, without using critical thinking processes to sort out what makes sense from what does not. Often our faith is a lot about magical thinking, is based on unconscious assumptions, or is the concretization of concepts or stories that were meant to be metaphors. The fatherly and bearded God appropriate to a child is not appropriate to an adult living in the twenty-first century. Losing this God may be difficult, but it is a good thing.

Putting together a new theology, which is simply a framework within which we understand our experience of God and discipleship, is a lengthy process and cannot be hurried. Generally the undertaking involves shattering old assumptions and taking a hard look at our beliefs to determine what kind of truth will stand the test of time and trial. Again, faith is a process, and the more we learn, experience, and listen, the deeper and closer we will get to God. We need to continually test our truth. In this journey, it is useful to have a guide who is at least a little bit ahead of us on the road and who seems to have useful advice. Our soul will do the searching. Then if we catch up, we can pass by this guide and find a new mentor, always remembering that our faith is healthy if it can stand to be questioned.

Christian Meditation and Contemplative Prayer

All great religious traditions have developed forms of meditation to facilitate spiritual growth and healing. Christian traditions have focused on various forms of prayer and meditation on the Word, the effect of which is often enhanced by the practice of fasting. Few if any conversion experiences have happened on a full stomach! This is probably because in order to allow God in, we have to empty ourselves, physically and spiritually, so that we can experience the necessary longing to be filled with something Other.

Meditation on the Word can be as simple as reading the Daily Office or some piece of scripture and reflecting on what God might be saying to us through it. Sometimes it is useful to attempt to "step into" a story and "be" one of the characters. Meditation of this sort is an experiential exercise in which we allow the scripture—or any piece of good writing, for that matter—to work within us, rather than working over the material by theologizing, exegeting, or philosophizing about it.

Christian meditation is in general about placing ourselves before God, becoming silent, and listening. It is actually the beginning of, and becomes, contemplative prayer, a form in which we stop asking for something for our self or for others, offer our self to God, and simply listen for God's will for us. Morton Kelsey, in his book *The Other Side of Silence: A Guide to Christian Meditation,* does a good job of laying out a map for this practice. When I'm up against it, I usually go to my office, get down on my knees and silently say, "OK, God, help." This, of course, usually only happens after I have hit my head against a brick wall until it is bloody. However, God (laughing, I'm sure, but always patient) always replies in some way. The response may come in silent words that race across my mind, or it may be a solution that suddenly jumps off the page that I have been reading (usually having nothing to do with the author's purposeful content).

Finally, God often speaks through angelic beings, although their wings are usually invisible. These are usually ordinary folks who in some special way enable a personal epiphany. Angels are everywhere. We just have to look around, and take notice.

Active Imagination

Active imagination is a technique developed by Carl Jung, a contemporary of Freud's, and the developer of what has come to be known as ego psychology. Jung himself was apparently a mystic, and certainly he began as an unbeliever. He struggled with the concepts of good and evil and developed his own relationship with the numinous, which he called the Self (note the capital *S*).

Active imagination involves allowing the mind to create a story that has a beginning, a middle, and an end. In this practice, we sit and meditate on a picture, or even an object like a window or a door. When using this technique with spiritual seekers, some guides start with a series of drawings that are specifically designed to facilitate the process by offering the unconscious an entrance, sort of like a beginner's lesson. Strangely enough, once the unconscious is invited in this way, it reveals itself.

Recording the story is an important part of the practice. It can be done at the end of the adventure, using first person and present tense, in the same way it is best to record a dream. Once we become adept with the practice, we can write as the story is unfolding. Of course, the story, similar to a dream, will be a metaphoric representation of the message our Self—or what many of us would call the God within—is trying to communicate. After the story is recorded, further meditation and perhaps some spiritual direction will unfold the meaning.

Eastern Meditation

Forms of Eastern meditation all focus on the breath as an entrance into the practice. They may also use chanting, bowl gongs, bells, drums, or other instruments to help focus and clear the mind. Native Americans and many other cultures use drums and rattles. Sitting with one or both knees, or at least both feet, on the ground with the back straight is important as it provides necessary grounding and allows energy to move freely up and down the spine. Other practices, such as some forms of yoga, involve assuming certain postures in addition to the breath work. These postures are often ones that, unimpeded, the body will assume by itself in prayer. They are the body's attempt to clear its energy pathways.

Sufi spiritual practices (from the mystical tradition of Islam), Zazen (from the Buddhist faith), and Kundalini yoga (from the Hindi faith) are but a few of the powerful forms that often lead to ecstatic experience and enable paradigm shifts called satori—"ah-ha," enlightenment, or conversion experiences. Most if not all of these forms are best used under the tutelage of a mentor or spiritual teacher. Meditation mentors or masters for these disciplines can suggest to students the particular practices that are appropriate to their stage of the spiritual journey, teach them to perform the practices properly, and enable students to avoid nasty consequences. Some forms of practices, with the exception of Zen meditation because of its use of physical grounding practices, produce a wide variety of unsettling psychological phenomena, body movements, and uncomfortable physical sensations and experiences and can be actually dangerous for the unprepared or novice meditator.[1]

Spiritual Guidance

Here we should talk a bit more about spiritual mentoring or spiritual guidance, sometimes known as spiritual direction. In all contemplative pursuits, it is wise to work with a mentor who has walked the walk before you and knows the pitfalls and hard places. At times in my own journey, I actually thought I was going crazy but had the good fortune to have a spiritual guide who would simply sit with me and tell me to not be afraid because something holy was happening. Spiritual guides can prescribe helpful practices, such as reading the Psalms. Traditionally, spiritual guidance also helps an individual distinguish between messages from the ego and messages from God. The spiritual guide questions the spiritual sojourner in order to discern what is his or her own agenda (born out of conscious and unconscious processes, family messages, and desires of the ego) and what is God's agenda. And the spiritual guide, much like Rainer Maria Rilke in his *Letters to a Young Poet,* aids the sojourner to "live the questions now" so that "someday far in the future you might live into the answer."

Journaling

Journaling is also an excellent way to enable the spiritual life. It is different from keeping a diary of daily occurrences; rather, it is about recording our dreams, screams, prayers, questions, observations, and ah-ha experiences. In short, the journal is a place to talk to self and to God. Journals are private places and should be kept private. They are a place to be yourself, with all your light and darkness, grief and joy, anger and delight, misspelled words, improper grammar, and poor penmanship. Journals should preferably be kept in a book with numbered pages, so that we are less inclined to rip out offending entries, and they should be written in ink, so that we can't erase a "mistake" that might actually be a communication from the unconscious mind to the conscious mind. If you really have to alter an entry, put a single line through it. You will often find that the word you crossed out is the key to what your unconscious mind—or God—was saying to you. Many resources available on the Internet and in bookstores describe journal exercises and techniques. Journaling is a worthwhile discipline to develop, because it provides an emotional outlet, a place to work through problems and questions, and historical record of emotional-cognitive synthesis, personal growth, and the answers to prayers.

Dream Work

Journals are a great place to do dream work—Freud's "royal road to the unconscious" or what Episcopal priest and Jungian analyst John A. Sanford calls "God's forgotten language." Biblical characters learned a lot from their dreams—remember Jacob and Daniel—and so can you. Begin by keeping a pad and a pen by your bedside. If a dream wakes you up, discipline yourself to turn on the light and write it down, even if it means you have to get up and go into another room to avoid disturbing your partner. When you wake up in the morning, ask yourself what the last image was that you had in your mind. Write it down, even if you can only remember a fragment. The action of writing will bring back additional pieces of the dream. Don't obey the little devil that sits on your shoulder and asks, "Oh, why don't you go to the bathroom, brush your teeth, or take a shower first?" By the time you have completed that activity, your conscious mind will have suppressed the dream contents. Always record dream content in the first person, present tense, and remember that often the persons, places, and things in your dreams are really representations of parts of yourself. A Jungian therapist, gestalt therapist, existential therapist, or experienced spiritual guide can help you learn to discover the meaning of this particular form of communication that is most often from the unconscious to the conscious but sometimes comes directly from God.

∽

All meditation and forms of contemplation, be they Christian, Eastern, Native American, or some aboriginal form of shamanic practice, open a door and begin a journey from which there is no turning back. In these practices we place ourselves before the Holy, offer our life to God, and wait to grow into the answer. Sometimes the passage is dangerous. Therefore, be forewarned, take courage, and discover the peace of God.

PART 5

LOOKING TOWARD THE FUTURE

As a congregation moves more deeply into recovery following an experience of clergy misconduct, it begins to become more future oriented. The chapters in this part help afterpastors and lay leaders think about next steps, sometimes in congregations that will never fully recover. Ideally, congregations continue to grow healthier and are able to call a new pastor who will support that growth, respond to the victim/survivor with care and respect, and discover more resources, deeper insights, and greater strengths for ministry.

Even as congregations work toward healing, the wider church—both as judicatory and denomination—has work to do. The goal is clear: consistent, faithful, appropriate, and healing response to clergy misconduct. In the end, wisdom, courage, commitment, and healing can be manifest throughout the church.

26

MANAGING SITUATIONS
THAT MIGHT NEVER BE GOOD

Matthew Linden

MOST CLERGY, JUDICATORY OFFICIALS, AND CONSULTANTS who have worked with congregations affected by clergy sexual misconduct say it takes a decade for a motivated congregation to recover its vitality. Healing and recovery take time. Some congregations recover more quickly than others, especially when the lay leaders and judicatory use sound practices during disclosure and the period afterwards. Other congregations, however, never fully recover. Instead, they go through a series of short-term pastorates as the overall condition of the congregation continues to deteriorate. Many of these congregations were not all that healthy to begin with. Some have endured more than one instance of clergy misconduct within the past 25 years, which usually means that the unhealthy dynamics within the system were not effectively dealt with after the first episode. Others experienced a disclosure process that was handled poorly by both the lay leaders and the judicatory. Many congregations are independent or have minimal ties to any middle judicatory, so the lay leaders and afterpastor have few resources and little support when handling disclosure and the period afterwards. Finally, many afterpastors do not always know when accepting a call or appointment that sexual misconduct has occurred during a previous pastorate, so they take steps that seem reasonable but, because of the unique history of the congregation, are actually counterproductive. In this chapter I will discuss the dynamics afterpastors experience in situations where it seems unlikely that a congregation will ever recover.

Entering the Twilight Zone

Afterpastors are often ill prepared for what they will encounter. Many assume that strong pastoral care skills, experience in helping a congregation work through a devastating crisis like a fire, or a history of advocacy on behalf of survivors of sexual abuse will provide a sufficient foundation for ministry in settings where misconduct has occurred. However, it is common in some circles to describe afterpastor ministry as "The Twilight Zone"—things are not always as they seem. The relationship between the clergy and the congregation may appear to be going smoothly, with rising attendance and remarkably conflict-free board meetings. Then one Sunday there is significantly lower attendance than usual. The following morning the minister receives a call from a judicatory official concerning a letter listing half a dozen grievances that leave the minister wondering if the judicatory had mistakenly telephoned the wrong church. Criticism of the minister escalates, the accusations having little relationship to actual job performance. The pastor and family may begin to use terms like "spiritually oppressive" to describe the overall climate of the congregation. It is not unusual for an afterpastor to begin to doubt if accusations against the offending pastor were credible and begin to take drastic self-protective measures. Overall, afterpastors work in settings where they cannot always trust their gut feelings or prior experience.

The anxiety afterpastors experience becomes easier to manage when "The Twilight Zone" is understood as a combination of several systemic conditions that are both the result of and a contributing factor to clergy misconduct. Three of these are (1) an erosion of appropriate professional boundaries, (2) regression on the part of congregational leaders that severely impedes their ability to make thoughtful, nonreactive decisions, and (3) perhaps most importantly, the replacement of official structures by informal networks for both disseminating information and making decisions. As puzzling and anxiety producing as the dynamics might be in a congregation where clergy misconduct has occurred, afterpastors can understand these dynamics and take steps to manage the situations they are in.

Appropriate Professional Boundaries

Rarely does clergy misconduct occur immediately after a pastor is appointed to or installed in an otherwise healthy congregation. The overall culture—especially the unspoken norms—prevents such behavior from taking place. Perhaps the most important of these unspoken norms are the professional boundaries between the minister and congregants.

Appropriate professional boundaries are necessary to preserve the overall health of any system. Therapists do not socialize with their clients. Investors do not go on gambling junkets with the managers of their investment portfolios. Teachers do not discuss their difficulties with another teacher in the presence of students. For clergy, however, the lines are not always easy to see. Pastoral ministry fosters a level of intimacy unlike other professional relationships. We play a variety of roles in our relationships with congregants. We may have a working partnership with the church school superintendent *and* preside over her wedding and sit with her family at the hospital when the decision is made to disconnect life support from her father. Clergy also have to manage conflict between various leaders, knowing that actions and decisions in one situation can be influenced by confidential information disclosed in another. Congregants also learn confidential information about their ministers, often through their secular employment. For example, a lay leader might also be a receptionist at the office of the pastor's physician and have access to the pastor's medical history. Difficult as boundaries might be to identify in a congregation, they are essential to protect both the integrity of the clergy/congregant relationship and the system that provides the context.

One of the first things afterpastors notice is the absence of boundaries. They often sense intuitively that the expectations and rules are somehow different in this congregation. Parishioners may casually divulge personal information, implying a level of trust the pastor has not earned. Congregants may give signals that they expect the pastor to reciprocate with the same level of self-disclosure and complain that he or she is distant, aloof, or uncaring. One telltale indicator of breached boundaries is the expectation that the pastor will somehow know without being told that a parishioner is in need of pastoral care. These expectations belie the overall lack of trust the congregation demonstrates toward the pastor in other areas. Mixed signals indeed!

It is helpful for afterpastors to "go to the balcony" on a daily basis, reflecting on each encounter and asking such questions as, What does that conversation tell me about this place? Another good practice is to listen carefully as people describe their relationship with previous pastors. It is not uncommon to hear details about a pastor's personal life that could be known only if the pastor had disclosed them. This information will give the afterpastor some idea about the unwritten rules and cultural norms of the congregation.

Afterpastors need to understand that working in a system where appropriate professional boundaries do not exist can be very seductive, especially when the pastor feels lonely, isolated, and unappreciated. Boundaries fall away slowly and subtly, their erosion a mutual effort by the minister and congregation. One of the things the afterpastor needs to avoid is using a supportive parishioner as a confidant, especially in matters concerning relationships and conflicts with other parishioners. The temptation to do this is particularly strong in congregations affected by clergy sexual misconduct, because conflict and anxiety tend to be chronic—and often focus on the pastor. However, a pastor's turning to parishioners for support not only exacerbates conflict, but leaves the afterpastor vulnerable when the power dynamics of an unstable congregation change.

The congregation can be extremely resistant to reestablishing boundaries, even in situations where the relationship between the absence of boundaries and misconduct is obvious. Reestablishing appropriate professional boundaries requires persistence and often involves violating the congregation's cultural norms. Symbolic actions by the pastor can go a long way toward restoring appropriate professional boundaries. Sometimes wearing a clerical collar or jacket and tie when performing pastoral duties will reinforce—in the minds of both the parishioner and minister—the professional nature of the relationship. A minister might also request that he or she be addressed by title and last name, even if the minister has always gone by Pastor Pat or Reverend Ralph. Some afterpastors refrain from socializing with parishioners, putting in only a brief appearance when they are invited to members' homes. They also make a point of never drinking alcohol in the presence of a member. Another suggestion, if possible, is that the pastor live in a neighborhood or township different from the congregation's, especially if the congregation is in a small town. This will help keep conflicts between the minister, the minister's family, and the congregation from carrying over into other contexts such as school or community organizations. The stress on clergy families in these settings cannot be underestimated.

Regression among Congregational Leaders

Congregational consultant Peter Steinke refers to mature leaders as "the immune cells" of any church or family system. Their capacity to respond in a nonanxious and thoughtful manner encourages a congregation to maintain its integrity in the midst of internal and external threats. A congregation needs effective lay leaders to preserve its identity, mission, and core values in the face of a traumatic experience. Their nonreactive stance enables the congregation to respond in ways that will do no further damage to the already fragile community.

One of the insidious effects of clergy misconduct is what it does to lay leaders. When news first breaks, many leaders are paralyzed by shock and disbelief. It is not uncommon for lines to be drawn between those leaders who believe the charges brought against the ordained leader and those who do not. As families begin to transfer their membership and weekly offerings drop, leaders may begin blaming the victim or the judicatory official who processed the complaint. When this happens, the most objective leaders may withdraw from their positions. Those who remain band together to "save the church at all costs," often with a handful of people assuming much of the financial burden. Though they may be successful in bringing a level of stability to the congregation, they often lack the objectivity needed to provide thoughtful, nonreactive leadership. The crisis hits too close to home; the church is too important in their lives to consider questions related to long-term sustainability.

The afterpastor should resist labeling individual leaders as "dysfunctional," "undifferentiated," or "clergy killers." Leaders in any congregation that has survived clergy misconduct will regress. Their inability to make healthy decisions usually has more to do with the length of time their family has been involved with the congregation or the importance it has in their lives than any innate inability to deal with stress. To the extent possible, the afterpastor should try to be empathetic toward these wounded leaders, although they might continue to be difficult to work with.

In general, the afterpastor needs to focus on the overall health of the congregational system instead of the functioning of individuals. Afterpastors are left with a dilemma, however. They are not automatically given the trust necessary to lead. At the same time, most of the lay leaders will lack the objectivity to provide vision and direction. This creates a stalemate in which the clergyperson's attempts to provide leadership are sabotaged by those who cannot see past the next monthly financial statement. In order for a congregation to move beyond this impasse, the afterpastor needs to identify potential leaders currently on the margins of congregational life; develop trusting, spiritually focused relationships with them; and encourage them to faithfully develop the skills needed to answer God's call to them. The best potential leaders are those who have credibility with the existing leaders and some degree of emotional objectivity about the congregation. The grown children of long-term members or people who "married into" the congregation are often good candidates for leadership. As new leaders emerge, the afterpastor has to accept that they will be the ones who get the credit for returning the congregation to health. Any attempt by the afterpastor to assume center stage can derail the process.

It takes a year or two before an afterpastor knows a congregation well enough to begin identifying and equipping potential leaders. Attempting this too early can result in selecting inappropriate people—potential leaders who do not have credibility with the current leaders and wider membership and who therefore will not be accepted. Even when the right people are identified, it may take another year or so before existing leaders will be open to receiving the new person's leadership. Clearly, developing new leaders requires that the afterpastor be patient.

Informal Networks

Parking lot meetings and telephone grapevines are a fact of life in congregations. There is always a meeting after the meeting. Difficult decisions made by the board will be second-guessed by those who turn down every invitation to serve as leaders. Such is the nature of congregational life just about everywhere. The difference in a congregation affected by clergy misconduct is that these informal networks replace official boards and committees by both disseminating information and overturning decisions made during official meetings in the presence of the pastor.

While this aspect of being an afterpastor is maddening, it begins to make sense when looked at from the perspective of the congregation. First, when a scandal involving the minister breaks, only a handful of leaders knows the "who, what, when, where, and how" of the situation. These leaders may believe it is better for the congregation to disclose as little information as possible, so most members are kept in the dark, their requests for information denied. As pieces of the story begin to surface or are leaked, a grapevine is established. This network remains in place long after the offending pastor is removed and may still be perceived as the only reliable source of information about the congregation. Second, members may have attempted to address the behavior of the offending minister through the congregation's or judicatory's official structure, only to be met with denials, accusations, and threats, often intended to protect the offending minister's career rather than address the interests of the local church. Members learned through painful experience that the official channels for confronting a clergyperson's behavior are blocked and efforts to address misconduct are not worth the energy. (One side effect of such an experience is that afterpastors often find appeals to congregational bylaws or denominational polity ineffective when trying to sustain decisions made by administrative boards, sessions, or vestries.)

Though a congregation's reliance on unofficial communication networks is understandable, it ultimately works against the congregation's best interests, creating a web of triangles where direct communication between people in conflict is avoided. This pattern of indirect communication—which began as a way of adapting to a recalcitrant pastor, stonewalling vestry, or unhelpful judicatory—soon becomes standard practice for any conflict within the congregation, including situations that do not involve the pastor at all. The result is a congregational environment where anxiety is ever present and seemingly minor disagreements quickly become major flare-ups.

The afterpastor needs to "de-triangle" the system, but this is almost impossible to accomplish when the congregation has lost all confidence in the pastoral office. Judicatory officials may be even less effective in working directly with the congregation due to lingering mistrust. The best person to handle the task of reestablishing open communication is somebody outside both the congregational and judicatory system. A consultant retained by the governing board is probably the best option. If a congregation lacks the financial resources for a consultant, they might consider asking the judicatory if grants are available. When funding is not available, it is probably better for the congregation to contact an experienced clergy or layperson from another denomination than to use someone from the judicatory staff. Another option might be to select a mature and capable layperson who is currently on the margins of the congregation and consequently not part of any existing triangles.

Some Cautions

The work of afterpastors may be the most stressful of all ministries. As someone who has served as afterpastor in one congregation and dealt with a devastating fire in another, I can say unequivocally that ministry in the aftermath of a fire is a walk in the park compared with being an afterpastor. The afterpastor must never underestimate the difficulty of serving in such a setting. Here are some of the common pitfalls.

- ATTEMPTING TO BYPASS RECOVERY THROUGH EVANGELISM, CHURCH GROWTH, OR OUTREACH EFFORTS. Most pastors cannot bring about congregational growth without the help and support of the members. Even those pastors with exceptional evangelistic gifts will find that people they bring in will not be assimilated into the congregation and will be perceived as "the pastor's people." The cost of premature growth is often forced termination or a congregational split.
- ATTEMPTING REDEVELOPMENT TOO EARLY. A common mistake is to begin redevelopment within a year or two of the disclosure. For at least five years,

the goals should be reestablishing appropriate professional boundaries, developing spiritually mature lay leaders, and establishing open patterns of communication. Attempting redevelopment before these things are accomplished is usually ineffective.

- Underestimating the potential for stress and burnout. The potential for health problems, divorce, or an episode of sexual misconduct is significantly higher for afterpastors than for pastors in other settings. It is best to negotiate and make arrangements with the judicatory for professional coaching or counseling prior to accepting a call or appointment as an afterpastor. *The afterpastor should not expect the congregation to assume financial responsibility for any agreement made with the judicatory.*
- Participating in a clergy support group where no one has experienced being an afterpastor. Congregations where clergy misconduct has occurred are unique settings. Sound pastoral practices that are effective elsewhere are often benign at best. Pastors with no experience in these settings often have trouble even believing some of the things that are routine for afterpastors. Their advice may not be helpful. It may be also quite demoralizing.
- Going into a congregation without a back-up plan. It is common for congregations affected by misconduct to arbitrarily reduce salary, stop paying the pastor's pension or health insurance premiums, and refuse to pay utilities on the church-owned parsonage, regardless of the requirements of denominational polity or the pastor's contract. An afterpastor needs to negotiate a back-up plan with the judicatory before accepting a call or appointment as an afterpastor.
- Taking responsibility for things beyond the pastor's control. The congregation's image in the wider community and its relationship with the judicatory are two things an afterpastor cannot change.

At some point during the slow recovery process, an afterpastor asks, Will things get better? I think a more productive question is, to quote Jack Nicholson, "What if this is as good as it gets?" The difference in phrasing shifts the focus from conditions within the congregational system to the pastor's own functioning within that system. The average tenure for an afterpastor is around three years in a recovery process that often takes ten years or more. Afterpastors need to accept that they may not complete the entire process with the congregation and would be wise to define faithful ministry as helping the congregation move from one stage of recovery to the next. Staying in that setting too long can be harmful for both the afterpastor and the congregation.

Is there ministry beyond being an afterpastor? Yes. In fact, the experience of being an afterpastor teaches principles about congregational systems and dynamics not ordinarily learned in other settings. The results are often greater sensitivity and improved effectiveness in later ministries. The congregation may not become healthy during the pastor's tenure. However, the afterpastor will be able to leave knowing that she or he provided responsible and faithful pastoral leadership.

27

PREPARING TO CALL
A NEW PASTOR

Dan Smith and Mary Sellon

"THANK GOODNESS, THAT'S OVER. Now we can put it behind us and get on with things." This is the siren song luring a congregation as it begins to look to the future following clergy misconduct. People will want to believe that once the offender has been removed and an appropriate response made to the victims, that particular chapter of its life is concluded. It is not. And to believe and act as if it is sets up a congregation for repeat occurrences of clergy misconduct.

Often, a congregation does initial work around healing and declares things "back to normal." The problem is that normal for that system may still be unhealthy. Professional boundaries may be nebulous, lay leadership ineffective, and communication practices poor. Interims begin the work of restoring health, but it takes many years for healthy changes to pervade a system. And until a system changes, it is vulnerable to and even invites further victimization. The task of calling a new pastor provides a congregation with a mechanism for taking its next step towards restoring systemic health. A strong, healthy leader, such as a skilled interim pastor, can help the church continue to move forward. At the same time, the future health of the congregation demands that the search committee itself learn and model healthy relational practices as it engages in that selection process.

Clergy misconduct violates the congregational system at the same time as it violates individuals. Misconduct by a pastoral leader skews a congregation's understanding of what church is supposed to be, while establishing or further anchoring unhealthy patterns of relating. Though the event itself is over, congregations will typically exhibit one and usually more of the following systemic traits:

179

- Preference for pastors with poor personal boundaries
- Absence of spiritually mature, self-differentiated laity in key leadership positions
- Informal decision making by a few supplanting formal decision-making structures
- Indirect patterns of communicating that promote secrecy
- Estrangement from the denominational system/structure

Alone, any of these traits can subvert a congregation's missional purpose. In combination, these systemic traits create a closed and isolated community where a clergy leader can have free reign to abuse his or her power. As those traits become more firmly entrenched, congregations turn inward and lose the outward-focused mission that is their fundamental purpose. The right next pastor must be able to help establish and hold appropriate boundaries, focus on the development of spiritually mature lay leaders, strengthen lines of accountability and decision making, develop patterns of clear and open communication, and close the rift between church and denomination. The search committee's challenge lies in developing a process that will surface the person able to attend to these systemic issues.

The right pastor will not appear magically from thin air. And hard as it may be to believe, if the right next pastor did magically appear, the majority of the congregation would fail to recognize the rightness of the fit. The personality of that person and the work that pastor sees as important may be very different from what the congregation has come to believe is not only normal, but desirable.

The search committee, if it is to recognize the right next pastor, must learn to look through new lenses. Committee members will need to set aside their biases and personal desires and educate themselves about their congregation, the unique challenges the congregation faces, and what is needed at this point in its journey for the faith community to truly be faithful. They then must find the leader who can help the congregation take those next steps.

A Search Committee Models Health

In its work together, the search committee supports the ongoing recovery process by putting into practice what it learns about healthy congregational relationships. As the group learns about healthy boundaries, decision making, and communication, it takes the opportunity to apply those learnings in its work together. In this way, the committee models a new way of being for the entire congregation. The committee serves the congregation by fulfilling the tasks assigned *and* by practicing right relationship as it does them.

A basic step in practicing right relationship is designing how the committee will work together. What are the covenant agreements that will guide how they do their work and relate to one another? What can each member count on from the others? How will they handle disagreements?

The search committee also needs to mutually agree on how they will relate to the congregation. What information will they share with the congregation and how? Will the congregation be trusted with the thinking and struggles of the committee or only with the decisions? Will the committee speak with one voice, or will individuals be free to share their personal opinions outside of committee meetings? Having these conversations before the committee launches into its work helps establish the relationships needed to do its work effectively.

In modeling recovery, the committee must resist becoming mired in problems and stuck in nonproductive feelings. Fully aware of and acknowledging the wounds and the factors that contributed to its problems, committee members must discern the future God has in mind for them. They must keep in mind what within the congregation may need to shift in order to avoid repeating the problem. Committee members need to commit themselves to creating a community among themselves that is both faithful and safe.

Qualities Required of Committee Members

Members of the search committee have responsibility for making one of the most important decisions made in the congregation's life in recent years. Through a task force, the congregation has already been doing important work in initial responses to the misconduct. The search committee now has a task that will significantly affect the future health of the congregation as a new pastor is selected. Serving on the committee is both a high privilege and a demanding responsibility, and the work requires committing a significant amount of time and energy. Members will need to become resident experts on the dynamics surrounding clergy misconduct, the impact of misconduct on the congregational system, and the shifts required for recovery and health. Congregations that do not understand and learn from their history tend to repeat it.

More demanding than the time requirements, the role requires emotional maturity, spiritual strength, and wisdom. The members' job is to function not as representatives of groups or caucuses, but as stewards serving the missional well-being of the entire faith community. They must listen deeply and with compassion. They may become targets of the anger and frustration felt by members of the congregation. They must remain grounded and not take those expressions of feelings personally.

As the congregation or board discerns who might best serve on the search committee, the following questions may be helpful: Who do people turn to when they need trusted personal or spiritual advice? Who has the emotional maturity to hold the heat of the strong feelings that will be evoked in the congregation during this time? Who possesses a deep sense of what church is supposed to be about?

Each member will need to examine his or her heart, asking: Am I willing and able to fill the role required of a member of this committee? Under these circumstances, am I one of the right people to serve the congregation in this role? Can I step into what is required of me in this process?

As part of the covenant agreements early in the life of the committee, members should talk about what they need from each other for the sake of their own emotional and spiritual well-being. Agreements need to be made not only about how they will hold each other accountable, but how they will support each other in their work.

Connecting with the Judiciary

A common hallmark of congregations that have experienced clergy misconduct is estrangement from their denominational and judicatory support staff. The committee needs to make an honest assessment of its attitudes toward and relationship with the judicatory. A church over time or at the urging of an offending pastor may have increasingly separated from its denomination. The estrangement may seem to center around theology or stands taken on social issues. It may center around the judicatory's urging for financial support for denominational mission and ministry beyond the local church. Perhaps there is a pervading sense that the judicatory has not dealt fairly with the congregation, promising resources not faithfully or adequately delivered.

An even stronger negative attitude toward the judicatory may develop in response to the recent pastoral misconduct. Blame may be placed on the judicatory for what has happened in the church. "How can we trust them? If they'd been doing their job, this never would have happened!"

This "separatist" attitude is often a reflection of the inclination of the pastor or a series of pastors and may have been nurtured by pastors who themselves did not violate the congregation. The net effect, however, was to contribute to the conditions that made the congregational system more susceptible to misconduct. The pastor who does engage in misconduct welcomes that distance from the denomination or judicatory, which minimizes "authorities" looking over his or her shoulder.

A congregation that desires to move to new levels of health after clergy misconduct would be wise to partner with its judicatory. Judicatories generally have significant wisdom, provide a steadying presence, and can help connect churches with helpful and much needed resources. Working collaboratively and in good relationship with the judicatory allows the call process to progress more smoothly and yields the best results. As the search committee models a new level of openness to and partnership with its denomination, the congregation takes another step toward recovery and health. The committee is then well positioned to begin its work—first, educating itself, and second, developing a profile of the next right pastor.

Stage One: Education

After gathering, the committee's first task is educating itself about three things:

1. The denominational and/or church policies that guide its work as a committee
2. The dynamics of clergy misconduct
3. The congregation

What's Our Task?

Each congregation has its own procedures for a search committee to follow. For some, these procedures are clearly spelled out by the denomination. A congregation not responsible to a judicatory body follows procedures and policies established by the congregation. The first task of the committee is simply to become familiar with the procedures governing its work and reach a commonly held understanding of those procedures. This understanding should also be discussed with the congregation's governing board, so there is clarity between them about the committee's task. Helpful questions include:

- What is our committee's task as defined by denominational or, in the absence of such directions, congregational guidelines?
- What judicatory representatives do we work with or through?
- What is that person's role and what is the committee's role?
- What is the process?
- To whom do we answer?
- What is the scope of our responsibility?
- What is *not* the work of this committee?
- Where does our work end and another group's work begin?

Given the recent boundary violations and the likely possibility that boundaries in the congregation are in need of bolstering, it is especially important for the committee to be clear about its work. The committee must establish (if necessary) and follow recommended policies and procedures both in its own work and in its communication with the congregation.

What Happened Here, and How Can We Prevent It from Happening Again?

A search committee in a congregation that has experienced clergy misconduct faces a special and challenging task. It must educate itself about congregational customs and expectations that make a congregation vulnerable to misconduct. Dangerous norms, practices, and expectations may be the very ones that parishioners have become accustomed to without any awareness of the dangers.

In settings where clergy misconduct has occurred, it is common to find a preference for ways of living together that made and will continue to make that community vulnerable to abuse by someone in a position of power. A series of pastors who were available 24/7 and were open about the intimate details of their lives may have created a culture of very lax boundaries. Lone-ranger pastors who do it all themselves may have unwittingly weakened the power of lay leaders. Disagreements with denominational leadership can leave a congregation isolated. Education provides the committee with new lenses through which to view what has happened in the church and what is needed from its next leader.

The committee needs to operate with a common framework for understanding the dynamics of clergy abuse and how that applies to the congregation *now*.

Even though the entire congregation may have received some education on clergy misconduct, the responsibility shouldered by the search committee demands a higher level of training. If the congregation is working with a response team or consultant, such resources can be enormously helpful in assisting the search committee to design an educational strategy for itself.

The search committee needs a deep understanding of what happened in the congregation. What made it possible? How is the congregation different now? How does the way the congregation functions make it more vulnerable than other congregations to further instances of misconduct? What is known about the journey back to health? Even if all members of the committee have already received this sort of training and understand what happened in their congregation, the committee needs to have this conversation as it begins this phase of the work.

Who Are We as a Congregation?

Finally, the search committee must educate itself about the congregation. How is the church organized? What are the various programs and ministries? What is the average worship attendance, and what have been the trends in attendance across the past 10 years? What is the budget? What are the pertinent facts of its history? What values undergird life together in the congregation? Does the congregation have a vision and mission statement? What are the gifts of this congregation? The challenges? Denominational guidelines and resources can also provide guidance about what information to gather to develop a congregation profile.

The profile must report that clergy misconduct has occurred in the congregation. Rather than emphasizing the details, however, which will be shared in the interview with the candidate, the profile focuses on how the congregation has been affected by the misconduct and the patterns in the congregation that need to be shifted. For instance, one committee discovered a problematic pattern of congregants having free access to the parsonage, located next door to the church. This committee also found that the congregation had a pattern of communicating indirectly that led to frequent misunderstandings. Additionally, the group surfaced a congregation-wide habit of small groups convening to negate decisions made in committee. This search committee needed to incorporate this information in its profile. It is important for a committee to share with a candidate whatever it has learned about the unique system that is the congregation.

Stage Two: Developing a Profile of the Right Next Pastor

After educating itself about the congregation and unique challenges it faces, the committee is ready to develop a profile of the right next pastor. This should encompass both a description of the person's qualities and skills, and what the committee is asking that person to do. The profile provides the essential tool for deciding who to interview and in interviewing, who to finally select.

The committee needs to allow ample time for the development of the profile. Some faith communities use the development of the profile as a way of engaging the congregation in continuing healing and education on the dynamics around clergy misconduct. Gatherings that allow the committee to share its working version of the next pastor's profile and its rationale for the profile open the process and put information and power in the hands of the people. Gatherings, as opposed to mailings to the congregation, invite congregational participation, support members' ongoing education, and nurture the healing of relationships within the congregation.

The profile should include specific personal qualities, the "being" of the person, such as spiritual and emotional maturity, strong personal boundaries, and emotional intelligence. The right next pastor will possess both self-awareness and the ability to self-manage. This person will derive his or her sense of self from within, rather than looking to others for a sense of self-worth. He or she will have a life beyond working with the church. The right next pastor will be an excellent listener, interested in truly understanding what another is saying.

A helpful profile outlines the knowledge base the person needs to have to effectively serve the congregation, such as an understanding of the dynamics of power and the issues underlying clergy misconduct and congregational recovery. The profile needs to specify required areas of demonstrated skill, such as communicating effectively, managing conflict, and developing spiritually mature lay leaders.

In addition to developing a profile of the personal qualities, knowledge, and skills required in the new pastor, the committee must be able to articulate what it is asking that pastor to do across the next several years. What is the assignment? What areas does the congregation need the pastor to focus on? What are the benchmarks that will mark appropriate development in those areas? What areas of the church do not need his or her primary attention? A congregation might set a guideline that the pastor should conduct no more than three counseling sessions with an individual, referring the person at that point to a professional counselor or therapist. Clarity about the assignment will help the committee surface the person with the right gifts and interests.

The search committee may wish to set expectations around boundaries. This is the time to be clear about such expectations, including the pastor taking off at least one full day (24 hours) each week, a full weekend each quarter in addition to vacation time, and all allotted vacation time each year. The committee might specify the pastor will work no more than three or four evenings in a given week and will swap time blocks if he or she must work during normal time off. Of course, it can be tempting for a committee in a badly burned church to overreact and go overboard in monitoring the pastor's hours. Boundaries set for the pastor out of distrust rather than out of caring support can have a detrimental effect on the relationship between the pastor and congregation.

Final Thoughts

After educating itself and creating profiles of the congregation and the needed pastoral leader, the committee needs to design an interview process. Within the first few minutes of an interview, people tend to develop strong feelings, positive or negative, about a candidate. While remaining open to intuition, it is important to focus on the needs of the congregation and whether the candidate meets those needs. There are many excellent resources available to educate a committee on how to interview candidates.

In the interview, the committee must talk honestly and candidly with the candidate about the misconduct that has occurred. Preparing to talk about the misconduct with the candidate calls, once again, for the committee to practice and model healthy conversations and relationships. Ignoring or hiding the misconduct builds a climate of secrecy that only creates problems over time.

Learning to openly share the story, both the details of what happened and the steps that have been taken toward recovery, is an important part of the healing process. An ultimate goal for the congregation will be for the people to own their own history and be able to frame even this part of their story as a journey of faith. A significant step towards that is the search committee learning to talk about the misconduct both in the written profile and in conversation with the candidate. This requires the committee to take time as a group, perhaps with the help of an outside resource person, to learn how to tell their story. The committee will need to learn what must be included and ways to tell the story that serve the long-term health and development of the congregation.

Background checks are considered a responsible practice in any pastoral transition. Judicatories will have followed their own processes for screening candidates regarding past misconduct. The committee is encouraged to ask about that screening and augment it when members feel it is needed. Companies exist that specialize in clergy background checks. Their services range from making written inquiries of educational institutions, employers, organizations, and supervisors to checking public records. Such companies work with congregations and judicatories to serve their specific needs. (See "Calling a New Pastor" in appendix A, "Resources.")

The selection of a new pastor presents a congregation with the opportunity to take the next step in recovering its health. The work is not easy. Much will be demanded of the members who serve on the search committee. But no work will have greater impact on the future of the church. Those who say yes to the call to serve in this capacity can find strength in knowing they are not alone. God is with them, working through them to bring healing and hope to their congregation.

28

What's Ahead
for the Victim?

Patricia L. Liberty

As I ENTERED MY SECOND DECADE OF WORK with survivors of clergy sexual abuse, I encountered a curious phenomenon: some of my earliest clients were returning for additional support and healing work. Well into their recovery, the presenting issues of spiritual and religious struggle, and sexual and relationship difficulties were often accompanied with a sense of frustration, failure, and dread. They had already spent years in therapy, attended retreats, and dealt with the anger, depression, sadness, and loss that are the heart of recovery from clergy sexual abuse. Now they were facing those issues again from a different perspective, as well as identifying new areas in need of healing.

It is important to note that the healing journey for each survivor is unique; survivors' pain and work is not easily categorized or identified. The majority of my work is with adult women survivors who were exploited as adults. The information that follows is drawn from work with that group and may not as accurately describe the recovery of those whose experiences of exploitation are substantively different. In addition, my work with survivors is not clinical; it is pastoral and advocacy based. However different the healing journeys, though, the women I have worked with have raised remarkably consistent issues.

A New Rhythm

Survivors identified a difference in the rhythm of the work they now faced that was qualitatively different from their earlier work. In the early phases of recovery, trauma is often the focus. Clinical treatment addresses issues of personal safety, restoration of basic function, and acute grief. The time line for this phase of recovery is affected by numerous factors, including the presence or absence of an ecclesiastical complaint process, the level and quality of disclosure in the congregation, and the level of family disruption.

The pastoral role with survivors in this phase is primarily to provide support, a venue for religious and spiritual reflection, and encouragement to continue clinical work. The client's overall movement is from victim to survivor. As time and work continue, victims of clergy sexual abuse gain perspective and a renewed sense of worth.

As survivors returned in the second decade of recovery, they identified a diminished sense of urgency about the work needed. Their pain was deep, but not as raw or acute. They expressed a yearning for deeper wholeness. The acute crisis phase and its attending energy were past, and they expressed a desire for further theological reflection, deeper spiritual healing, and sexual and relational healing.

As noted elsewhere in this volume, spirituality and sexuality are the last arenas of healing, and the survivors who returned in their second decade of recovery bore witness to that truth. (See chapter 11, "Victims/Survivors.") However, often survivors needed first to express their feelings of frustration and failure at having such significant pain so long after the abuse. The pastoral role in this time is to affirm the ongoing nature of the healing journey and assure the survivors that they are "not crazy" and their feelings are in fact quite understandable.

A profound consequence for women who are exploited as adults is that they mistrust their feelings and bodies, perceptions of reality, and decision-making capacity. Healing those core identity issues is one of the tasks of long-term recovery, and it is especially difficult when the predominant message from the church (as well as family and friends) is that they "should be all better by now." Pastoral support and advocacy can help ground survivors in the legitimacy of their own perceptions and needs as they attend to this phase of their healing. Often women who are cycling back into issues in the second decade are no longer in therapy. As in all phases of support and pastoral care, it is important for pastoral supporters to know their limits and know when a referral is appropriate.

Religious and Spiritual Issues

A second long-term healing issue is religious participation and spiritual practice. This issue is expressed in many ways, and many experiences raise it for survivors. Sometimes the religious life-cycle events of family and friends cause a predicament for survivors. Attending weddings, funerals, and baptisms, as well as adolescent membership rituals, may precipitate feelings of loss as well as anxiety and stress, especially if members of the church where these services are held know her identity or the abuser is still in a position of authority.

A more subtle expression of religious and spiritual pain often surfaces in the survivor's simultaneous desire for and fear of a faith community. Most survivors are alienated from the church where the exploitation occurred and from the church as whole. As time goes on, they may feel a deep longing to participate in community accompanied by a deep fear. The loss of worship, sacramental expression, fellowship, study, and nurture can draw a survivor back to an institutional religious setting. Helping her negotiate her own feelings, consider options, and establish a sense of inner safety while validating her hypervigilance is an important pastoral support at this time.

Healing for Relational and Sexual Issues

A third area in need of long-term healing is relational and sexual. Survivors almost universally report difficulties with emotional and sexual intimacy in the aftermath of clergy sexual abuse. Anecdotal evidence from my work with survivors suggests that the divorce rate is 40 to 70 percent. Several factors figure prominently: differing frameworks for understanding the experience, relationship vulnerabilities that may have predated the abuse, new sources of conflict and tension as a result of the exploitation, financial strain resulting from treatment costs, and possible changes in employment.

While shame is associated with all forms of sexual exploitation, the shame of clergy sexual abuse is qualitatively different because of its connection to the divine. Survivors speak of feeling "evil," "dirty," and "condemned" by God and a sense that their very physical body is somehow repulsive to God (and often to them). Their "sin" is often perceived not as their behavior but as their very essence. Since offending clerics often co-opt God into their abusive behavior (e.g., "God knew how much I needed you," "What we are doing here is holy"), survivors are cut off from a sense that healthy sexuality is a gift of God. As a consequence, sexual activity often connects them to feelings of worthlessness, shame, guilt, and sin.

Not only do survivors struggle with their own sense of bodiliness, they also face profound relational struggles. While women who are recovering from the abuse are learning to divest themselves of blame, their spouses or partners may still be talking about the exploitation as an affair. These differing frameworks cause tremendous strain and conflict in a relationship. Women are trying to stop blaming themselves for the abuse, and spouses or partners are still blaming them. It is important to note that the primary impact for spouses and partners is in the marital relationship. For the spouse, the exploitation *is* an affair, because that is how he or she experienced it. Spouses also may struggle with the loss of religious community and support, but such losses are usually secondary to the relationship issues. The costs of individual and couple counseling adds to the financial strain that may already have been present because of prior employment issues or the change in employment that is a direct result of the abuse.

Often it was because of family or relationship strain that women originally sought out the counsel of a trusted religious leader—counsel that became abuse. Difficulties with aging parents, developmental issues with children, ordinary relationship challenges, as well as more acute problems of unemployment, domestic violence, or substance abuse may lead a woman to seek help from her pastor. If the presenting issue was not addressed when the woman first sought help, it remains *and has been exacerbated* by the abuse. When the acute recovery phase is over, the original problem still needs attention. As one survivor said, "I went to my pastor for help, and what I got was sex."

In addition, new relationship stressors are introduced as a direct result of the exploitation. To the extent that the victim/survivor is known in the congregation and community, there is loss of privacy, rumor, speculation, and blaming of all parties involved. In rural areas or small towns, survivors and their families are often driven from their homes to seek privacy in a new community. The stress of uprooting a family, changing employment, and seeking new residence is often enough to shatter an already fragile system.

Survivors who were church employees report being fired or resigning from their positions as a result of the exploitation. This happens even when the offending pastor is removed. (Other clergy, educators, musicians, and support staff in the congregation may also be fired or resign.) The financial impact of a lost career or employment adds to the mounting stressors in the relationship.

It is important to note that these issues often surface long after the ecclesiastical process is over, the financial support for counseling is spent, and the church has moved through (however well or poorly) that chapter of its history. These are the "invisible" chapters of recovery that are largely unknown to and unseen by judicatory officials, church leaders, and members. The ongoing pain of survivors and the invisibility of their struggle is a profound commentary on the church's failure to truly support survivors in their recovery.

Reason for Hope

While the long-term recovery issues are profound, a thread of hopefulness weaves through them all. Survivors who are faithful to their recovery through the years develop remarkable strength, tenacity, and insight. They are among the most faithful, courageous, and insightful people I know. Their capacities for theological reflection and spiritual discernment are hard earned and serve them well. Survivors often know more about the theology of forgiveness, reconciliation, and restoration than the religious leaders who try prematurely to push them into it. Their sense of justice born of righteous indignation (and fueled by the church's sellout to cheap grace) is both gift and grace. As a result, they have a low tolerance for hypocrisy and can spot a phony a mile away. As one survivor commented at an "Is Nothing Sacred?" retreat, "One thing that happened as a result of the abuse is that I now have a bullshit-o-meter. By the time I realized I needed one, it was too late to save me from Rev. Jones. Now, I don't leave home without it." Often survivors also develop a great sense of humor as well. Survivors raise up a vision of religious leadership that is authentic and human. Their faithfulness to their own journey is a witness of faithfulness, integrity, and strength.

There is a lot of hard work and heartache ahead for survivors in the long term. Some survivors say recovery is forever. Pieces of the pain return, sometimes when least expected. However, as the journey goes on, with each hurdle crossed, survivors discover more resources, deeper insights, and greater strengths. Gradually the individual moves from victim to survivor to victor.

29

WHAT'S AHEAD
FOR THE WIDER CHURCH?

Patricia L. Liberty

WHEN I STARTED WORKING in the field of clergy sexual abuse intervention in the late 1980s, I assumed that denominations with hierarchical or connectional polities would be more effective in responding to complaints of clergy abuse than those with congregational polities, because officials in connectional systems would have the power to intervene. Conversely, I assumed churches with congregational polity would be at a disadvantage in responding due to lack of centralized ecclesiastical authority. Both assumptions were wrong.

Within several years, it was clear to me that differences in polity did not yield substantive differences in responses to clergy misconduct. There was something deeper, and more troubling, at work than the limits of denominational polity and ecclesiastical authority. One of the most chilling aspects of working in this field for almost 20 years is the institutional evil I have encountered while addressing clergy misconduct. I have seen just about every expression of denominational polity used to obfuscate the issue, deny its severity, blame the victim, keep the secret, and protect the power of the clergy. I discovered that despite differences in theology, organization, and understanding of mission, the one thing shared by all denominations is desire for self-protection that is based, in part, in patriarchal authority. Such authority is not specifically male, for there are numerous instances of women officials making the same dismal response as their male counterparts. Rather, denominational structures focus on using the power of the system to protect the system, instead of protecting the vulnerable and making a just response to those hurt by religious leaders.

While important and substantive changes in denominations' responses to clergy misconduct are evident in the past decade, there is more work to do. Policies and procedures, training for response teams, assessment and treatment for abusers as well as care for survivors are primary areas needing attention in most denominations. (See chapter 16, "Judicatory Leaders," for further discussion.)

Policies and Procedures

When the crisis of clergy sexual abuse surfaced over 20 years ago, the church responded by writing policies and procedures. Many were written hastily and with heavy influence from the legal profession. There is a difference between a policy and a procedure. The policy is the statement that names the behavior as abusive and sets forth the basis for response. The procedure sets the course of action to be taken when the policy is violated. It is important to note that legal advice is an important component in an effective response to complaints of clergy misconduct; however, it is not *the* most important. The lawyers need to be on the bus; they do not need to be driving.

A policy statement should be clear and concise and reflect the church's theological basis for naming the behavior as wrong. Recognizing that clergy misconduct is a misuse of the power and authority of the role as well as a violation of trust are key components of a policy statement.

A procedure should outline clear steps to be taken, beginning with how complaints are filed and the ecclesiastical official to whom they are directed. Procedures should be updated regularly to reflect changes in standards of practice, including new clinical information and treatment modalities and new case law. Much has been learned in the past 20 years, and that learning needs to be reflected in policies and procedures on misconduct.

Policies and procedures should also clearly address the needs of the accused clergy, the victim, and the congregation or other setting where the abuse occurred. Many policies and procedures overfocus on clergy, which is understandable, given that it is the behavior of a pastor that provokes the allegations, investigation, and adjudication. Ultimately a decision must be made about ministerial fitness in the aftermath of allegations of abuse. However, focusing exclusively on the accused does not address the healing needs of those who are directly affected by the abuse.

When FaithTrust Institute in Seattle (formerly the Center for the Prevention of Sexual and Domestic Violence) published the landmark training program "Clergy Misconduct: Sexual Abuse in the Ministerial Relationship" in 1991, guidelines for effective policies and procedures were included. Few policies I have reviewed implement all the recommendations, particularly those suggesting suspension of the accused minister, ongoing disclosure to the congregation, disclosure to future congregations, and inclusion of survivors on committees that hear complaints and work with survivors. It is not coincidence that these recommendations are often ignored by denominational structures. Silencing the voice of survivors in the process helps protect the power of the clergy and keep the secret. Survivors who are well along in their healing process make a valuable contribution to the process of hearing and responding to complaints, however. They keep the process honest by reminding decision makers that ministry is a privilege and not a right and that the damage done by abusive clergy is long last-ing and far reaching. Survivors provide a helpful corrective to denominational leaders who are quick to reinstate abusive clergy.

Suspension or leave of absence at the time an allegation is made and ongoing disclosure are cornerstones of good procedure. It is tempting to assume (as I did many years ago) that differences in denominational polity prevent or complicate suspension and disclosure, but the notable exceptions to these tendencies span denominational lines. Congregations with free-church polity have policies that in-clude suspension and disclosure, and connectional churches with the ecclesiasti-cal authority to suspend clergy and disclose misconduct do not always do so. Suspension and disclosure are not issues of polity but of perspective, education, and commitment to due process for victims and churches. When clergy privilege is dismantled—when the "secret" is told through structured, appropriate, timely, and ongoing disclosure—the healing journey for victims and congregations is much easier.

Another difficulty is that even within denominations, the policies may differ from region to region, and there may be significant variations in implementa-tion. National guidelines for policies may or may not be adopted, depending on denominational requirements. Even in highly connectional systems, there is some difference from region to region in how policies are written and how the goals of the process are understood. In addition, lack of communication among regions is still an issue, although the loopholes that allow abusive clergy to move within their denomination are getting smaller. In many denominations, clergy are required to return to the region where their credential was removed or sus-pended to request reinstatement. In cases where clergy credentials are termi-nated, there is great variation in how that information is communicated; however, I have seen numerous cases where clergy credentials were removed, and the individual relocated and assumed a "retired" clergy role without conse-quence, because the local church was not informed. These "retired" clergy often serve as volunteer ministers of visitation or in other roles where they have access to vulnerable individuals. Widespread dissemination of information regarding removal of credentials is essential if these loopholes are to be eliminated.

Lack of communication between denominations is a huge issue. There are many instances of abusive clergy losing credentials in one denomination and moving to another denomination without detection. The onus is on the receiv-ing denomination to track down all recommendations and references. Denomi-national leaders need to ask their colleagues why this individual left the ministry in the former denomination or district, and they need to ask specifically about misconduct or disciplinary actions. The policy and procedure for receiving clergy from other denominations must specify that such inquiries will be made. This reduces the reluctance of denominational officials to ask such pointed questions.

Once a complaint is received, the procedure is invoked to begin the re-sponse process. The procedure should set forth a flow chart of events that covers all the possible outcomes and identifies the roles that are needed. One of the biggest mistakes I see in the adjudication of complaints is having too few individuals playing too many different roles in the process. Those who adjudicate the complaint should not conduct the investigation. The advocate for the complainant should not be a support person for the accused. As simple as that seems, it is surprising how often there is considerable overlap in the distinct roles needed for the procedure to be well executed.

Guidelines for gathering and assessing evidence, conducting disclosure meetings, reporting findings to the congregation, and assisting the congregation in its healing work must be delineated in the procedure. The services and supports available to complainants and the length of time those services are offered as well as subsequent support for healing should also be part of the procedure.

The policies and procedures form the "operations manual" for responding to complaints of clergy sexual abuse. A plan for all affected parties, the nature of the intervention(s), along with suggestions for reading, resources, and consultation should be part of every manual. Consistency from region to region within denominations and commitment to communication are essential goals that remain on the horizon for many denominations.

Training for Response Teams

A policy and procedure is only as good as those who implement it. A response team is a group of individuals with special training who (1) provide support to the accused and his or her family, (2) provide advocacy for the complainant and support for her or his family, and (3) handle congregational disclosure. (See chapter 17, "Response Teams," for further discussion.) If those individuals do not have sufficient training, they will be ill prepared for the intensity and complexity of working with the parties involved in a complaint. I have seen well-written policies have poor outcomes because of poorly trained response teams, and I have seen mediocre policies occasion good outcomes because of top-notch response teams or ecclesiastical officials. Standardizing the training and utilization of response teams is a major task for most denominations.

The most successful response teams use a recruitment and screening process separate from the usual judicatory nomination structure. Potential team members are recommended by a denominational leader (clergy or lay) or a local church pastor and fill out an application form that includes references. Individuals are then interviewed by those responsible for the work of the response team. New response team members attend several basic training sessions and then join the already established team for advanced training. Teams that meet regularly for training and team building, even when there are no active cases, tend to have better outcomes for their work. Longer terms of service are helpful, because they eliminate the rotation that would take them off the team just as they are becoming most effective. When a case comes to the team, new members are paired with an experienced team member for additional on-the-job training. Full membership on the response team comes only after this training and a probationary period.

Response team members are cross-trained and can serve in any of the above areas, although many team members specialize in and prefer to serve in specific areas. I have discovered that cross-training for response team members prevents polarization within the team and creates understanding of all the parties involved in the complaint. It is as important that advocates for complainants understand the need to support the accused as it is for congregational intervention specialists to understand the dynamics of advocacy. Many a response team has splintered over differing perspectives regarding the needs of the various parties involved.

A special word about advocates for the complainant is needed. The word *advocate* comes from the Latin word *advocare* meaning "to amplify." The role of a true advocate is to stand with the victim and support the victim's voice. Too often advocates, in their enthusiasm, further victimize complainants by speaking for them and making them invisible in the process. In many procedures, the "advocate" is really a liaison between the complainant and the adjudicating committee. In such instances, the role should be identified as "liaison" and not "advocate," because the role of advocate is clearly more than translating the policy and transmitting information. The role of the individual assigned to the complainant should be explained carefully to avoid further damage to the complainant and to keep the complaint process moving toward adjudication.

Assessment, Treatment, and Evaluation

Most of the mistakes made in the assessment, treatment, and evaluation of offending clerics (also discussed in chapter 24, "Responding to the Offender and Family") are made because the seriousness of the offense is minimized. If denominational officials believe the clergyperson has had an affair, then traditional client-centered talk therapy is seen as an appropriate treatment. In many cases, clergy referrals to therapy have focused on the pastor's personal unhappiness, past relationship failures, and professional dissatisfaction and burnout, to name a few issues. While those concerns may indeed be present for accused clergy, they are not the main issues to focus on in treatment, because they do not address the exploitive nature of the behavior. If the goal of treatment is to determine fitness for ministry, the accused minister must understand his behavior in the context of the professional role. If the accused does not understand that the professional behavior was a betrayal of the role and a misuse of the power and authority of the office, then he will remain at risk in the professional role.

An appropriate treatment plan depends on proper assessment. At the time of the complaint, the accused pastor should be sent to an assessment professional for diagnosis and treatment recommendations. Someone other than the assessing professional should provide the treatment. The original assessor should conduct a follow-up evaluation at the conclusion of treatment. This format of assessment, treatment, and evaluation provides a much fuller picture of the issues surrounding the abusive behavior and the possibility of redeployment in ministry. The liability risks for deploying clergy with a history of misconduct, should they offend again, are staggering. Since there are no guarantees that behavior will not happen again, redeployment is extremely risky.

Years of experience bring me to the "one strike and you're out" approach to dealing with abusive clergy. I have not always thought this way. What changed my mind is the witness of survivors who say that the distinction between "wanderer" and "predator" is finally false. In their experience, even those considered to be wanderers (needy, unreflective types who step over boundaries without any awareness that they are doing so) have predatory aspects to their behavior. They may not be full-fledged sociopathic predators, but the grooming techniques, isolating strategies, and unwillingness to take responsibility for their abuse are predatory behaviors that differ only in degree from those of sociopaths. The witness of survivors, combined with the liability issues mentioned above, make redeployment a nonviable option.

Compassion for Survivors

The church has a long way to go in its ministry with survivors. The specific healing issues are explored in some detail in other chapters of this book. (See chapter 11, "Victims/Survivors"; chapter 22, "Remembering the Victim"; and chapter 28, "What's Ahead for the Victim?") Suffice it say the church continues to fail survivors in their healing work. The church needs to make more money available for therapy through time as well for spiritual direction and other healing work. It is curious to note that the main intervention offered by the church is therapy. It is a crucial component to healing, but the longer-term issues such as spiritual healing and relational healing are rarely addressed. Financial support for couples counseling, family counseling, and spiritual work are needed for the long term. While most denominations will protest, saying such funds are not available, consider the costs born by the church for the assessment and treatment programs for offending clergy. Matthew 6:21 comes to mind: "For where your treasure is, there your heart will be also." The church's commitment to survivors will be adequate when the money and energy they expend for abusive clergy is equal to what it offers survivors.

The church in its many denominational expressions has come a long way in the past 20 or so years, but there is still a long way to go before there are consistent, faithful, appropriate, and healing responses made to the ongoing incidences of clergy misconduct. Fortunately, the steps that will enable churches to respond in this way are clear.

30

INVITING THE PRESENCE OF GOD

Candace R. Benyei

THE CHURCH IS SUPPOSED TO BE THE MANIFESTATION of Jesus' work in the world, the "bride" of Christ. If the good news that Jesus spoke about is that the realm of God is among us, then God's reign is here already, and the gathered church is supposed to be the agent of maintaining, if not creating, that reality. Jesus asks us to touch everyone, including lepers, the woman with the bloody flow, prostitutes, and tax collectors—even if society considers them untouchable, ritually unclean, or hateful. He asks us to treat all as equals, be they slaves, women, the poor, or princes. Like the Jewish prophets before him, he rails against social injustice and turns over the tables of the moneychangers in the Temple who have turned spiritual seeking into commerce. And knowing that laws are promulgated by the dominate and favored majority, he challenges society to look at and change the cause of transgression, rather than simply stone the woman caught in adultery.

Our Work as Disciples

The symptom of an unjust society that this volume has been concerned with is the abuse of individuals by clergy. From Jesus' perspective, the church's job, that of creating and maintaining the kingdom of God among us, is not merely to punish and demonize wrongdoers, even though certainly there are many who deserve to be stoned. Rather, our work as disciples is to change our church systems and our theological thinking, so our religious institutions and our belief systems no longer support abuse by members of the cloth.

Changing Our Systems

Clergy misconduct may be one of the major factors—if not the major factor—in the decline of religious institutions today because of its far-reaching effects on the families of faith touched in this way. From a systems perspective, clergy sexual abuse (or any other form of abuse) is an abuse of power, made possible by a structure that has always tended to be authoritarian.[1] Throughout human history, absolute power all too frequently has brought about absolute corruption. Ultimately the temptation to have what one wants without constraint or consequence becomes too great, and abuse is manifest.

Jesus, even in the beginning of his ministry and newly baptized, was fully aware of this. When, in the desert, the Tempter said to a hungry Jesus, "If you are the Son of God, command these stones to become loaves of bread," Jesus, aware of the danger, responded, "One does not live by bread alone, but by every word that comes from the mouth of God." And when the Tempter showed him all the kingdoms of the world and their splendor and said to him, "All these I will give you, if you will fall down and worship me," Jesus said to him, "Away with you, Satan! For it is written, 'Worship the Lord your God, and serve only him'" (Matt. 4:3-4, 8-10). The problem with absolute power is that the temptation is to use it to serve ourselves, instead of God and our neighbor.

Clergy, by virtue of their position as recognized agents of the church and those upon whom the finger of God has rested in their ordination, are vested not only with the power and persuasion of their hierarchical position but also with the power inherent in being identified as a God stand-in.[2] We need to reorganize our church systems, so that they are not clergy centered, but congregationally centered, with appropriate checks and balances to vested power. How do we do this?

We need to rewrite our canons and our constitutions toward the end of preventing, to the best of our ability, power abuse. We need to thoughtfully develop, stringently use, and publicly promulgate recognized, published, operational, and ethical procedures for reporting, investigating, and processing allegations. And then we need to educate the people in the pews about the same. We need to forget the window dressings, canonical changes, letters of intent, and unused and unpublished protocols that are all too frequently the current rage; craft sincere, thoughtful, and operational methodologies that we are willing to employ; and then insist that they be strictly adhered to. We need to abandon the strategy of "pluck and move" and the desire to do political or collegial favors for transgressors.

We also need to stringently screen our potential clergy candidates, so that we can prevent psychologically inappropriate applicants from entering the process. Being a charismatic preacher is *not* the only credential needed for ministry. Having the courage to be a prophet, to stand up and be counted as against injustice, even when this is inconvenient, may be.

Finally, while it is human nature for individuals to idolize people whom they perceive as holy, even to the point of holding them blameless for obvious misdoings, clergy can mitigate the effect by doing their own inner work. Their goal should be to not need—so they do not encourage—the adulation. Clergy often report feeling powerless and may consequently have a covert need to be looked up to. However, felt powerlessness is actually an illusion born of an unawareness of how and why we make our choices and is usually complicated by an impoverished sense of self. We often give away our power in order to get something else. We accede to the wishes of others, frequently unhappily, in order to curry favor, avoid rejection, or gain special attention or recognition. We need to remember that standing on a high pedestal (or pulpit) always invites a serious fall. And if we fear a serious fall, it is hard to fess up to our faults. Jesus realized this while standing on the Temple roof with the Tempter, and he gave us an example of what to do.

Changing Our Theology

While these suggestions may seem to portend a tremendous work, actually the greater task is to change our theology and belief systems so that they, of themselves, do not support abuse. We need to stop believing that sex is sinful and should not be talked about. This is a Christian mistake that emerged from the thinking of St. Augustine and his doctrine of original sin.[3] Jewish authors of the story of God and Adam and Eve in the Garden of Eden never prefigured the notion that sex is sinful, nor has such an unfortunate myth regarding sexuality ever been part of Jewish thinking. Further, not talking about sex is dangerous, because whenever we cannot talk about something, it becomes a secret, and as we have seen in the previous pages, secrets have great power and can be ultimately destructive, even for generations. We need to be able to talk about sex and sexual abuse, openly.

We need to examine the dearly held fantasy that the church community is the "good family" we never had and that, while clergy misconduct is "out there," it is "Not in My Church."[4] Certainly it is more comforting to believe that such an awful thing could not possibly threaten our sanctuary. However, sweeping reality under the narthex carpet only rots the fiber. Abuse can happen in any church. And when it happens, it needs to be clearly and adequately dealt with.

We need to better develop our theology of forgiveness, both of ourselves and others. Forgiveness is not something that happened 2,000 years ago with Jesus' death on the cross. And forgiveness is not about looking away from transgressions in which others are being hurt and abused. Nor is forgiveness achieved by saying a few prayers. Instead, forgiveness from the perspective of Jesus is the hard work of owning our own sin and brokenness, in both the big places and the little places, making what restitution we are able, and giving up the rest to God, who forgives what we cannot fix. Even the apostle Paul recognized, "I do not understand my own actions. . . . I can will what is right, but I cannot do it. For I do not do the good I want, but the evil I do not want is what I do" (Rom. 7:15, 18-19).

Only after owning and letting go of our own sin and accepting God's forgiveness for ourselves can we turn and forgive others. True forgiveness, or radical mercy, is about forgiving others for what they cannot fix, while at the same time interceding to keep them from continuing an abusive action. In short, forgiveness is a difficult act of faith, requiring from us the practice of discipleship. This is the radical mercy that Jesus teaches and asks us to follow in his Sermon on the Mount when he says, "Blessed are the merciful . . . ,"[5] and in the Great Commandment, "Love your neighbor as yourself." If we cannot love ourselves and accept forgiveness for ourselves, we cannot love and forgive our neighbor. The inability to fulfill this commandment precludes the ability to do the work of healing.

Finally, we need to let go of the Christian tendency to believe we have the corner on *the* Truth, so that we can admit that we also make mistakes—the first step in correcting them. This is actually a theological problem born of a community that historically has seen its path as the only way up the mountain. Thinking that one has grasped the whole Truth lends only a false sense of security, prevents true spiritual seeking, and inhibits the discovery of other choices, including those choices that lead to creating ethical behavior. Neither preacher nor congregant authentically practices his or her faith if the walk does not match the talk. Faith is evidenced by the way one lives out one's faith in the world, not by what one says in the edifice on the Sabbath. It is important to remember that God chooses us not to be kings, but to be servants of all. God empowers us all to be priests, to study and understand God's word, and God asks us all to be deacons, table servants of God's holy banquet for all people.

Reason for Hope

If we can effectively deal with these difficulties, then the gathered church will be able to begin the kind of ministry that Jesus envisioned, a ministry to heal the world and create the realm of God among us. Only when we fully accept and understand our own brokenness will we be able to mend ourselves and help heal another. Only when we fully recognize the log in our own eye will we be able to help remove the splinter from the eye of our neighbor.

The good news is that it is not an impossible task. If the realm of God among us is the same one that Jesus taught about, our job as disciples of Jesus of Nazareth is to promote and maintain a society that treats all individuals with respect, celebrates differences, abuses no one, and responds to injustice from a responsible perspective. That is, it is our obligation as disciples to change the cause of the problem rather than punish the symptom. As Marie Fortune has said, "Justice requires courage." But with wisdom, courage, and commitment, healing can be manifest.

RESOURCES

Books, Videos, and Web Sites

General Resources

Congregational Resource Guide, www.congregationalresources.org.

A joint effort of the Alban Institute and the Indianapolis Center for Congregations, the Congregational Resource Guide (CRG) helps congregational leaders identify resources they need to gain insight into challenges and to encourage transformation in their faith community. It is frequently updated, and more information on many of the resources in this appendix is available there.

Cooper-White, Pamela. *Shared Wisdom: Use of the Self in Pastoral Care and Counseling*. Minneapolis: Fortress Press, 2004.

Includes detailed discussion of countertransference issues and has a case study involving a narcissistic pastor on the "slippery slope" toward boundary violations. Also includes a chapter on clergy sexual abuse.

Gonsiorek, John C., ed. *Breach of Trust: Sexual Exploitation by Health Care Professionals and Clergy*. Thousand Oaks, Calif.: Sage Publications, 1995.

Provides information and research on sexual exploitation; includes firsthand accounts by victims and discussion of support groups and therapy; describes innovative work being done to deal with perpetrators; and addresses risk management, prevention, and boundary training.

Hopkins, Nancy Myer, and Mark Laaser, eds. *Restoring the Soul of a Church: Healing Congregations Wounded by Clergy Sexual Misconduct.* Collegeville, Minn.: Liturgical Press, 1995.

Sexual misconduct by clergy violates trust and inflicts deep wounds. Pastors called to serve congregations in the wake of these crises need to understand what happened to victims, the perpetrator, and the congregation.

Horst, Elisabeth. *Questions and Answers About Clergy Sexual Misconduct.* Collegeville, Minn.: The Liturgical Press, 2000.

This 40-page booklet presents a brief overview of common misunderstandings and offers clear and understandable explanations of the basic issues and dynamics involved.

Mennonite Central Committee. *Crossing the Boundary: Sexual Abuse by Professionals.* Akron, Pa.: Mennonite Central Committee, 2000.

Resource packet explains the pattern of abuse by professionals and discusses ways to prevent and address it. Available from Mennonite Central Committee, listed under "Organizations" below.

Sperry, Len. *Ministry and Community: Recognizing, Healing, and Preventing Ministry Impairment.* Collegeville, Minn.: The Liturgical Press, 2000.

Highlights the interplay of personality dynamics and organizational dynamics for eight of the most common forms of ministry impairment and how they can be recognized, treated, and prevented.

Advocacy

Block, Heather. *Advocacy Training Manual.* Winnipeg: Mennonite Central Committee Canada, 1996.

A training manual for advocating for survivors of sexual abuse by a church leader or caregiver. Available from MCC Canada and MCC U.S. See organizations listed below.

Mennonite Central Committee. *Expanding the Circle of Caring: Ministering to the Family Members of Survivors and Perpetrators of Sexual Abuse.* Akron, Pa.: Mennonite Central Committee, 1995.

Compiled by Esther Epp-Tiessen, this booklet addresses the needs of these "secondary victims" through storytelling and informative articles. Also speaks to how the church can minister to them.

Public Education Work Group of the Task Force on Sexual Exploitation by Counselors and Therapists. *It's Never OK: Information for Victims and Victim Advocates on Sexual Exploitation by Counselors and Therapists.* St. Paul: Minnesota Coalition Against Sexual Assault, 1998.

This resource defines sexual exploitation by counselors, describes options available to victims of sexual exploitation, and presents methods of choosing counselors who are not exploitative. Geared toward persons who have been sexually exploited as adults. Available for download at www.advocateweb.org. Search for "It's Never OK."

Calling a New Pastor

Oswald, Roy M., James M. Heath, and Ann W. Heath. *Beginning Ministry Together: The Alban Handbook for Clergy Transitions*. Bethesda, Md.: Alban Institute, 2003.

Covers the transition period between the announcement that one pastor is leaving and the time when another pastor is well settled. Includes extensive guidance for the search process and welcoming the next pastor, and identifies two organizations that conduct background checks:

Oxford Document Management Company, 655 West Highway 10, Anoka, MN 55303, (763) 971-0124 or (800) 801-9114, www.oxforddoc.com

Professional Research Services, 4901 W. 77th Street, Suite 135, Edina, MN 55435, (800) 886-4777 or (952) 941-9040, www.prsnet.com

Conflict Management

Dobson, Edward G., Speed B. Leas, and Marshall Shelley. *Mastering Conflict and Controversy*. Portland: Multnomah Press, 1992.

Explains how to discern the root cause of a controversy, how to deal with and minimize inevitable conflict, and how to turn conflicts to good.

Leas, Speed B. *Moving Your Church through Conflict*. Washington, D.C.: Alban Institute, 1985.

This how-to manual written for clergy and lay leaders discusses what to do when conflict arises and spells out appropriate responses to different levels of conflict. Available only as a download from the Alban Institute Web site, www.alban.org.

Mayer, Bernard. *The Dynamics of Conflict Resolution: A Practitioner's Guide*. San Francisco: Jossey-Bass, 2000.

This guide goes beyond observable techniques to offer a close look at the creative internal processes—both cognitive and psychological—that successful mediators and other conflict managers draw upon.

Dynamics of Clergy Misconduct

Cooper-White, Pamela. *The Cry of Tamar: Violence Against Women and the Church's Response*. Minneapolis: Fortress Press, 1995.

This comprehensive, practical assessment of various forms of violence against women challenges the Christian churches to examine their own responses to the cry of Tamar in our time. Author describes specific forms of such violence and outlines appropriate pastoral responses.

Fortune, Marie M. *Is Nothing Sacred? The Story of a Pastor, the Women He Sexually Abused, and the Congregation He Nearly Destroyed.* Cleveland: United Church Press, 1999.

Considered a standard reference about clergy sexual abuse, this case study is a guide for congregations on preventing and finding solutions for sexual abuse by clergy against congregants. Selected Book of the Year by the Academy of Parish Clergy.

Irons, Richard, and Jennifer P. Schneider. *The Wounded Healer: Addiction-Sensitive Approach to the Sexually Exploitative Professional.* Northvale, N.J.: Jason Aronson Inc., 1999.

Based on assessment of 150 practicing professionals who were referred for professional evaluation because of sexual misconduct, the book is divided into three parts: "Toward an Understanding of Sexual Exploitation," "Categories of Sexually Exploitative Men," and "Healing the Wounded."

Mennonite Central Committee. *Understanding Sexual Abuse by a Church Leader or Caregiver.* Akron, Penn.: Mennonite Central Committee, 2001.

Includes stories and information focused specifically on pastoral sexual misconduct and abuse. Includes a section on the issue of power and abuse of power. An excellent resource to prepare Christians to respond appropriately when confronted with the reality of sexual abuse.

Poling, Nancy Werking, ed. *Victim to Survivor: Women Recovering from Clergy Sexual Abuse.* Cleveland: United Church Press, 1999.

A compendium of survivors' stories that provides a poignant inside perspective on the experiences of victims/survivors as they call upon the church to be a safe place for all people.

Rutter, Peter. *Sex in the Forbidden Zone: When Men in Power Abuse Women's Trust.* Los Angeles: Jeremy Tarcher, 1989.

This classic in the field, based on over 1000 in-depth interviews, examines abuse from a helpful psychodynamic perspective of both the betrayer and the betrayed.

Ethics for Church Leaders

Fortune, Marie M. *Sexual Violence: The Sin Revisited.* Cleveland: Pilgrim Press, 2005.

Originally published in 1983 as *Sexual Violence: The Unmentionable Sin,* this book is an updated combination of Fortune's experiences as a church educator, advocate for sexual abuse survivors, and pastor that answers a difficult question: How do we respond to sexual violence?

Gafke, Allen, and Lynn Scott, eds. *Living the Sacred Trust: Clergy Sexual Ethics.* Nashville: General Board of Higher Education and Ministry, United Methodist Church, 2000.

Written from a family systems perspective, *Living the Sacred Trust* includes practical and theoretical guidance about needs of families, offenders, and congregations. Developed for the United Methodist Church, but much of the material is relevant for other denominations.

Gula, Richard M. *Ethics in Pastoral Ministry.* Mahwah, N.J.: Paulist Press, 1996.

Suitable for both Protestants and Catholics, this book addresses theological foundations regarding the minister's character and virtue, professional duties, power in the pastoral relationship, sexuality, confidentiality, and a proposed code of ethics.

Sexual Ethics for Church Professionals

A 90-minute video with nine dramatized situations portraying compromising pastoral situations. Each vignette is followed by a panel discussion by a group of professionals who examine pastoral, ethical, and legal issues. Includes facilitator's guide and copy of *Ministry and Sexuality* by G. Lloyd Rediger. Prepared by the Seventh-day Adventist Church. Contact General Conference Ministerial Continuing Education, PO Box 66, 403 E. Hwy. 67, Keene, TX 76059, (800) 982-3344 or (817) 341-3643.

Understanding the Sexual Boundaries of the Pastoral Relationship

A 35-minute video developed by the Roman Catholic Archdiocese of St. Paul and Minneapolis about sexual abuse and sexual harassment in the church. Clearly addresses harassment as a separate issue. Applicable for audiences other than Roman Catholics. Includes study guide. Contact Office of Communications, Archdiocese of St. Paul and Minneapolis, The Chancery, 226 Summit Ave., St. Paul, MN 55102, (651) 291-4411.

Family Systems

Benyei, Candace R. *Understanding Clergy Misconduct in Religious Systems: Scapegoating, Family Secrets, and the Abuse of Power.* Binghamton, N.Y.: Haworth Press, 1998.

This volume, written by a teaching psychologist, family therapist, and minister, is a complete explanation of the family systems perspective with regard to religious institutions and clergy misconduct, and includes a comprehensive glossary.

Friedman, Edwin. *Generation to Generation: Family Process in Church and Synagogue.* New York: Guilford, 1985.

This very technical book by a student of Dr. Murray Bowen and a leader in the family therapy field is an exhaustive study of systems thinking in all aspects of religious institutions.

Oswald, Roy M., and Robert E. Friedrich Jr. "An Evening of Historical Reflection." In *Discerning Your Congregation's Future: A Strategic and Spiritual Approach*. Bethesda, Md.: The Alban Institute, 1996.

The authors provide detailed instructions for a group process that will help congregations examine their history. A useful tool for uncovering behavior patterns in a congregation.

Steinke, Peter L. *How Your Church Family Works: Understanding Congregations as Emotional Systems*. Washington, D.C.: Alban Institute, 1993.

————. *Healthy Congregations: A Systems Approach*. Bethesda, Md.: Alban Institute, 1996.

Drawing on the work of Bowen, Friedman, and his many years' counseling experience, Steinke shows how to recognize and deal with the emotional roots of such issues as church conflict, leadership roles, congregational change, irresponsible behavior, and the effects of family of origin on current relationships.

Grief

Kübler-Ross, Elisabeth. *On Death and Dying: What the Dying Have to Teach Doctors, Nurses, Clergy, and Their Own Families*. New York: Simon and Schuster, 1969.

This classic, one of the most important psychological studies of the twentieth century, was the first to discuss the five stages of death: denial, anger, bargaining, depression, and acceptance.

Powell, Trevor. *Free Yourself from Harmful Stress*. New York: DK Publishing, Inc., 1997.

Powell helps readers identify symptoms and sources of stress and develop skills for managing it. Includes detailed short-term action plans for breaking destructive behavioral patterns and discussion of a "grief wheel" that can help congregation leaders and members understand their response to clergy misconduct.

Personal Wellness

Benyei, Candace R. *How To Get There From Here: Creating God Among Us*. Philadelphia: Xlibris Corporation, 2001.

A liberation theologian and psychologist guides individuals and communities in the examination and rebuilding of their spiritual understandings, so they may withstand life's storms.

Foster, Richard J. *Celebration of Discipline: The Path to Spiritual Growth*. New York: Harper & Row, 1978.

A practical guide to deepening the inner life through the classical spiritual disciplines of meditation, prayer, fasting, study, simplicity, solitude, submission, service, confession, worship, guidance, and celebration.

Grof, Stanislav, and Christina Grof, eds. *Spiritual Emergency: When Personal Trans-formation Becomes a Crisis.* Los Angeles: Jeremy P. Tarcher, 1989.

A series of articles address the pitfalls and promises of spiritual practice.

Johnston, William. *Christian Zen: A Way of Meditation.* San Francisco: Harper & Row, 1979.

An Irish Jesuit's integration of his long experience of Zen meditation with Christian thought and practice.

Jung, Carl Gustav. *Modern Man in Search of a Soul.* New York: Harvest/Harcourt Brace Jovanovich, 1933.

This introduction to the thought of Carl Jung examines dream analysis, the primitive unconscious, and the relationship between psychology and religion.

Kelsey, Morton T. *The Other Side of Silence: A Guide to Christian Meditation.* New York: Paulist Press, 1976.

A comprehensive practical manual for the inward journey.

Melander, Rochelle, and Harold Eppley. *The Spiritual Leader's Guide to Self-Care.* Bethesda, Md.: Alban Institute, 2002.

An ideal companion for clergy, lay leaders, and others who would like guidance about how to make changes in their personal life and ministry but do not want to read a text-heavy book about self-care. Includes journal-writing suggestions, personal reflection questions and activities, guidance for sharing the discovery process with another person, an activity for the coming week, and suggested further resources, such as novels, videos, and Web sites.

Rilke, Rainer Maria. *Letters to a Young Poet.* New York: Vintage/Random House, 1986.

Classic statements of creative process and spiritual development.

Sanford, John A. *Dreams: God's Forgotten Language.* New York: J. B. Lippencott, 1968.

The author draws on modern psychologists who, in their search for ways to help individuals find healing and wholeness, have discovered what the Bible knew all along but Christians had forgotten.

Woods, Richard, ed. *Understanding Mysticism.* Garden City: Image/Doubleday, 1980.

Notable essays on various dimensions of mysticism and the mystical experience.

Prevention

Ask Before You Hug: Sexual Harassment in the Church

Churches are called to be communities of welcome, hospitality, and respect. This 31-minute training video presents six different situations that portray a range of inappropriate behavior in church settings. Offers suggestions on how to act and react appropriately. Video, available from EcuFilm, (800) 251-4091.

Bless Our Children: Preventing Sexual Abuse

The story of one congregation's efforts to include sexual abuse prevention in their children's religious education program. Intended for use with *Hear Their Cries,* below. Video, available for purchase or rental from FaithTrust Institute, (877) 860-2255, www.faithtrustinstitute.org.

Friberg, Nils, and Mark Laaser. *Before the Fall: Preventing Pastoral Sexual Abuse.* Collegeville, Minn.: Liturgical Press, 1998.

Addressed to church and seminary leaders concerned with the formation of people for ministry. It describes the risk factors that lead people to act out sexually and the necessary foundations for personal health and successful life in ministry.

Grenz, Stanley J., and Roy D. Bell. *Betrayal of Trust: Sexual Misconduct in the Pastorate.* Downers Grove, Ill.: InterVarsity Press, 1995.

Examining sexual relationships between male pastors and female congregants, this book offers guidelines for helping a pastor recognize susceptibility to sexual misconduct and for preventing such misconduct from occurring.

Hear Their Cries: Religious Responses to Child Abuse

An award-winning documentary about the role of pastors and lay leaders in preventing, recognizing, and responding to sexual abuse. Intended for use with *Bless Our Children,* above. Video, available for purchase or rental from FaithTrust Institute, (877) 860-2255, www.faithtrustinstitute.org.

Love: All That and More

An award-winning video series and six-session curriculum for youth on healthy relationships. Includes three videos, 50-minute lesson plans, handouts, and facilitator guides. Available from FaithTrust Institute, (877) 860-2255, www.faithtrustinstitute.org.

McClintock, Karen A. *Preventing Sexual Abuse in Congregations: A Resource for Leaders.* Herndon, Va.: Alban Institute, 2004.

Shows congregations how to protect children and vulnerable adults, prevent sexual harassment either by clergy or of clergy, and strengthen clergy families by raising awareness of the occupational and emotional risks inherent in pastoral ministry.

Melton, Joy T. *Safe Sanctuaries: Reducing the Risk of Child Abuse in the Church.* Nashville: Discipleship Resources, 1998.

Full of helpful information and guidelines for churches that are committed to providing safe and nurturing ministries for children. Includes sample forms and training sessions.

————. *Safe Sanctuaries for Children and Youth: Reducing the Risk of Abuse in the Church.* Nashville: Discipleship Resources, 2004. Available as DVD and video.

Following up on the Safe Sanctuaries manuals, this DVD/video is designed for training and raising awareness in congregations. The three key segments address why and how to develop and implement a policy to reduce the risk of abuse in your church and provides necessary forms to use in the process.

————. *Safe Sanctuaries for Youth: Reducing the Risk of Abuse in Youth Ministries.* Nashville: Discipleship Resources, 2003.

Another excellent guide for reducing abuse in the church. Includes suggested process and tools for developing and implementing employment policy; basic procedures for safe ministry with youth; how to develop a congregational plan to respond to allegations of abuse; suggested training model for youth ministry workers; service and stories of healing; sample forms.

Mennonite Central Committee. *Making Your Sanctuary Safe: Resources for Developing Congregational Abuse Prevention Policies.* Akron, Pa.: Mennonite Central Committee, 2005.

Packet provides guidelines for congregations developing abuse prevention policies in church settings. Includes information on screening volunteers and sample policies used by Mennonite and Brethren in Christ congregations.

Peterson, Marilyn R. *At Personal Risk: Boundary Violations in Professional-Client Relationships.* New York: W. W. Norton & Company, 1992.

Addresses boundary violations through the lens of the professional-client relationship, drawing examples from law, medicine, religion, education, and psychotherapy. Covers social context of relationships, power differentials, characteristics of boundary violations, and healing for client and professional. Includes early signs of impending trouble and steps for restoring breached boundaries.

Preventing Child Sexual Abuse Program

Prevention curricula designed for Christian education settings. The following three resources are designed for specific age groups and a church-school format. Available from FaithTrust Institute, (877) 860-2255, www.faithtrustinstitute.org.

Reid, Kathryn Goering. *Preventing Child Sexual Abuse Ages 5–8.* Cleveland: United Church Press, 1994.

Reid, Kathryn Goering, with Marie M. Fortune. *Preventing Child Sexual Abuse Ages 9–12.* Cleveland: United Church Press, 1989.

Voelkel-Haugen, Rebecca, and Marie M. Fortune. *Sexual Abuse Prevention: A Course of Study for Teenagers.* Cleveland: United Church Press, 1996.

Reducing the Risk II: Making Your Church Safe from Child Sexual Abuse.

A complete and practical kit that includes reference book, detailed training manual, and DVD with six video presentations, and assists in developing strategies and policies for churches. Items may be purchased separately. Christian Ministry Resource, (800) 222-1840, www.christianministryresource.com.

A Sacred Trust: Boundary Issues for Clergy and Spiritual Teachers

A facilitator's guide with four videotapes: Part 1: "Boundaries, Power, and Vulnerability"; Part 2: "Dating, Friendships, Dual Relationships, Gifts"; Part 3: "The Pulpit, Transference, Hugging and Touch, Intimacy"; and Part 4: "Personal Needs and Self-Care, Red Flags, Final Reflections." Guide includes background information, discussion questions, exercises, and handouts. Available from FaithTrust Institute, (877) 860-2255, www.faithtrustinstitute.org.

Smith, Harold Ivan. *Singles Ask: Answers to Questions about Relationships and Sexuality,* rev. ed. Minneapolis: Augsburg Fortress, 1998.

A comprehensive, helpful resource for single adults that does not shy away from tough issues.

Training Curriculum on Sexual Abuse by Clergy

A comprehensive trainer's curriculum that includes background and scope of the problem, factors in boundary crossing, ethical analysis, prevention, and intervention. Includes two videos with study guides, *Not in My Church* and *Once You Cross the Line,* educational brochure, detailed trainer's notebook, and workshop manual. Available from FaithTrust Institute, (877) 860-2255, www.faithtrustinstitute.org.

Trauma

Hermann, Judith. *Trauma and Recovery: The Aftermath of Violence—from Domestic Abuse to Political Terror.* New York: Basic Books, 1997.

A classic in the field for understanding post-traumatic stress disorder, this book surveys the recent history of psychological trauma and discusses recovery for victims. Finds similarities between the experiences of war veterans and sexual assault victims in an easy-to-read format.

Hudson, Jill. *Congregational Trauma: Caring, Coping, and Learning.* Bethesda, Md.: Alban Institute, 1998.

Addresses uncommon, tragic crises that strike congregations and require special caring, coping, and learning skills. Includes tested strategies; helpful checklists; worship and healing resources; and advice on obtaining judicatory support, engaging the media, and dealing with anniversaries.

Organizations

AdvocateWeb

A nonprofit organization providing information and resources to promote awareness and understanding of the issues involved in the exploitation of people by trusted helping professionals. Offers extensive, free online resources for victims, survivors, and their families, friends, victim advocates, and professionals. Includes e-mail peer support groups and Web discussion forum. AdvocateWeb, PO Box 202961, Austin, TX 78720, www.advocateweb.com.

The Alban Institute

2121 Cooperative Way, Suite 100, Herndon, VA 20171, (800) 486-1318, www.alban.org.

Alban Institute is an ecumenical organization that supports congregations through consulting services, research, workshops, and educational resources. They offer a variety of helpful seminars on topics such as conflict, congregations, and clergy self-care.

Bridgebuilder

PO Box 300939, Austin, TX 78703, (512) 342-8684 (voice) or (512) 527-9827 (fax).

Established by congregation consultant Peter Steinke, Bridgbuilder is an intervention process for churches in conflict. This structured, tested process has been used in more than 200 congregations.

Center for Media Literacy

3101 Ocean Park Boulevard, #200, Santa Monica, CA 90405, (310) 581-0260, www.medialit.org.

Dedicated to a new vision of literacy for the twenty-first century: the ability to communicate competently in all media forms, print and electronic, as well as to access, understand, analyze, and evaluate the powerful images, words, and sounds that make up our contemporary mass media culture.

Church Mutual Insurance Company

The leading insurer of worship centers and related organizations in the United States. Offers booklets, posters, videos, checklist and inventory forms, sample background screening and release forms, and other safety materials by mail or online. Church Mutual Insurance Company, PO Box 357, 3000 Schuster Lane, Merrill, WI 54452-0357, (800) 554-2642, www .churchmutual.com.

FaithTrust Institute

> 2400 N. 45th Street, #10, Seattle, WA 98103, (877) 860-2255, www
> .faithtrustinstitute.org.

> An organization dedicated to preventing domestic violence and sexual
> abuse, formerly known as the Center for the Prevention of Domestic and
> Sexual Violence. They offer workshops on sexual abuse in the ministerial
> relationship, clergy boundaries, and victim recovery.

Interfaith Sexual Trauma Institute

> Saint John's Abbey and University, Collegeville, MN 56321, www.csbsju.edu,
> isti@csbsju.edu.

> The Institute promotes the prevention of sexual abuse, exploitation, and
> harassment through research, education, and publication. Currently ad-
> ministered by Saint John's University School of Theology/Seminary, the
> ISTI Web site continues to be a resource of education and outreach.

Interim Ministry Network

> 5740 Executive Drive, Suite 220, Baltimore, MD 21228, (800) 235-8414,
> www.imnedu.org.

> An organization dedicated to the health and wellness of congregations.
> Focus is prevention of unhealthy practices before they take root, mainte-
> nance of congregational health during times of stress or change, and
> restorative care when it is required.

International Critical Incident Stress Foundation, Inc.

> 3290 Pine Orchard Ave., Suite 106, Ellicott City, MD 21042, (410) 750-
> 9600, www.icisf.org.

> ICISF is an international foundation that educates first disaster response
> teams such as medics and firefighters, to debrief, support, and reduce the
> risk of post-traumatic stress disorder in first responders. Their model of de-
> briefing can be used in congregations as well.

Lombard Mennonite Peace Center

> 101 W. 22nd S., Suite 206, Lombard, IL 60148, (630) 627-0507, www
> .lmpeacecenter.org.

> LMPC works to encourage the nonviolent transformation of conflict in rela-
> tionships in homes, workplaces, schools, churches, and throughout our
> world. Programs and resources address ways of resolving conflicts and
> building healthier relationships.

Media Education Foundation

> 26 Center Street, Northampton, MA 01060, (800) 897-0089, www.mediaed
> .org.

> Produces and distributes video documentaries to encourage critical thinking
> and debate about the relationship between media ownership, commercial

media content, and the democratic demand for free flow of information, diverse representations of ideas and people, and informed citizen participation.

Mennonite Central Committee

A relief, service, and peace agency of the North American Mennonite and Brethren in Christ churches. Search "Resources and Publications" on their Web site to reach an extensive online bibliography with advanced-search capability. In the U.S., contact (717) 859-1151 or toll free (888) 563-4676. In Canada, contact (204) 261-6381 or (888) 622-6337. www.mcc.org. See also www.mcc.org/abuse for more specific information on abuse, and www.mcc.org/canada/womensconcerns/prof_misconduct.html for information about resources produced by the Women's Concerns Network.

The Nathan Network

The Nathan Network's mission is to serve the church by providing support for those engaged in preventing or responding to misconduct. Resources include training and empowerment, education, policy dialogues and proposals, individual and systemic wellness tools, spiritual support, and more. Contact (877) 285-8659, or visit www.nathannetwork.org.

The National Catholic Risk Retention Group

Creator of VIRTUS, best practices programs designed to help prevent wrongdoing and promote "rightdoing" within religious organizations. The VIRTUS programs empower organizations and people to better control risk and improve the lives of all those who interact with the church. For VIRTUS programs and services, contact: 321 S. Boston Ave., Suite 900, Tulsa, OK 74103, (888) 847-8870, www.virtus.org.

Restorative Justice

This relatively new approach to justice works to resolve conflict and repair harm. It encourages those who have caused harm to acknowledge the impact of what they have done and gives them an opportunity to make reparation. It offers those who have suffered the harm the opportunity to have their harm or loss acknowledged and amends made. Not yet commonly used in cases of sexual abuse or exploitation, it may have promise in some cases. Organizations such as Center for Restorative Justice and Peacemaking (2ssw.che.umn.edu/rjp), Prison Fellowship International Restorative Justice Online (www.restorativejustice.org), Restorative Justice Consortium (www.restorativejustice.org.uk), and The Centre for Restorative Justice (www.sfu.ca/crj) provide more information.

Safe Church Network

Similar to the Nathan Network (see the entry above), the Safe Church Network works with congregations of the Episcopal Church and the Evangelical Lutheran Church in America in New England. A contact list is available at www.safechurches.org.

CRITICAL INCIDENT STRESS MANAGEMENT

E. Larraine Frampton

THE CRITICAL INCIDENT STRESS MANAGEMENT (CISM) process can be helpful for first responders to trauma, victims, faith community leaders, and congregations. Two of its main objectives are to mitigate stress effects of trauma and to speed the recovery process. I have used CISM, specifically one component—Critical Incident Stress Debriefing (CISD), after a disclosure of a traumatic event such as clergy sexual abuse. Response teams, and leaders, can use this process for debriefing victims or members. It is not considered therapy. It is a safe process designed to allow people to articulate their initial thoughts and feelings to accelerate the recovery process. In order to ensure the proper use of the CISD process, facilitators should receive education from someone certified in CISM. You can contact the International Critical Incident Stress Foundation (www.icisf.org) to locate a CISM member near you.

Critical Incident Stress Management

Jeffrey T. Mitchell, professor of emergency health services at the University of Maryland, and George S. Everly, professor of psychology at Loyola College, also in Maryland, developed process models to prepare and debrief professional responders and people affected by trauma. CISD was developed for crisis and trauma intervention (such as child abuse and fires) as well as a wide diversity of settings and constituent groups, and is applicable to traumatic events such as clergy sexual abuse.

The following seven-step process for CISD is only one element of CISM crisis intervention. CISM also includes preparation of first responders for mass disasters, individual support, a three-step immediate small-group defusing, and a decompression, demobilization technique for very large groups after mass disasters.

In general, CISM starts at the cognitive level (facts), moves deeper to the emotional level by inviting participants to share personal reactions, and then moves back up to the cognitive level (cognitive–affective–cognitive). I use it for disclosure meetings where members will hear for the first time that their pastor has been removed from office and has sexually abused a member of the congregation. It is an accepted fact in the therapeutic world that sexual abuse is traumatic. Clergy sexual abuse is also traumatic and needs to be addressed through a process that will help members recover.

CISD's Seven Steps

These are the seven stages in crisis incident stress management as developed by Mitchell and Everly. I have applied the steps to debriefing congregations after the disclosure of clergy sexual abuse at a congregational meeting. The congregation is to be divided into small groups (not to exceed 12 members per group). A trained facilitator is to be assigned to each group. The facilitator may or may not be a member of the response team.

When the debriefing of small groups immediately follows the disclosure, a meal or snacks and beverages can be made available and served in between the disclosure and the debriefing meetings. I try to keep the group meetings around two hours. It is not recommended to have breaks during the debriefing process, because breaks interrupt the cognitive–affective–cognitive process, and facilitators simply cannot regain the flow. Other interruptions—such as using cell phones and pagers, or leaving early—are discouraged. If some participants know they have to leave early, it is almost better to have them meet with a response team member at another time. Facilitators do need to allow individuals to take care of personal needs such as going to the bathroom. Individuals who need to leave the group are asked to step out and return quietly.

1. Introduction
- Facilitator introduces herself and describes her role in the process and in the faith community.
- Facilitator explains what CISD is and why it is done.

     CISD is used as an early intervention strategy to give individuals an opportunity to articulate their thoughts and express their emotions, so that the recovery process can immediately begin. CISD is educational. It provides information about what members might feel in the weeks to come and tells them how they can take care of themselves. Members can begin to support each other, even though they may be in different emotional places. It also allows for follow-up meetings to continue the recovery process.

     Group establishes ground rules.

     Confidentiality is vital and should be agreed upon by all participants. Other helpful ground rules include: speak only for yourself; do not interrupt or judge others; if you have a lot to say, make an appointment with a response team member or therapist; do not take notes. Inform individuals who do not feel safe that they can make an appointment with a response team member.

2. Facts
Facilitator asks members to state their names, how long they have been attending the church, and what role(s) they have or how they participate in the life of the congregation. A member may choose not to speak, but everyone should have an opportunity.

3. Thoughts
Facilitator asks members what their first thought was when they heard about the abuse. Members will often begin to move into their feelings at this point. Some thoughts might be: "I can't believe this is true." "My pastor would never do a thing like this." "The victim(s) is (are) lying."

4. Reaction
This is the affective period, when members begin to express their feelings. Facilitator asks members what is the worst part about the clergy sexual abuse. Members might comment that their beloved pastor abused and victimized a member(s); they are not safe from abuse even in their own congregation; the congregation will be thought of as the place where sexual abuse occurred; they will lose members.

5. Symptoms
This step provides transition back into the cognitive mode. Facilitator asks individuals to talk about any personal distress they are experiencing as a result of the clergy abuse. Personal distress symptoms can be emotional, cognitive, physiological, and spiritual. (Examples are listed below in step 6, "Teaching.")

6. Teaching
* Facilitator expands on the symptoms expressed in step 5 with additional reactions and symptoms typical in traumatic events. Reactions can encompass physical, cognitive, emotional, behavioral, and spiritual symptoms. Common physical reactions are feeling numb, headaches, gastrointestinal problems, fatigue, apathy, and changes in blood pressure. Common cognitive reactions are an inability to process thoughts, difficulty articulating ideas, and interrupted thought process. Common behavioral symptoms can include not wanting to come to worship, avoiding recovery meetings, discontinuing financial support to the congregation, and blaming others such as victims or judicatory leaders for upsetting their congregation. Common emotional reactions are shock, grief, anger, confusion, cynicism or negativity, and emotional withdrawal. Common spiritual reactions are confusion about one's relationship with the pastor and God in light of the trauma, anger at God, doubt, and a sense of betrayal.

- Facilitator normalizes reactions by explaining that they are results of the trauma of clergy sexual abuse and are the first step in the recovery process.
- Facilitator teaches stress management by encouraging proper self-care and seeking spiritual nurturing and prayer.
- Facilitator informs members that they can seek outside professional therapists if symptoms persist or they feel the need to talk further. A list of therapists with their contact information can be provided at the end of the large group reentry meeting. (Therapists should be consulted before their names are offered.)
- Facilitator encourages members to come to recovery meetings and to continue their regular congregational participation, so they can heal and the congregation can recover.

7. Reentry
- Facilitator will thank members for attending. Confidentiality is reinforced. The facilitator will adjourn the small-group meeting to the large-group meeting.
- The judicatory leader or response team recovery leader will give an overview of what will happen next in the process and when the next recovery meeting is scheduled. He or she also explains the role of the recovery team and the length of time the team will be working with the congregation. Finally, the meeting facilitator states that after a year, the congregation will be reassessed to determine how its recovery is progressing and if it is ready to call a new clergyperson. (See chapter 17, "Response Teams.")
- A familiar religious prayer or ritual that is spiritually soothing is used to close the meeting.
- As members leave, leaders hand out an information sheet with therapists' names and contact information, as well as the names and contact information of recovery response team members, and the date, time, and place of the next recovery meeting. (This information is also posted in a highly visible place and published in newsletters.)

Conclusion

I find that using CISM immediately after the disclosure can accelerate the recovery of congregations. At the very least, this model provides an opportunity for members to express their feelings in a safe setting, to understand their reactions, and to receive encouragement to care for themselves. Participants are also invited to recognize that the spiritual strength that has upheld them in the past will be with them as they recover. In addition, ground rules for communication can be established to lessen rumors and, we hope, reduce conflicts. Future recovery meetings can be scheduled, giving the congregation a sense of hope.

NOTES

Foreword

1. Judith Herman, *Trauma and Recovery: The Aftermath of Violence—from Domestic Abuse to Political Terror* (1992; repr., New York: Basic Books, 1997).

2. For more about this resistance movement, see Peter Rutter, *Sex in the Forbidden Zone: When Men in Power Abuse Women's Trust* (Los Angeles: Jeremy Tarcher, 1989); Marie Fortune, *Is Nothing Sacred? When Sex Invades the Pastor-Parishioner Relationship* (San Francisco: Harper & Row, 1989); Pamela Cooper-White, "Soul Stealing: Power Relations in Pastoral Sexual Abuse," *The Christian Century* (February 20, 1991): 196–99.

3. Research summarized in Marie Fortune, *Clergy Misconduct: Sexual Abuse in the Ministerial Relationship Workshop Manual*, rev. ed. (Seattle: Center for the Prevention of Sexual and Domestic Violence, 1997); Pamela Cooper-White, "Sexual Exploitation and Other Boundary Violations in Pastoral Ministries," chap. 16 in *Clinical Handbook of Pastoral Counseling*, eds. Robert J. Wicks, Richard D. Parksons, and Donald Capps (New York: Paulist Press, 2003), 3:342–65.

4. Pamela Cooper-White, "The Use of the Self in Psychotherapy: A Comparative Study of Pastoral Counselors and Clinical Social Workers," *American Journal of Pastoral Counseling* 4, no. 4 (2001): 5–35.

5. For example, Chilton Knudsen, "Pastoral Care for Congregations in the Aftermath of Sexual Misconduct" (unpublished paper, Episcopal Diocese of Chicago, 1993). See also Knudsen, "Understanding Congregational Dynamics," in Nancy Myer Hopkins and Mark Laaser, *Restoring the Soul of a Church: Healing Congregations Wounded by Clergy Sexual Misconduct* (Collegeville, Minn.: Liturgical Press/Interfaith Sexual Trauma Institute, 1995), 75–101.

6. Nancy Myer Hopkins, "Symbolic Church Fights: The Hidden Agenda When Clerical Trust Has Been Betrayed," *Congregations: The Alban Journal* (May/June 1993): 15–18.

7. Knudsen, "Trauma Debriefing: A Congregational Model," *MCS Conciliation Quarterly* (Spring 1991): 12–13.

8. Nelle Morton, *The Journey Is Home* (1985; repr., Boston: Beacon Press, 1986).

Preface

1. Edwin H. Friedman, *Generation to Generation: Family Process in Church and Synagogue* (New York: Guildford Press, 1985), 221.

Introduction

1. Darlene K. Haskin, "After Pastors in Troubled Congregations," in *Restoring the Soul of a Church: Healing Congregations Wounded by Clergy Sexual Misconduct* (Collegeville, Minn.: The Liturgical Press, 1995), 155.

2. See Chilton Knudsen, "Understanding Congregational Dynamics," 79ff in *Restoring the Soul of a Church,* for a vivid rendering of this phenomenon.

3. See chapter 7 in Candace R. Benyei, *Understanding Clergy Misconduct in Religious Systems: Scapegoating, Family Secrets, and the Abuse of Power* (New York: The Haworth Pastoral Press, 1998), for a through discussion of scapegoating dynamics in betrayed congregations.

Chapter 3

1. Marie Fortune, *Clergy Misconduct: Sexual Abuse in the Ministerial Relationship* (Seattle: Center for Prevention of Sexual and Domestic Violence, 1992), 43.

2. Legal proceedings against the Roman Catholic Church rising from failure to acknowledge the harm done by priests who abused children in the church and to take appropriate steps to prevent further harm have been extensively covered in the media. Less widely covered are suits for sexual misconduct and breach of fiduciary duty against clergy who sexualized professional relationships with adult female church members. See among other case law 150 N.J. 550, 696 A. 2d697 in which the New Jersey Supreme Court found for the plaintiff, stating that the First Amendment guaranteeing separation of church and state does not insulate a member of the clergy from actions for breach of fiduciary duty arising out of sexual misconduct.

3. Fortune, *Clergy Misconduct,* 45.

4. Ibid., 46.

5. Ibid., 48.

6. Ibid., 65.

Chapter 8

1. For details about diagnostic critieria for PTSD, search for "309.81 DSM-IV" on the Web.

Chapter 9

1. Conrad W. Weiser, *Healers—Harmed and Harmful* (Minneapolis: Fortress Press, 1993), 135–42. Weiser observes that because of his position in the congregation, a minister cannot maintain a neutral role in relation to congregants, as therapists are required to do in relation to clients. He suggests further that a minister's poor management of transference and countertransference can cause failures in minister-congregant relationships, "most frequently resulting in either sexual or destructive though immaculate affairs" or in "professional burnout or depression."

2. Peter L. Steinke, *How Your Church Family Works: Understanding Congregations as Emotional Systems* (Bethesda, Md.: The Alban Institute, 1993), discusses this phenomenon at length.

3. Edwin H. Friedman. *Generation to Generation: Family Process in Church and Synagogue* (New York: The Guilford Press, 1985), 52–54.

Chapter 10

1. See Hopkins and Laaser, *Restoring the Soul of a Church*, for a fuller discussion of closed religious systems.

2. Robert J. Kearney, *Within the Wall of Denial: Conquering Addictive Behaviors* (New York: W. W. Norton, 1996).

Chapter 11

1. "Broken Symbols: Child Sexual Abuse and the Priesthood," *Today's Parish* (September 1992): 9–13.

Chapter 12

1. Alan J. Roxburgh, "Pastoral Role in the Missionary Congregation," in *The Church Between Gospel and Culture: The Emerging Mission in North America*, eds. George R. Hunsberger and Craig Van Gelder (Grand Rapids: Erdmann's, 1996), 330.

2. Gerald A. Arbuckle, "Gospel Communities in Rapid Change: A Spirituality of Grieving into Newness," in *The Hidden Spirit: Discovering the Spirituality of Institutions*, eds. James F. Cobble Jr. and Charles M. Elliott (Matthews, N.C.: CMR Press, 1999), 63.

3. Ronald W. Richardson, *Creating a Healthier Church: Family Systems Theory, Leadership, and Congregational Life* (Minneapolis: Fortress Press, 1996), 133.

4. Ibid., 134.

5. Frank A. Thomas, *Spiritual Maturity: Preserving Congregational Health and Balance* (Minneapolis: Fortress Press, 2002), 32.

6. Friedman, *Generation to Generation*, 212.

7. Thomas, *Spiritual Maturity*, 31.

8. Friedman, *Generation to Generation*, 229.

9. Thomas, *Spiritual Maturity*, 31.

10. E. Dixon Junkin, "Up from the Grassroots: The Church in Transition," in *The Church Between Gospel and Culture*, 312.

11. Ibid., 313.

12. Arbuckle, "Gospel Communities," in *The Hidden Spirit,* 64.

Chapter 14

1. "The Baptismal Covenant," *The Book of Common Prayer and Administration of the Sacraments and Other Rites and Ceremonies of the Church: According to the Use of The Episcopal Church* (New York: The Church Hymnal Corporation, 1979), 304–305.

Chapter 15

1. Others have observed the reactions of clergy to colleagues' misconduct. Jan Winebrenner and Debra Frazier observe in *When a Leader Falls: What Happens to Everyone Else* (Bethany House Publishers, 1993) that colleagues often feel hurt and confused, and have increased self-doubt upon learning of another clergyperson's "fall from grace." Kevin McDonough dramatically suggests that in the responses of clergy colleagues, one can see, as in the central event of Christianity, both signs of life and signs of death in church and ministry. (See "The Effects of the Misconduct Crisis on Non-Offending Clergy," in *Restoring the Soul of a Church.*) And Candace R. Benyei has noted that colleagues, especially those of lesser status—seminarians, interns, associates—and those who may have witnessed or have knowledge of misconduct, are exposed to coercive attacks by other clergy, are readily scapegoated, and endure career setbacks as a consequence of reporting another cleric's misconduct (see Benyei, *Understanding Clergy Misconduct in Religious System* (Haworth Pastoral Press, 1998).

2. Richard Allen Blackmon, "The Hazards of the Ministry" (PhD diss., Fuller Theological Seminary, 1984).

3. Jeff T. Seat and others, "The Prevalence and Contributing Factors of Sexual Misconduct Among Southern Baptist Pastors in Six Southern States," *The Journal of Pastoral Care* 47, no. 4 (Winter 1993): 363–70.

4. In the 23 states that have criminal statutes related to sexual contact between a psychotherapist and client, the lion's share list clergy among possible therapists, although the clergyperson must be performing whatever that state defines as "psychotherapy," and how psychotherapy is defined varies from state to state. Clergy who counsel in a church may be open to prosecution, but they are typically able to claim they were doing "spiritual" or "pastoral" counseling. In both Minnesota and Texas, however, it is a felony for clergy who are providing spiritual counseling or guidance to have sex with a counselee. All that is required is that the clergyperson have a private meeting with the person at some point. Simply being a member of a congregation does not qualify as "receiving spiritual counseling," and conversely, counseling nonmembers is not treated the same way as counseling members.

Clarifying that clergy are guilty of a crime when they have sex with a counselee has dramatic impact in helping victims be understood, healing victims' marriages or partnerships, and the like. Therapeutically, there is nothing more powerful than identifying the clergyperson as a criminal and the victim as the victim of a *crime.* Those who are serious about protecting victims of clergy misconduct, particularly sexual abuse, should examine their state's statutes in this regard.

5. "The Ordained Minister's Code" (Cleveland: United Church of Christ, 2003).

6. "Vision and Expectations: Ordained Ministers in the ELCA" (Chicago: Evangelical Lutheran Church in America, 1990).

7. "The Ordained Minister's Code."

8. "Code of Professional Practice" (Boston: Unitarian Universalist Ministers' Association, 1998).

Chapter 19

1. A discussion of First Amendment issues (the constitutional right to free exercise of religion and to be free of government establishment of religion) is beyond the scope of this book, but expertise is required to deal with issues related to church/state separation, which often arise when cases are brought in court. The U.S. Constitution, and most state constitutions, goes to great lengths to protect churches from government interference. Congregations should seek an attorney who is familiar with these issues as they relate to clergy misconduct cases or who has a strong relationship with a legal consultant who is familiar with the issues.

Chapter 25

1. See Stanislav Grof and Christina Grof, eds., *Spiritual Emergency: When Personal Transformation Becomes a Crisis,* in the "Personal Wellness" section of appendix A, "Resources."

Chapter 30

1. See Benyei, *Understanding Clergy Misconduct in Religious Systems,* 63–65.

2. J. H. Bloom, *The Rabbi as Symbolic Exemplar: By the Power Vested in Me* (Binghamton, N.Y.: Haworth Press, 2002).

3. See Elaine Pagels, *Adam, Eve, and the Serpent* (New York: Vintage, 1988).

4. *Not in My Church* is an award-winning, dramatic video of one church faced with a betrayal of trust by its minister and is available from FaithTrust Institute. (See appendix A, "Resources.")

5. See Matthew 5:7 and the chapter on this verse in Benyei, *How To Get There From Here: Creating God Among Us* (Philadelphia: Xlibris Corporation, 2001), 63–70.

CONTRIBUTORS

CANDACE R. BENYEI is a published author, poet, liberation theologian, spiritual director, research scientist, and teaching family therapist. She received her M.P.S. from New York Theological Seminary and her Ph.D. in clinical psychology from the Union Institute, with research conducted in group family of origin work with clergy couples. She maintains a private practice of psychotherapy, spiritual direction, and congregational conflict resolution, and lives with her family on a horse farm in Redding, Connecticut.

NANCY BIELE is the convener of the Minnesota Council of Churches Committee to End Sexual Misconduct in the Religious Community, an interdenominational committee founded in 1987 to respond and advocate within religious institutions to end sexual exploitation. She serves as a trainer, consultant, and advocate supervisor for churches and denominations aiding in policy and procedure development, denominational training, and advocacy. She is also the director of a faith-based social service agency in Minneapolis.

RICHARD B. COUSER is an attorney with D'Amante Couser Steiner Pellerin in Concord, New Hampshire. He is the author of *Ministry and the American Legal System* (Fortress Press, 1993), a comprehensive guide for pastors and lay leaders of churches and religious organizations. He is also past president of the Christian Legal Society, a national organization of Christian attorneys. Much of his practice involves counseling churches and religious organizations.

E. LARRAINE FRAMPTON is an ordained minister in the Evangelical Lutheran Church in America. Her doctor of ministry degree work was exploring religious issues that affect sexual abuse. She has served in many settings, including congregations, judicatory staff, hospice care, and the Division for Ministry, ELCA. Her mission is to help keep the church safe and sacred, so the gospel can be heard and lived. She provides response team workshops and works with congregations in conflict.

NANCY MYER HOPKINS has a family systems background and for over 15 years has been consulting with and training laity, clergy, and judicatory officials to help traumatized congregations recover from leadership trust betrayals. She was coeditor of *Restoring the Soul of a Church* and author of *The Congregational Response to Clergy Betrayals of Trust*, both published by Liturgical Press. Nancy lives in Maine with her husband of 50 years, Harold, and two mildly neurotic pets. Nancy and Harold have six adult children, five sons- and daughters-in-laws, and six brilliant grandchildren.

PATRICIA L. LIBERTY is cofounder and director of Associates in Education and Prevention in Pastoral Practice, an ecumenical and interfaith resource that assists individuals and organizations in the aftermath of clergy sexual abuse. She is nationally known for her advocacy work with survivors of clergy sexual abuse and is a leader of the acclaimed retreat "Is Nothing Sacred?" A United Church of Christ minister, she serves as a consultant to churches and judicatories around the country and lives in Rhode Island.

MATTHEW LINDEN, a graduate of Syracuse University and the Theological School at Drew University, is a United Methodist pastor in the Greater New Jersey Annual Conference. He spent four years as an afterpastor and is currently appointed to the Belford United Methodist Church in Belford, New Jersey. He is married and has three sons.

LOREN D. MELLUM serves as senior pastor of Trinity Lutheran Church in North Branch, Minnesota. He attended the Lutheran Bible Institute of Seattle; Christian Theological Seminary, Indianapolis; and Trinity Lutheran Seminary, Columbus, Ohio. He is currently a doctoral student at Luther Seminary, St. Paul, Minnesota, where he is studying congregational leadership and mission. He has served congregations in Iowa, Indiana, and Ohio.

DEBORAH J. POPE-LANCE is a licensed marriage and family therapist and a Unitarian Universalist minister with three decades of experience in parish, interim, and counseling ministries. Currently, she provides therapy to individuals and relationships, consults with clergy and congregations on the ethics of ministerial practice and congregational life, and teaches at Andover Newton Theological School. As a coach to afterpastors, she has helped hundreds of clergy do their best work in the aftermath of misconduct.

GLENNDY SCULLEY has served Lutheran denominational offices and organizations since 1985, and since 2001 has been bishop's associate for rostered ministries in the Minneapolis Area Synod of the Evangelical Lutheran Church in America. Beginning in 2000, she has had responsibility for judicatory response to clergy misconduct. Glenndy and her husband, Michael, have been married for 25 years, and live with their pampered dogs, Louie and Frankie, and cat, Smokey.

MARY SELLON is a United Methodist Church minister who has served in a variety of settings, including redeveloping congregations and new starts. A certified professional coactive coach, she currently works as a coach and consultant to clergy and congregational teams. She is coauthor of *Practicing Right Relationship* (Alban, 2005) and *Redeveloping the Congregation* (Alban, 2002).

DAN SMITH is a United Methodist Church minister who has resourced congregations in a variety of ways. He has served as pastor, district superintendent, and judicatory executive, and is currently a coach and consultant. He is a certified professional coactive coach who works with clergy and congregational teams, and is coauthor of *Practicing Right Relationship* (Alban, 2005) and *Redeveloping the Congregation* (Alban, 2002).